Eagles, Donkeys, and Butterflies

RECENT TITLES FROM THE HELEN KELLOGG INSTITUTE FOR
INTERNATIONAL STUDIES

Scott Mainwaring, *general editor*

The University of Notre Dame Press gratefully thanks the Helen Kellogg Institute
for International Studies for its support in the publication of titles in this series.

Kevin Healy
*Llamas, Weavings, and Organic Chocolate: Multicultural Grassroots Development
in the Andes and Amazon of Bolivia* (2000)

Vikram K. Chand
Mexico's Political Awakening (2001)

Ruth Berins Collier and David Collier
Shaping the Political Arena (2002)

Glen Biglaiser
Guardians of the Nation? (2002)

Sylvia Borzutzky
Vital Connections (2002)

Alberto Spektorowski
The Origins of Argentina's Revolution of the Right (2003)

Caroline C. Beer
Electoral Competition and Institutional Change in Mexico (2003)

Yemile Mizrahi
From Martyrdom to Power (2003)

Charles D. Kenney
Fujimori's Coup and the Breakdown of Democracy in Latin America (2003)

Alfred P. Montero and David J. Samuels
Decentralization and Democracy in Latin America (2004)

Katherine Hite and Paola Cesarini
Authoritarian Legacies and Democracy in Latin America and Southern Europe (2004)

Robert S. Pelton, C.S.C.
Monsignor Romero: A Bishop for the Third Millennium (2004)

Guillermo O'Donnell, Jorge Vargas Cullell, and Osvaldo M. Iazzetta
The Quality of Democracy (2004)

Arie M. Kacowicz
The Impact of Norms in International Society (2005)

For a complete list of titles from the Helen Kellogg Institute for International
Studies, see http://www.undpress.nd.edu

Eagles, Donkeys, and Butterflies

AN ANTHROPOLOGICAL STUDY
OF BRAZIL'S "ANIMAL GAME"

Roberto DaMatta
and Elena Soárez

Translated by Clifford E. Landers

UNIVERSITY OF NOTRE DAME PRESS

NOTRE DAME, INDIANA

Manufactured in the United States of America

Translated by Clifford E. Landers from *Águias, burros e borboletas:
Um estudo antropológico do jogo do bicho,* by Roberto DaMatta and Elena Soárez,
published by Rocco, Rio de Janeiro, Brazil, 1999.

Library of Congress Cataloging in-Publication Data

Matta, Roberto da.
[Aguias, burros e borboletas. English]
Eagles, donkeys and butterflies : an anthropological study of Brazil's "animal
game" / Roberto DaMatta and Elena Soárez ; translated by Clifford E. Landers.
    p.   cm. — ("From the Helen Kellogg Institute for International Studies")
Includes bibliographical references and index.
ISBN 0-268-02580-0 (pbk. : alk. paper)
1. Bullfights—Social aspects—Brazil.   I. Soárez, Elena.   II. Helen Kellogg
Institute for International Studies.   III. Title.   IV. Series.
GV1108.6.B6M3813   2006
791.8'20981—dc22

                                                    2005032956

∞ *This book is printed on acid-free paper.*

This book is dedicated to the memory of our grandparents

Emílio Lourenço de Souza

and

Emerentina Perdigão da Matta

The people, however, the real people, those who do not know how to read and write, have a very different rule for interpreting their dreams. Extracting a tooth is a death in the family. I have never understood the relationship between one thing and the other, but there must be one. The voice of the people is the voice of God. Dreaming of excrement brings a fortune; about a dead person brings health; raw meat is a sign of crime. How did the public discover those equivalencies?

There is still no sure interpretive theory for dreams applied to the Animal Game, but one is being essayed, despite the difficulties.

—LIMA BARRETO

———

Etelvina, I hit the lottery,
I won five hundred *contos*
I don't have to work any more . . .
—WILSON BATISTA AND
GERALDO PEREIRA

———

Thus these are more than themes, more than the bare bones of institutions, more than complex institutions, even more than systems of institutions divided, for example, into religion, law, economy, etc. They are whole "entities," entire social systems, the functioning of which we have attempted to describe. We have looked at societies in their dynamic or physiological state. We have not studied them as if they were motionless, in a static state, or as if they were corpses. Even less have we decomposed and dissected them, producing rules of law, myths, values, and prices. It is by considering the whole entity that we could perceive what is essential, the way everything moves, the living aspect, the fleeting moment when society, or men, become sentimentally aware of themselves and of their situation in relation to others. In this concrete observation of social life lies the means of discovering new facts, which we are only beginning dimly to perceive. In our opinion, nothing is more urgent or more fruitful than this study of total social facts.

—MARCEL MAUSS

CONTENTS

PROLOGUE AND
ACKNOWLEDGMENTS

I believe in part this book began to be written at 31 Nilo Peçanha Street, in Niterói, when I was eight years old and my maternal grandmother, Emerentina, asked me for a hunch for the "animal game." I don't know why I said "elephant," choosing one of the possible animals, and gave the matter no further thought.[1] At the end of the afternoon, to my surprise, I received from a delighted Emerentina money that allowed me to buy a handful of coveted chocolate bars at the corner store. The elephant headed the list, I was informed amid smiles and pats on the head![2]

I don't remember the taste of the chocolate, but I still carry inside me the gratifying sensation of having made my grandmother happy and of feeling capable of "hitting in the animal game"—because a child's hunch is a very good one, as they taught me—discovering, after all, something in which everyone could participate freely and equally.

Beginning with that episode, the animal game penetrated my heart and I began, despite Dumbo and Tarzan films, to look upon the elephant as a potential source of money, the money that was always so lacking in our family of public servants: mere "ashamed poor," as that same grandmother would say in her more pessimistic moments.[3]

Grandmother Emerentina Perdigão da Matta inspires part of the research in this book. That research began when I was a boy in the 1940s,[4] was expanded at the National Museum of the Federal University of Rio de Janeiro between 1970 and 1980,[5] and was fully executed in the 1990s, when Elena Soárez, then my student in the National Museum's Post-Graduate Program in Social Anthropology, became interested in the subject, carried out detailed and competent field work, and wrote the master's thesis that is the basis of this essay.

This book is therefore the result of a complex collaborative process, representing two anthropological experiences and reflecting two perspectives—female and male—speaking by way of three generations and perhaps discussing two different ways of facing life: my grandmother Emerentina's and our own.

Emerentina's life was marked by reversals of fortune. She got married in Manaus, at seventeen, at the turn of the century, to a merchant from

Maranhão, Carlos de Azevedo Perdigão, after a two-week courtship that profoundly displeased a deserted fiancé. She was the mother of two boys (Kronge and Marcelino) and was pregnant with a girl, Maria de Lourdes, who was to become my mother, when her husband was shot to death by the former fiancé in a bar in the city. Without the wealthy husband who had given her everything, Grandma began "taking in sewing," and pawned the jewels that were the keepsake of a happier time, of a Manaus made rich by the rubber boom that by then was heading toward bust.

But that terrible turnaround did not embitter her. She remade her life, marrying a justice of the peace, Raul Augusto da Matta, like her a widower with two children (Amália Leopoldina and Renato, who was to become my father), rebuilt her life and had other children. All told, my grandmother had fifteen children, of whom I met only four! The others I knew only through my mother's stories, for they died of some implacable and fatal disease while still children, youths, or young adults. They were all embedded in an idealized Manaus, along with the rosary beads, in the prayer book, in a few photographs, and in the empty spaces of Grandma's black embroidered shawl.

Despite this disturbing familiarity with the worst type of death, that of her children—Grandma Emerentina used to say that she "was born to bury children"—I don't picture her as lachrymose or bitter. Just the opposite; I keep the image of her as a happy, energetic matron, perfumed and vain in her black dress, the scarlet ribbon of the congregation of the Sacred Heart of Jesus on her gentle and loving bosom, fingernails painted, giving orders to her husband, her children, the maids, and the "rambunctious grandchildren," and telling an errand boy to place a bet in the animal game for her based on her favorite hunches, a bet she would check religiously at the end of the day.

While Mom equated suffering with fate, Grandma went on living her life, still with the strength to survive widowhood and the loss of her oldest son. My mother, whose life was to all appearances more stable, alternated between crying for no reason and the redeeming euphoria of the piano she always played skillfully, while Emerentina, despite everything she had experienced, was a model of steadiness.

But I want to believe—and this book helped me to become aware of it—that it was the game that impelled her and provided the model she needed to confront adversity. After all, in life as in the game, one can't foresee the outcome. To Emerentina, gambling wasn't a test of affirmation of personality or some simple effort to get rich. It was a means of renewing the joy of living, an exercise in recapturing generous expectations, a defense against chaos, and a way to give order to the banal, unforeseen facts of daily life: those things that, depending on their interaction, make days the same or profoundly different. To her, poker, roulette, and above all the cheap, domestic, and pacific animal game—which her sons and daughters-in-law sometimes considered a "vice" but about which my grandfather Raul never once complained (he called himself "a man forever in love")—were an act of hope.[6]

It was probably this reading of life as something tenuous, the warp and woof of events that appeared and disappeared with the ease of a game that, I choose to believe, enlivened my grandmother's existence, allowing her to bear all the tragedies as well as the small loss of money in the weekly card games, which she never missed and on which she blew the back pay that, in true Brazilian fashion, she was entitled to after Raul's death. At that time, Emerentina again displayed an admirable personality. Upon receiving the money, which an uncle and I went to get from the bank, Grandma gave each of us a small gift and later devoted herself—over the family's objections—to spending the entire sum on her favorite activity: gambling, which as she liked to say, showed that "money and shit are the same thing."

This attitude, by the way, is totally consistent with the aristocratic vision of gambling, as codified in the famous treatise *Il Cortegiano,* by Baldesar Castiglione (1528), an employee of the Duke of Urbino, who meditated on gambling not through the prism of modern morality—in which the act of gambling is seen as "a suicide without death," as an unconscious self-destructive compulsion, or as a functional mechanism aimed at managing social tensions and personal frustrations—but as a means of social affirmation independent of money.[7] The aristocratic life style is more concerned with elegance of behavior than with the mere objective of emerging victorious and pocketing the "vile metal."[8]

In the bourgeois world, money is transformed into capital and into an instrument of the saving of souls and of the exploitation of labor. The desacralization of the most important fetish of the capitalist system is perhaps the fulcrum of great gamblers' philosophy of life and has been a pacifying element of my own ambitions of wealth. Especially when I write these notes surrounded by my beloved grandchildren, who are our real treasure (and our main source of hunches!), as my sorely missed grandmother knew.

I believe that Grandma's fascination with games of chance had its origin in a fact revealed by Elena Soárez's research, according to which there is a tie, hidden but direct, between order and disorder.[9] This mysterious link enables every form of order to dissolve into chaos and every form of disorder to be fitted into classification and cosmos, relativizing the rationalist ideal espoused by Enlightenment values of controlling, programming, and predicting everything.

All this is to say that the idea of studying that most Brazilian animal game was not born merely in the good schools I attended, or in the brilliant sociological theories I read, but on the wide porch of an old rented house in Brazil. Its rooms had many doors, it lacked running water, there was an enormous somber skylight and Aunt Amália saw ghosts who asked for her prayers, there was no electric refrigerator and the bathroom, as my Uncle Mário put it, was a block away!

Nor was studying the animal game a theme suggested by some professor attuned to Brazilian social life. No! The idea of penetrating the logic, history, and sociology of the game, collaborating with Elena Soárez's research, came to me the morning I served as the innocent source of a hunch and from the hopes of life styles of those who shaped me and who live on inside me.

If structuralist methodology, so out of fashion today, provided the yardstick by which I attempt to interpret the world, the rhythm was given to me by those Emerentinas and by the mythical city of Manaus that Lulita, my beloved mother, idealized brilliantly at the piano on the days that my enthusiasm for music and my father's eloquent silence were the most emphatic testimony to my unconditional admiration for her art.

It was those women who awakened my interest in Brazil—from Carnival to authoritarian rites; from processions to popular and literary heroes; from the idea of space to conceptions of nature; from popular music, which makes the world lighter and more beautiful, to the rhetoric of violence that embodies it and makes it terrible.

Because of all that, I was quite gratified and happy when Elena Soárez took seriously the project of studying the animal game. Using notes, newspaper articles, books, and other materials that she had collected, she produced the master's thesis that is the basis of this essay. Elena thus demonstrated that the younger generations were sensitive to a theme that lay at the heart of my sociological studies, at the same time that she helped characterize what I called "the Brazilian dilemma" (see DaMatta, 1979), inspired by Gunnar Myrdal's classic study of race relations in the United States. But if in America the dilemma lay in the intransigence typical of a society with an egalitarian creed that, for that very reason, has an antipathy toward hybridism and mixing, in Brazil the dilemma was found in our inability to conclude stages, break with styles, separate motives and feelings, and, at the extreme, become conscious of hierarchy.

Intrinsically, it is an issue with two sides. On one hand, one must do like everyone else: characterize the emergency of modernity in Brazil by delimiting it in relation to its centers. On the other, one must undo what everyone else has done, by reflecting at greater length on a possible, parallel, and differentiated modernity: a singular, Brazilian-style modernity.

Another cause for delight stemmed from the fact that Elena's work opened a dialogue with the assuredly most original and courageous part of Lévi-Strauss's work: that dedicated to the understanding of the "savage mind" and of totemism.[10] But with an important new element: if for Lévi-Strauss, who articulated the question, animals are "good to think" and thus are good to classify; to challenge and reinforce the social order; to prohibit, to ritualize, and to curse; and to establish limits, as argue, respectively, Mary Douglas (1976), Stanley Tambiah (1985), Edmund Leach (1983), and Robert Darnton (1985), none of them said that animals are also good for gambling! This is because no one had explored the intriguing relationship between animals and numbers in the context of a sphere that hitherto has escaped a serious sociological scrutiny: games of chance.[11]

By having taken on this ideological side of the animal game—the system of beliefs that shapes it and gives it strength—Elena Soárez's research reveals that the use of animals as symbolic operators is not limited to tribal societies of Australia, Africa, North America, or the Amazon but is also present among us, Brazilians, who, not without ambiguities, have adopted the Western paradigm and cyclically renew our promises of living in accordance with the compass of rationalism, compartmentalization, statistical indexes, progress, and historical linearity. This essay conclusively demonstrates that the animal game is a style of coping with uncertainty and, as such, can arise wherever there is the desire to break with the framework of a holistically organized universe. Rather than a proof of moral weakness and historical and social inferiority, it expresses a particular style of dealing with inequality and with processes of change imposed from above. In essence, this "modern totemism" studied here for the first time suggests a reading of the world as a place full of enchantment, despite the setbacks of a history that has also produced—*comme il faut*—tragedy, frustration, and suffering.

Speaking of tragedy, frustration, and suffering, I want to state emphatically that the aim of this volume is to understand the animal game as a culture and as a system. Nothing in its pages seeks to justify or render the organization of the animal game palatable, defensible, or sympathetic. The network that joins and separates the game's bankers, as well as its execution and the decrying or judging of its life style, are not topics of this work, which focuses on the symbolism of the lottery. This note is important because our sympathy, our curiosity, as well as our acute awareness of the originality of the lottery, must be clearly distinguished from any complicity with crime and criminal activity. This book is a study of a particular type of lottery, not an endorsement of gambling, or a license of legitimacy for those who take advantage of its powerful symbolic force. This, as Kipling said, is another story.

The ensuing essay is divided into five parts. Its point of departure is an "Initial Hunch and Finishing Touch" in which I attempt to discern the place (as both subject and object) of the animal game in the process of Brazilian modernization. Four chapters follow, in which the history of the game is reconstructed, its expressive dimensions characterized, its practices explained, and the symbolism of its animals studied. The text ends with a detailed description (an ethnography) of this social universe.

With the exception of "Initial Hunch and Finishing Touch," of my authorship, all the chapters were written by Elena Soárez. In these parts of the book my contribution consisted of modifying the language, broadening the scope of certain lines of argument, clarifying ideas, and editing passages important to an academic thesis but superfluous in a book intended for a wider public. I mention these facts because, as a more experienced and better-known author, I wish to reiterate that Elena was not a mere research assistant but an imaginative and competent coauthor whose project resulted in this text.

One more thing: some readers may ask why this book does not end with a "conclusion." I was often asked this question in relation to my essays about Carnival, soccer, and house and street in Brazil. The answer I gave then is equally valid now: how can one "conclude" things like Carnival, soccer, nostalgia, and "Brazil"?

If "conclusion" means end, how can one don the robe of arrogance and perorate conclusively about institutions that, when all is said and done, are— even when viewed as moribund—more alive than we ourselves, which transform themselves before our very eyes, which take on new forms and change position even as we attentively study them, which help us be what we are?

Despite the moral questions they raise, these institutions are fundamental to constituting that Brazil with a capital B that is embedded in our hearts.[12]

I wish to thank, on behalf of Elena Soárez, colleagues in the Post-Graduate Program in Social Anthropology (PPGAS) of the National Museum, especially Professor Afrânio Raul Garcia Júnior, who in my absence was indefatigable and dedicated as the director-godfather of the thesis, as well as the National Museum, the National Center for Research (CNPq), the CAPES, and the Ford Foundation for the help she received in the form of fellowships for study and research. When we decided to collaborate to produce a text, Elena also had the support of the Reverend Edmund Joyce, C.S.C., Chair of the Department of Anthropology of the University of Notre Dame, which I have the honor of holding and which provided resources for the more in-depth investigation that resulted in this book.

Along with these individuals and institutions, mention must be made of Jacqueline Muniz, Elizabeth Morais, and Fábio Gavião, who made so many creative contributions to her work. In addition, Elena cannot overlook the secretariat of the PPGAS of the National Museum and all those who helped her during the time of the research that resulted in her master's thesis.

For my part, I would like to thank the University of Notre Dame, the institution that welcomed me and has shown confidence in my work, as well as all my friends and colleagues. At Notre Dame, Patrick Gaffney, Karen Richman, Frederico and Joana Xavier. In Brazil, Ilana and Armando Strozenberg, Lívia Barbosa, Ricardo and Silvana Benzaquen de Araújo, who listened to me and offered encouragement as I was working on this text. My brother, Renato Augusto da Matta, went to the trouble to send me an important notice concerning the topic; Valter Sinder and Vânia Belli were fundamental because of their intellectual help and brotherly encouragement; Enylton de Sá Rego was a highly valuable interlocutor; Affonso Romano de Sant'Anna made in passing, as is typical of generous friends, an important bibliographical suggestion; Alberto Dines was exemplary in the rapidity with which he responded to a last-minute appeal by sending me texts about the cabbala; Fernão Mesquita and Fernando Mitre, my journalist supporters from the *Jornal da Tarde,* sent an important file about the current status of the game. Brian Owensby, of the University of Virginia, sent me valuable bibliographical references, and the editor José Mário Pereira, besides sharing my enthusiasm for the project, placed at my disposal two fundamental texts of Jorge Luis Borges.

By inviting me to take part as a key speaker in the 15th Meeting of the Brazilian Anthropological Association in Vitória, Espírito Santo, and in the Groupe de Réflexion sur le Brésil Contemporain, at the Maison des Sciences de L'Homme, in Paris, in April and May, 1998, respectively, Mariza Corrêa (then president of the Brazilian Anthropological Association) and Afrânio Raul Garcia Júnior, associate director of the group, left me in their debt for the suggestions and encouragement from the listeners, among whom I wish to mention specifically Marcos Lanna and Márcio Silva in Vitória and, in Paris, Ignacy Sachs, José Sérgio Leite Lopes, and Lygia Sigaud.

No one among them is responsible for what is said here, but to all we express our gratitude.

Finally, I must mention the invisible yet crucial participation of Celeste, my wife and my life's companion, who with much love, enormous patience, and inexpressible generosity, both at Notre Dame and in Niterói, has laid the foundation for the life and work of an incorrigible hunch player.

RDM
Jardim Ubá, June 1998

Initial Hunch and Finishing Touch

The Bichos Are More Important than the Bookies

Institutions critical to the understanding of Brazil, like Carnival, soccer, *cachaça* (Brazilian rum), and the animal game (*jogo de bicho*) have, for all practical purposes, been banned from intellectual consideration. One can count on the fingers of both hands the number of studies about Carnival,[1] there are extremely few sociological works about soccer,[2] there is nothing historical and sociological about cachaça[3] as a gift (along with *cafezinho* and Sunday luncheon), and about the subject of this book—the animal game— alongside sparse academic works,[4] there is a file that speaks less about it and much more about how the "elites" view that lottery. In the discussion, these institutions always appear as proof of ignorance and the expression of our perennial tendency toward corruption and crime, as signs of "cultural backwardness" and symptoms of a recalcitrant "false consciousness," those indelible marks of political and social weakness and the absence of civilization.

Everything happens as if a good part of our intellectual elite, that part permanently fascinated with reforming the world and admirably faithful to its ideologies, were irresistibly enthralled by bankers but harbored a formidable disdain for the animals (*bichos*). Mistaking apples for oranges, it has emphasized the most apparent and the least important, ignoring that which permits and legitimizes the social and political power of the undertaking: the bichos. Or rather, it ignores the system of the animal game—the symbolic operator—which, like a gift, irrevocably links bichos and bookies.[5]

In this way, much of what has been written about Carnival, soccer, and the animal game serves more to block than to enhance understanding of these institutions, which in the case of social sciences means confronting them candidly, without prepackaged notions and moralizing intentions aimed at correcting the system, for its major objective is to produce a translation of a singular, localized set of institutions into the universalistic language of comparative sociology, into what an ingenuous confidence in the natural-sciences model has pompously termed "anthropological theory."[6]

II

The comprehensive approach assumed in this essay respects but refuses to repeat that trivial, normative exercise in pigeonholing and proposes instead to examine the relationship between the animal game and Brazilian society. This is also a problematic posture because it suggests on one hand the existence of concrete things like cachaça, Carnival, and the animal game, and on the other, a thing still more concrete called "Brazilian society." In reality, what we perceive as "Brazil" or "Brazilian society" cannot constitute anything relatively complete without the presence of these institutions. In other words, without Carnival, cachaça, soccer, and the animal game our perception is incomplete—and let me add to that list other uninvited guests of official sociology equally basic to our view of ourselves as a dynamic system struggling with itself: *umbanda* (an Afro-Brazilian religion), roguishness (*malandragem*), popular music, the naysayer (*espírito de porco*), the beach, gossip, hitting on women (the *cantada*), clientelism, lies, and the ingenious solution (*jeitinho*).[7] Without them—I reiterate—it would scarcely be possible to construct what we trivially call Brazilian "reality" or "identity."

It is important to note that identities are made up of a cultural collage and, in the case of Brazil, those institutions have served as stays for a relatively integrated vision of ourselves. I say "relatively integrated" to emphasize that in Brazil it is not the set of "modern" institutions and values, instituted and proclaimed with independence from Portugal or the advent of the republic, that has served as the main source of our identity. In fact, to the disappointment of many observers of the national scene, the anthem, the flag, the school system, industries, parliament, the constitution, the apparatus of the state, the political regime, and the currency—above all, these last two—form a problematic whole, uncertain in their operation and in constant, radical transformation. But cachaça, popular music, Sunday lunch, soccer, and the animal game have displayed tremendous continuity, constituting for that very reason crucial sources of reference for the sketch or the finished portrait of Brazilian identity. And, without relatively fixed referents to remember, there cannot be the forgetting that—as Ernest Renan would put it—is at the heart of the forming of identities, whether individual, group, professional, regional, or national.[8]

To study the animal game, therefore, one must adopt a certain perspective, a place from which he can see the air he breathes and catch sight of his own nose. A place where he can make the attempt to read himself as a foreigner with distance and a healthy dose of skepticism, but without confusing diligent criticism with complacency, defeatism, or self-flagellation.

III

Thus it is absolutely crucial to verify that this group of institutions truly constitutional of our sociability is always seen from a factual, journalistic, or normative angle. In this view, social institutions exist only to guarantee the power of a given class over society—or, with the same result, to inebriate the always good but ingenuous public consciousness. The more these institutions consolidate the power of the dominant segments and intoxicate the people, the stronger and more omnipresent they become.

In this way, these institutions would be everything but what they say they are: festivals that permit the inversion of the world; tremendously imaginative classificatory operators that help to transform probability into certainty, impersonality into intimacy, poverty into wealth, and despair into hope; competitive, agonistic rituals that promote a positive union between society and the national state while generalizing and intensifying the experience with universal norms, with performance, and with equality; cosmologies that, by reintroducing magic to everyday life, permit the (re)enchantment of the world and, through the promise of a miraculous windfall, legitimize aspirations of victory and justice with a possible reshaping of social identity. Moreover, they are powerful codes of communication between social segments separated by political participation, education, and the brutally skewed distribution of goods and services.

In other words, the normative approach serves only a denunciatory or monitory function, forgetting the dimensions referred to earlier. Governed by utilitarianism or, to use the expression of Marshall Sahlins (1976a, 1995), in "practical reason," it confuses sensorial perception with empirical judgment and fails to see the arbitrary, symbolic interpositions between functional demands and their results.[9] In this type of reasoning, war, for example, would be the result of aggressive impulses, in the same way that the animal game would be the consequence of the ignorance of the masses eager to overcome the poverty in which they find themselves because of an unjust economic system. Without understanding that the impulse to surmount unfair material conditions and mere ignorance do not generate the animal game wherever such factors are present—and I presume that these conditions are universal in the capitalist system—this approach is blind in relation to culture: to the always singular, local, and arbitrary styles of effecting accommodations among the forces that act within and outside any social group. In this sense, the objective here is to read the animal game as culture,[10] attempting to go beyond the ideology of any group seen as a universe governed by political interests and universal economic necessities to see it also as a field laden with meaning. This field is translated as "life" and "fate," those dimensions of the world that for us Brazilians abound with contradictions, ambiguities, and dilemmas.

"Life" and "fate," without rejecting what exists—the scientific credo, liberalism, the power of money, the play of the market, probability, the democratization of consumption, globalization, high technology, and the reification of the subject as individual incarnated as citizen who would be exactly the same everywhere—also take seriously conspiracies, secret desires, political plots, coups, gifts and supernatural encounters, coincidences, misfortunes, miracles, intrigues, and uncontrollable forces. Put another way, it is a reading that, while not rejecting modern ideology, does not forbear the possibility of coexistence with unsuspected totalities and invisible relationships.

In the countries that founded modernity and rationalism (France and England), games of chance challenged individual liberty (and the idea of probability), and open a parallel, alternative path to a means of enrichment that dispenses with work. The moral and legal reaction to gambling, in the form of legislation, treatises, pamphlets, books, and plays, is an obvious way of resolving the paradox established by a double incentive—on one hand, that of getting rich by working; on the other, that of making money by speculating in the stock market or at the table, by gambling. Indeed, how to condemn the desire for easy money, even at the cost of being trivially and immorally misled, if the entire system is based on that very principle?

As a matter of fact, as early as 1898, in his history of gambling in England, John Ashton underscores precisely this point when he says: "When the drive for money increases and predominates over the technical . . . gambling is seen as the quickest way to riches and everyone gets involved in it, betting on the stock market, horse races, or something else, hoping to win, because, of course, if the person thought about losing, no one would be foolish enough to embark on the activity" (Ashton, 1969:2). The same point is repeated by the eighteenth-century French moralists studied by John Dunkley, when they evinced awareness of the paradoxical relationship between commercial risk, approved by the new bourgeois morality, and gambling as a vice and means of dissipating money, ambiguously disapproved of by the system (Dunkley, 1985:222ff.).

In the same fashion, in his classic and little-read *The Theory of the Leisure Class,* published in 1899, Thorstein Veblen associates the concept of "luck" and of "gambling" with a "predatory," "animistic," and archaic view of the world, which would project human attributes onto objects and natural beings such as animals and plants. To Veblen and the Victorians in general, this constitutes an undesirable "survival" and a clear regression to a state of primitivism, irrationalism, and superstition. This point is reiterated in the *Encyclopaedia of the Social Sciences,* when William Seagle observes the contradictory relationship between gambling and financial speculation and—intrepid and optimistic—points to belief in luck as an anachronism "in the machine age" (Seagle, 1948, vol. 5: 555–561). The hegemony of the notion of rational and moral progress lies at the heart of arguments against gambling in France, England, and the United States. Roger Caillois (1979) adopts the same point of view. Not to mention the thesis of Johan Huizinga (1950), in which the act of play—which liberates, invents, and disciplines, leading to respect for rules and engendering a space of one's own—would be a primordial element of the civilizing process itself.[11]

IV

In this work we set aside the moralizing view and study the animal game as one more manifestation of what I have called "the Brazilian dilemma" (see DaMatta, 1979). To this end, we take this modality of a game of chance to be an authentic and paradoxical "modern totemism."[12] Thus a system that is also framed by the tyranny of ready-made formulas, "how-to," and "know how" typical of Western rationality—which does not permit the mixing of nature and culture—unabashedly relates numbers, animals, things, feelings, and people through an elaborate system of hunches.

It all happens as if the animal game were capable of cannibalizing modern ideology. To an order based on the market, quantity, individualism, the "work ethic," impersonality, and utility, the animal game presents a dazzling alternative, at once public and domestic, open and hermetic. For it reiterates the possibility of achieving "the easy life" by resort to luck and without necessarily having to engage in work. "Work," *pace* the noble and much trumpeted "Protestant ethic," makes all of us, if not slaves, at least good sycophants and philistines ready to sacrifice festival and love for employment and the routine, for responsibility as punishment, and for a future that, why mince words, remains as uncertain as the bicho that may or may not "hit" tomorrow. Besides this, the animal game reaffirms that one can "hit" and "get rich" through an explicit and codified system of intuitions (or "hunches") relatively in harmony with modern rationality, which it contradicts and charms, although the system is impossible to demonstrate empirically. In reintroducing the possibility of a qualitative and sensitive vision of the world, this system displaces the explicit reading of nature and of society obedient to fixed, predictable laws.

Instead of compartmentalizing the world in order to better govern it, endowing it with fixed and quantifiable agendas, as would modern ideology, the animal game proposes to see it in a compact Brazilian manner, as "life" and "fate." It deals with a relational totality replete with intersections between that which legitimates and affords certainty to the modern vision—its prestigious science of numbers, which, say the oracles of the *Wall Street Journal,* the *Financial Times,* and the lauded Department of Economics of the University of Chicago, neither lie nor fail and possess a logic of their own[13]—and its Achilles heel: the universe of animals. This problematic area is attempting today to recover after a death struggle with a scientific utilitarianism that legitimated its destructive plundering by its conception of nature as a foreign territory to be mercilessly exploited and, worse yet, as the private property of colonial powers, nation-states, and the wealthy.[14]

But it is in its social history that the animal game becomes even more paradoxical and curious. For it is precisely the moment in which Brazilian society was formally ending slavery, instituting a free labor system, making a radical political change, and attempting to abandon nepotism, that this most Brazilian of lotteries appeared.[15]

This game that, surely more than any other popular agency, has been capable of integrating the legitimate capitalist desire of making a lot of money with little effort—isn't it precisely this that characterizes what is known as "speculation" and explains the fortune of many modern heroes from Rockefeller to Forrest Gump, not to mention Hillary Clinton?—with a universe of bichos that, by making memorable the lottery's random outcome, allows one to attribute moral significance to probabilistic series and thus reinstate a cosmos in which everything once again relates magically to everything else.

In fact, as Kavanagh (1993:113) reminds us, invoking Buffon, the chance event, such as the result of the roulette wheel or the winning bicho, reveals a terrible independence in the relationships between past and future. Placed outside of any determination, the result of the lottery is a hermetic event[16] that challenges the determinisms postulated by the Enlightenment and by the positivist ideas that followed them (see Berlin, 1990; Geertz, 1973: chapter 2; Sahlins, 1995; Todorov, 1993). Gambling casts doubt on the intriguing random relationship between structures and events. And the animal game, because it serves as a bridge between numbers and animals, redefines the entire question, reintroducing into a field delimited by modern probability the line of reasoning of sorcery, as was simultaneously disclosed by Henri Bergson (1932) and E. E. Evans-Pritchard (1937) when they point out that the problem of explanation through magic is not the rejection of causality and reason, for sorcerers know that the person died of tuberculosis or because of an accident. Rather, it is to discern, as Bergson says, "proximate causes," which helps in attributing "human significance" to certain facts of existence; or, as Evans-Pritchard discovered: to give "moral value" to accidental events, by explaining why that person and not this one was struck down by misfortune.[17] In this way, moral significance is attributed to a routine disrupted by disturbing facts, such as accidents or misfortunes, making it possible to positively relate the terrible indifference of chance and the social importance of the victim of an extraordinary event.

The animal game makes use of these same arguments, allowing the transformation of random, unpleasant, and seemingly meaningless events such as nightmares, accidents, and sudden deaths into "hunches" that give them order, structure, "moral value," and, perhaps, fortune. Deep down, I reiterate, we are dealing with a logic that allows the establishing of moral equivalents between events, persons, and social relationships in a "totemism" that in a truly Brazilian way is—and isn't—at the service of bourgeois-capitalist society.

This intrigues us still more when we learn that the inventor of that lottery, Baron Drummond, popularized the game in an effort to raise funds for an initiative consistent with the modern view of nature: maintaining a zoo. But if the zoo is the place modernity reserves for animals, where they are protected and serve—like objects in museums—as natural relics in the "artificial" atmosphere of the city, the animal game associated with them by the baron and immediately embraced by the people of Rio de Janeiro achieved the exact opposite. By means of the game, these animals leave their cages and, thus liberated, act upon the very lives of those who visit and admire them. But all of this can only be properly evaluated when one focuses on the system of the animal game and not merely on its bookies.

This orientation is not without consequences. From the outset it reveals that, instead of our producing a modernity made up of individuals possessing freedom and autonomy, of citizens who use rationality and the market as the critical determinant in their lives, we have engendered a modernity that has banks, stock market, capital, and everything else one might wish to throw into the mix, but also has its animal game. A game whose symbolism reintroduces, in a society formally marked by liberal and universalistic ideals and norms, an intense personalness and an unbridled particularism.

In fact, in a social universe that the republican elites intended to govern by means of impersonal, abstract, cosmopolitan norms, divination (re)emerges and with a system of hunches that unite the "modern" and the "archaic": algorithms, dreams and bichos, which confers upon them a new garb and awareness. It is a system that, furthermore, highlights a local way of interpreting dreams and unforeseen events that Brazilian modernity undoubtedly multiplied by freeing the slaves, "regenerating" the nation's capital city, demanding French elegance, persecuting the guitar and the serenade; by criminalizing the absence of collars and shoes, the *bumba-meu-boi* folkloric dance, the Catholic festival of Penha, Carnival street revelers and *candomblé* worship rites; and by opening its streets to automobiles, disciplining vagrancy, and creating laws founded on the individual and based on equality of political rights.[18]

In fact, while Freud in Vienna was discovering and seeking to exorcise the irrationality of dreams, distinguishing them from popular superstitions and considering them the "royal road" to study of the unconscious, in Rio de Janeiro Baron Drummond was doing the exact opposite, calling upon the oneiric universe as part of a popular lottery that boldly reintegrated the "primitive" and magical with the rational and utilitarian.[19]

All this at the dawn of the twentieth century, amid a powerful wave of political renewal, capitalism, and stock-market speculation, when all, former barons and former slaves alike, were legally transformed into citizens. At the moment when, for the first time in Brazil, the words "investment," "working capital," "interest," and "market" became popular terms and part of the vocabulary of newspapers,[20] the animal game brought to an urban milieu undergoing rapid social change a "forgotten" language of the hunt that emphasizes the premonitory value of dreams, expresses the whims of fate, and, at its extreme, postulates magical links of sympathy and honor between hunter and hunted.

In the full dawning of the republic, when the country tried to embrace an intensely liberal policy in the economic area, which generated the famous *encilhamento*[21] of 1890–91, a period of wild speculation, the Canudos rebellion broke out in the backlands, and in the Brazilian metropolis that was the Rio de Janeiro of the elegant, of the cosmopolite Bilac (who, like every good Brazilian had two sides and also played the animal game),[22] of con men and idlers, the talk was of "surrounding" and "hitting" renatured and "totemized" numbers in bichos that thus can be domesticated, pleased, observed, stalked, ambushed, pursued, and perhaps transformed into wealth.

To prove this ambiguous line by which Brazilian society unites the old and the new, one must mention that, just as occurs in the stock market and the marketplace, certain animals can be very "sought after," which causes their value to fluctuate. The greater the demand, the lower the prize. But let's not deceive ourselves. It's a matter of a two-edged logic. The modern price mechanism exists precisely because the volume of wagers is symptomatic of an excess of magical confidence, which shows that the "bankers" of the game, as the name indicates, trust as much in modern banking logic as in the bicho—the being emblematic of the power of the magical thinking that encompasses it.[23]

V

All of this seems to contain a serious sociological lesson, demonstrating that innovation never takes place in an ideological vacuum and that acceptance of the so-called "modern" is not done through a gradual abandoning of what we judge to be old and obsolete, but through impudent and confused syntheses that combine the old and the new, the cautious and the audacious, modern logic that divides and the "savage mind" that fearlessly guesses and generously generates determination and totalities.

Canudos and the animal game indicate not merely a simple desire to return to traditional ways or a wise and popular resistance to an imposed modernity; they represent a creative synthesis of the old and the modern. It is what Gilberto Freyre called "Brazilianisms," original and dramatic syntheses of elements old and new, from without and within, of things known and loved and of exotic institutional forms, often necessary, imposed legally or by authoritarian means from above, which in the end shape a modernity difficult to characterize with precision.

This modernity *sui generis* is so special that the elites, whose heads are filled with fixed historical and sociological models crystallized by the history of European bourgeoisie, have never fully understood or translated it. From this, doubtlessly, comes the disdain for the animal game, so base and so locally Brazilian, so absent from the theoretical universe of the LeBons, Lapouges, Marxs, Hegels, Webers, and Lukács, and the "dialectical," "political," "literary," and "economic" analyses as not even to merit mention.[24]

Less, therefore, than something reactionary, out of place, or candidly traditional, as would be trivial to state, these syntheses prove that Brazilian society is something alive and dynamic, and that it accepts by postponing and resists by merging. As could only be the case, it adopts the new in its own way.

VI

From this perspective, the animal game is the profound expression of local codes, but also a way of cannibalizing the reification of statistical tables, financial tools, and the laws of the market espoused by businessmen, administrators, intellectuals, journalists, and politicians. It is precisely because it assimilates so well the exogenous, that the animal game promotes a subtle and humble revolution by turning the entire system upside down.

If a banker can speak seriously about investment, if a politician elaborates a bill inspired in liberalism, the animal game represents a popular, cheap, and realistic version of these things[25]—whether to show that getting rich is not all that mysterious, for money is fickle and deep down is linked to excrement, the residual and means of exchange of the work relationship;[26] whether to rip aside the veil of monetary sacralization by joining animals to numbers, relativizing the modern proposition of separating the natural from the social; or whether to dislodge the official ideological axis by discovering that, within that institutional framework based on the family and personal relations, getting rich has much more to do with betting, hunches, well-informed speculation, and gambling than with work, study, and honesty. We know this much better nowadays, when an uncontrollable wave of speculative financial capital is said to threaten the entire "system" that paradoxically stimulates and refuses to hinder it.

In this sense, the animal game carnivalized capitalism in general and local capitalism in particular. A capitalism, furthermore, much more formal and political than economic,[27] in which bankers, landowners, industrialists, businessmen, and rulers have highly intimate relationships among themselves—ties in every way similar to the relationship between the bichos and the numbers.

This contradictory identity on the political and financial plane is expressed in what Raymundo Faoro called "dismemberment of opposing tendencies," forces that led the "promoters" to always demand "freedom for the enterprise, but not to forgo . . . official stimulus" (1975:433), a process that we are with great effort seeking to change. If we conceive the player in the animal game to be a humble speculator located at the opposite pole, it can be said that his actions are inspired by that same model, except that he replaces the state with the dream, liberalism with the bicho cosmology, and the system of connections and pull with hunches born of the affinities between player and bichos. This is exactly like the behavior of Camilo, the character in the story by Machado de Assis who played the animal game in search of a sympathetic link or an intimate relationship capable of domesticating the terrible and paradoxical indifference embedded in the bichos on which he bet.[28]

It is no exaggeration, then, to say that the animal game is a "totemic operator" that enables the appropriate absorption of the globalizing movements to which Brazil has been subjected. The result of this movement is the invention of a zone that permits the interaction between the global and the local, the universal and the particular, by balancing its tensions and conflicts.

Modern financial capitalism penetrated Brazil, producing a complex banking system and a highly original and paradoxical animal game, a popular and creative formula of "totemic capitalization" capable of attracting small investors and basest pennies, but which—like its big brother—also promises the gigantic, immediate, and magical growth of capital. The game certainly adopts and cannibalizes the capitalist promise of abundance and monetary success to effect a change in social position, but, unlike orthodox capitalism, makes no pact with the social indifference instituted by individualistic market-based reductionism. Because it is a system founded on the undaunted magical thought that links everything to everything else, the animal game is in fact an antidote to the impersonality and disenchantment of the world that, as Max Weber perceived, marked the modern ethos.[29]

Instead of the acceptance of a social dynamic rooted in the indifference inherent in massification, anonymity, and individual autonomy, the animal game suggests a holistic perspective of social reality by reading it as a system made up of hierarchized interdependent parts. It is a web capable of integrating people and animals, as well as real and virtual positions, with seemingly cold, discrete numbers in a boundless totality, in which everybody is encompassed by everybody else and the movement of each can affect the paths of the rest.

VII

The animal game also reveals a disturbing fact: how modern speculative capitalism, loosed upon a hierarchized society controlled by clientelistic, aristocratically modeled[30] elites related by family ties (who thanks to state credit incur no risk), was appropriated and interpreted by the society that adopted it. If the local elites are forever inclined to imagine that acculturation can be an instantaneous and linear process, with the "old" and the "local" (which are obviously no good) being without delay or reaction replaced by the "new" and the "universal," which are read as the spice of life and represent progress and the future, the study of such popular institutions as the animal game, soccer, and Carnival demonstrates subtle and unsuspected local adjustments.[31]

The set of exogenous institutions, which arrived here under the banner of being mere technically neutral instruments of modernization, cosmopolitanism, liberation, and innovation of values and customs, invariably assumed local expressions and in so doing took on new meanings. All the more so because the animal game, in contrast to its brothers and to the unbridled capitalist speculation of the time, was paradoxically stripped of legitimacy.

As a matter of fact, if soccer and Carnival gained ground and became part of the social scene of Rio de Janeiro and of Brazilian society in general, the animal game was intermittently outlawed and definitively marginalized in 1944, when the federal government decided to forbid it everywhere in the national territory. This prohibition, along with the repression suffered by all Brazilian popular institutions, proves once more the absence of understanding of society by its cultured, lettered, often somewhat foreignized elites predisposed to civilize it.[32]

The fact, however, is that illegalization placed the animal game in a special framework, helping to cement it in the Brazilian urban landscape as its most enduring and popular lottery-related activity. Just as occurred with the Afro-Brazilian religions, the prohibition of the animal game was an essential factor in its diffusion, acceptance, penetration, and generalization in popular consciousness. As if it knew that whatever is formally forbidden has a high transformative power, society kept the animal game in its interstices—in its social and ideological "woods," those zones safe from bourgeois norms. This once again confirms the disharmonious and often conflictual link between society and the national state or "government," as people say in Brazil.[33]

VIII

Instead, then, of reducing the animal game to an activity exclusively dependent upon the poverty of the popular sector or studying it as an institution dependent on the wiles of a group of audacious rogues and corrupt police officers, as is the conventional wisdom of orthodox analyses, we examine it in a Maussian mode, as a "total institution," an encompassing phenomenon with "juridical, economic, religious, and even aesthetic and morphological" dimensions (Mauss, 1990:3, 78–79). For us, then, the animal game is a classificatory system of totemic style that, paradoxically, arises in the urban world and characterizes a singular and contradictory process of modernization by not conforming to the patterns derived from the English, French, or American experience, which to this day are held to be universal and exemplary.

Our fascination with the animal game is not limited merely to the investigation of the networks of co-optation of lieutenants, of taking in bets, and to its clear power of producing wealth, prestige, and influence, by corrupting and buying souls. The activity forms a complex, integrated whole, a "trans" or "antimodern"[34] paradoxical totemic system that cannot be fully understood without the prominent role of its expressive supports, as proved by the wagers and the cast of animals. Besides the bookies, this body comprises, in a single plane of reality and in alphabetical order, domesticated and wild animals, both Brazilian and foreign; an abstract, artificial numerical system equally endowed with symbolic value;[35] and, in addition, objects, emotions, social acts, human types, ethnicity, desires, social calculations, money, symbols of power, and motivations, revealing that nothing is impossible to the immense creativity of the human spirit.

As an example of this creativity, the series of animals in the animal game convokes arbitrarily a whole in which mammals, reptiles, carnivores, and herbivores, appear as not only good to eat—as a sound functionalist would say—but also as "bichos." Or, as a follower of Lévi-Strauss would emphasize, the animals are "good to think," and further, as a Brazilian "eagle" would point out, are equally excellent vehicles for playing a hunch, hurting the "donkeys," duping the "butterflies," stirring up the "stags," and—hope springs eternal—for making a lot of money.

Grounded in a fixed set of 25 animals, listed in their alphabetical order in Portuguese, associated with 25 master or original numbers—which hierarchize and symbolize other numbers—and postulating equally stable relationships with qualities, types, and institutions situated in the dimension of time and society, the animal game operates like an inclusive and referential classificatory system, which makes it capable of digesting historical events, as occurs classically with the phenomenon of totemism.

This happens because, unlike traditional lotteries, the animal game operates with a finite list of numbers, imposing an arbitrary limit on the indeterminate list of digits. By choosing numbers from 1 to 25, this lottery reduces—just as happens in totemism—an infinite set to a constant and finite framework. These numbers are used as exclusive references and as encompassing units for other numbers, being divisors of 100 tenths, 1,000 hundredths, and 10,000 thousandths. The result is an elaborate and ingenious classification system that gives rise to a hierarchy of numbers. In it, the number 1 is associated with the ostrich (*avestruz* in Portuguese) as well as with the numbers 01, 02, 03, and 04. The number 2, that of the eagle (*águia*), represents the tenths 05, 06, 07, and 08; the 3, the donkey (*burro*) subsumes the numbers 09, 10, 11, and 12, until we come to the cow (*vaca*), which represents the tenths 97, 98, 99, and 100. In the animal game, therefore, the numbers both represent themselves and also encompass and symbolize—by losing their mere practical, impersonal, and objective function—other numbers, forming a hierarchy in which the 25 "reference numbers" (or "master numbers") have, just as occurs in society, "client numbers" or "subordinates" that refer to them. This permits multiple choices and combinations, making it possible to bet on the number 11, the horse, as well as on the tenths 41, 42, 43, and 44 that form the "clientele network" corresponding to that bicho-number.[36]

In the same manner, the animals taken as the focus of the lottery afford multiple points of intersection and present to those addressing them their own particular way of being and their perspective or point of view vis-à-vis the world, for as "bichos" they can be "nice," "indifferent," "skittish," "intelligent," "friendly," "brave," "strong," "difficult," etc., depending on the circumstances or the bettors.

In fact, it could be said that the animal game reinstates what Eduardo Viveiros de Castro calls "perspectivism," that is, "the conception common to many Amerindian peoples of the continent, according to which the world is inhabited by different species of subjects or persons, human and nonhuman, who apprehend it according to distinct points of view" (1996:115).[37] As occurs in societies we classify as "primitive," "savage," or "backward," in the animal game, the "bichos" establish a particular position through which they also see the world. Since the "bichos" are amalgamated into an equally fixed set of numbers, these numbers are also the founders of perspectives. Thus, for the player in the animal game, the eagle, the donkey, the horse, the cat, and the butterfly—as well as the reference numbers 2, 3, 11, 14, and 4—form positions through which the world can be viewed, for each of these "beings" possesses personality and "culture."

On a more profound plane, the animal game (like fairy tales, jokes, and the domain of advertising) reveals a residual, implicit perspectivism ready to emerge under certain circumstances. When this occurs, the world is transfigured and the modern universe based on the compartmentalization, indifference, and mutual autonomy of diverse "kingdoms," "spheres," and "domains" that constitute it yields to a contiguous space in which animals, numbers, and objects—as well as the living and the dead—think, act, choose, speak, and offer their particular view of the world in a never-ending dialogue. Instead of taking "nature" as the common denominator of all things, as Western cosmology dictates, everything is turned upside down and "culture" is taken as a dimension shared by all. In the elegant formulation of Viveiros de Castro: "While [modern cosmologies] find their support in the mutual implications between the uniqueness of nature and the multiplicity of cultures . . . , the Amerindian conception would suppose, to the contrary, a unity of the spirit and a diversity of bodies. The 'culture' or the subject would be here the form of the universal; 'nature' or the object, the form of the particular" (1996:116).[38]

This residual or implicit perspectivism in the animal game is one more point to alert us against linear views of history, recalling Tocqueville's wise admonition by which the modern and the traditional must be read not in opposition or as superimposed strata but as complementary styles of life ready, in certain circumstances, to emerge as "two distinct humanities, each of which has its particular advantages and inconveniences, its goods and evils that are proper to it" (Tocqueville, [1840] 2000:675).

In this way, the animal game pairs exotic tigers and camels, lumbering elephants, elegant stags, and majestic eagles with prosaic ostriches and banal housecats, dogs, rabbits, donkeys, and cows to form an authentic Brazilian zoology. It is a system of beings categorized as nonhuman and unsupernatural—which in Brazil we classify as "bichos"—endowed with a will of their own and inhabiting an interstitial portion of reality. It is a jungle, a backland,[39] or a "nature" that exists and does not exist in empirical time and space and establishes with human beings links replete with motivations and presages.

Although it is interstitial and at the threshold, to use an expression of the greatly missed Victor Turner, such a series is endowed with greater reality than all the books on zoology in the library of the National Museum. Precisely because they constitute an arbitrary set and are operators between the abstract impersonal universe of numbers, the exotic and opaque world of animals, and the contradictory domain of society, culture, and the supernatural, the bichos of the animal game are profoundly Brazilian. And, because they are "bichos" and not mere animals, they interact in Brazilian fashion with us, appearing in our fantasies, numbers, and misfortunes.

As totems of a system intended to transform anonymous lives into destinies and possibly to subvert social hierarchies, the animals are in fact "bichos!"—in other words, fantastic beings capable of prodigious feats.[40] And in our "capitalism" there is no prodigious feat greater than transforming a poor man into a rich one.

IX

If we in the era of radio, newspapers, a sharp rise in urban population, and political transformation engender our totemism, American society, which was born modern, has also rediscovered an equally fantastic zoology and an equally totemic system, with its Mickeys, Donalds, Minnies, Plutos, Goofys, and Toms and Jerrys.

On November 28, 1928, Walt Disney introduced to American movie screens the cartoon *Steamboat Willy,* "starring" Mickey Mouse. The decade of the 1920s was rich with this fantastic American zoology, which debuted in 1919 with the enormous success of Felix the Cat, created by Pat Sullivan and Otto Messmer. Later, after 1940 and Disney's extraordinary success, came Tom and Jerry, from MGM, and the Looney Tunes cartoons from Warner Brothers, which had various talented directors who gave the public Porky Pig (1931), Bugs Bunny (1938), and the Road Runner (1949). These were characters, it should be mentioned, drawn as "tough, insolent, and challenging"— tough beings from the urban universe, capable of representing "biting satires and shameless slapstick," brimming with contemporary elements and even strong sexual allusions—in open contrast to the asexual innocence of the "forest," typical of Disney (Sandler, 1998:165ff.).

In America, though, animals are good not for gambling but for reinforcing a lauded and successful American way of life. There, the dominant animals are the duck, the cat, and the mouse, animals equally popular in European folklore, significantly absent (with the exception of the cat) from the Brazilian animal game. Furthermore, American society seems to have a decided preference for minimal pairs that exemplify opposing, unavoidable, and seemingly "natural" forms of conduct, as is the case of the extremely successful series "starring" Tom and Jerry. Created by William Hanna and Joseph Barbera, they were born on the trail opened by Disney and were produced by MGM. But there are differences too. Tom and Jerry, the cat and the mouse, perhaps because they represent characters all too emblematic, with rigidly defined personalities, engaged in self-contained dramas in which one always attacks and tries to destroy the other, as their respective "natures" demand, were unable to reproduce themselves, while the universe begun by Disney has transformed itself into a powerful film and amusement-park conglomerate.

In Disney's world, the reproduction of the original characters represented by Mickey Mouse and Donald Duck created a Disneyland. This totemic world is inhabited by more than a hundred characters who, emerging from that womb, invaded American society (and, through it, the world), becoming exemplars of various types of temperament, professions, situations, and modular emotional states. Thus, besides Mickey, Donald, Goofy, and Pluto, there are Huey, Louie, and Dewey (Donald's nephews); the chicken Clara Cluck; Horace Horsecollar, the horse; Clarabelle Cow (the cow); Pegleg Pete (a cat of bad character); Scrooge McDuck, the millionaire miser who enjoyed significant success in Brazil; the cat Figaro; Daisy, the girlfriend or wife—never the lover—of Donald; Morty and Ferdie, Mickey's young twin nephews; Fifi the Pekinese; the bulldog Butch, Pluto's enemy; the Big Bad Wolf; Practical, Fiddler, and Fifer, the Three Little Pigs—who represent work and the Protestant ethic, in opposition to the total and partial idleness that doesn't produce results in American culture; the famous Gyro Gearloose; the Li'l Bad Wolf; Butch, Mickey's friend; cousin Gus Goose; Grandma Duck (Donald's grandmother); April, May, and June, Daisy's young nieces; Zé Carioca (the parrot who represents the American reading of Brazilians and was Donald's friend); Ludwig Von Drake (Donald's wacky schoolmaster); Millie and Melody (nieces of Minnie, Mickey's girlfriend or wife); Mickey's Uncle Mortimer and Aunt Agatha; Gladstone Gander, the "Lucky Duck," and others. These characters, like real human beings, have a place of birth (the majority were born in Mouseton or Duckburg, U.S.A.); have nicknames and noms de guerre; relatives, girlfriends, and mascots: Pluto, for example, is Mickey's dog, and Bolivar, a St. Bernard, is Donald's. They enjoy special properties and roles. It is known that Donald Duck joined the American navy, leaving his nephews in the care of Uncle Scrooge, and that he has several devices destined for Gyro Gearloose's ingenious experiments; while Mickey has a boat called Queen Minnie, in honor of his girlfriend.

It is nevertheless curious, and important to observe, that in the two largest mass societies of the Americas these "totemisms" arise when the system transforms itself, intensifying automation and compartmentalization, and establishing more precise borders between nature and culture, especially in respect to the limits of exploitation of the natural world.

But it's necessary to point out certain differences, for the American "totemic system" appears more encompassing and universal than the Brazilian, which is more profound and localized.

The American system appears to converge with society, to act by linking a countless number of established social objects and institutions—like the nation-state, the states, football teams, and certain industrial products—to animals, plants, natural phenomena, and supernatural or protohistoric beings, reaching every sphere of social life, with pets interacting intensely on individual psychology, as if without such ties identities could not be constructed.

As proof of this encompassment, suffice it recall that U.S. states have a state flower and a state bird: for Alabama, the camellia and the yellow woodpecker; for Indiana, the peony and the cardinal; and so forth. Professional baseball, basketball, and football teams are equally "totemized," associating themselves with tigers (Detroit Tigers), giants (New York Giants), cardinals (St. Louis Cardinals), pirates (Pittsburgh Pirates), twins (Minnesota Twins), falcons (Atlanta Falcons), bulls (Chicago Bulls), fishes (Los Angeles Lakers), heat (Miami Heat), redskins (Washington Redskins), wild horses (Denver Broncos, Baltimore Colts), bears (Chicago Bears), eagles (Philadelphia Eagles), lions (Detroit Lions), Vikings (Minnesota Vikings), dolphins (Miami Dolphins), "Celts" (Boston Celtics), rockets (Houston Rockets), warriors (Philadelphia Warriors), pistons (Detroit Pistons), etc., as at least one observer of North American popular culture, Arthur Neal (1985),[41] has noted.

In America, totemism is so broad that it even takes in the national state and the Republican and Democratic parties, represented, respectively, by the eagle, the elephant, and the donkey, even reaching into some units of the armed forces, whose associations with natural phenomena—it is worth remembering—were the point of departure for an original interpretation of totemism done by the American anthropologist Ralph Linton in 1924, as Lévi-Strauss tells us. It was Linton's totemic experience that led him to suggest the relationship between natural emblem and social identity, when he reminded us that during the First World War he belonged to the Rainbow Division, a unit that brought together soldiers from the most diverse American states. The fortunate name of the division—"Rainbow," a beneficent meteorological phenomenon that, without prejudice, joins various colors and appeared in the sky when the unit arrived in Europe—eased the construction of a social identity capable of integrating people of different social origins, allowing them to rapidly distinguish themselves from others (Lévi-Strauss, 1963:7).

In the political field, the equating of the two major parties with the elephant and the donkey was a proposal by the political cartoonist Thomas Nast, beginning in 1874, when the combative journalist drew for *Harper's Weekly* an elephant that represented the massive Republican vote and, in 1880, created the donkey as symbol of the Democratic Party, based on the fact that Andrew Jackson (twice elected president of the United States) had been called a jackass in the campaign of 1828.[42]

To confirm the observation that no native is a good exegete of his own symbolic system, I should say that when I confronted this "political totemism" I asked various Americans—professors, staff at the University of Notre Dame, students, and even leaders of the Democratic Party in New York— about the origin and significance of that association; I ran into a well-known, proverbial, and irritating native ignorance that revealed that, after all, the historical does not contradict the structural. If no one knew the origin of the symbols, everyone could still infer their meanings, indicating how the elephant and donkey are good for thinking about certain "qualities" of the Republicans and the Democrats, read here, respectively, by their size, historical grandeur, impetus, fidelity to certain ideals, perseverance, etc. One need not be a Lévi-Strauss to arrive at the sophisticated conclusion that the list of distinctive characteristics is endless . . .

The American case reveals an extensive and convergent system capable of encompassing all social activities and quite particularly the area of imagery, such as advertising, the media, and cinema. But the animals of the American symbolic system are not "bichos," and because of this they lack the mysterious, magical side present in the fantastic fauna of Brazil.

In American totemism the animals are stripped of enchantment and belong to society, possessing names of their own, automobiles, relatives, clothes, residences, mascots, and political preferences.[43] They are protagonists of episodes that dramatize in caricatural fashion basic aspects of life as represented in America.

It is as if in the society of egalitarian creed, tending more toward the revisionist, the rebellious, and the anarchical than toward the utopian and the revolutionary, relatively unhampered by traditional points of reference (like titles of nobility, family names, professional hierarchies, and birth), animals had the role of anchoring the system, legitimating it through naturalization. In America, perhaps because of this, the animals are paradoxically the same: whether in nature, whether in culture.

So we have the exhibitionist, neurasthenic, ambitious, activist duck, whose rash actions lead him to frustration and failure; there is the mouse of super good character, inventive and endowed with initiative, who despite his size solves every problem; and the dog incapable of doing harm to anyone. The American, in spite of everything, is a naïf averse to self-criticism (see Moog, 1955: chapter 6).[44] There is also a systematic and revealing set (relatively absent in Brazil) of parallel enemies, seen as naturally complementary—the cat and the rat, the coyote and the roadrunner, the canary and the cat, the three little pigs and the big bad wolf, the dog and the cat, and, last but not least, the elephant and the donkey—in permanent combat, as if to confirm that, in both the illusory society in which they are basic characters and the empirical realm of nature from which they were symbolically torn, conflicts are spontaneous, instinctive, and, above all, inevitable, calling for disciplinary action and strict repression. All of these "Toms and Jerrys" sustain the "totemic American truth," by which the difference between a cat and a rat is an excellent means of thinking about the contrast between John and Mary (and, by extension, between superiors and inferiors, the shrewd and the stupid, the successful and the losers, those favorable to the state and those opposing it), who as husband and wife fight like cats and dogs.

Not to mention the legion of animals that represent ideal or model behavior, "natural" and "spontaneous" examples of loyalty, courage, perseverance, and altruism that people should simply and serenely emulate. Many of these animals emerged from the pages of books, drawings, and newspapers to become transformed into Hollywood stars, receiving, until 1969, the Patsy—the coveted Oscar of animals—and other honors for bravery and exemplary conduct. Among them, to demonstrate this intriguing American attraction to nature read as a wellspring of human individual exemplary conduct, we should mention the chimps Bonzo, Cheetah, Stubbs, Timmy, and Judy; the elephant Sydney; the goose Samantha; Sophie the seal; the mountain lion Sir Tom and the lion Jackie; the tigress Patrina; Steer the stag; the lions Elsa, Zamba, and Clarence; Arnold the pig and Ben the bear; Rhubarb the cat; Esmeralda the seal; the dolphin Flipper; the horses Flame, King Cotton, Mister Ed, Fury, and naturally Trigger; Francis the talking mule; the dogs Faro, War Winds, Kelly, Shaggy, Higgins, Tramp, Jasper, Cleo, Lord Nelson, and naturally the canine superstars Rin Tin Tin and Lassie (see Lee, 1970).

As we are speaking of a majority of dogs and horses, it is worth remembering that between horses and dogs on the one hand and cats on the other, the cats, with rare exceptions, had an inescapable utilitarian function as rat chasers, while the dogs and horses, by being multifunctional, transcended these roles, for that very reason capable of being transformed into symbols of servitude, a basic element of the "conspicuous consumption" characteristic of the "leisure classes" (Veblen, 1965:136ff.). In other words, Veblen dissociates dogs and horses from their respective economic, utilitarian pigeonholes by suggesting that their "value" resides in their being symbols of consumption for the "leisure classes," as models of respectability, beauty, servitude, and aristocracy.

Everything takes place as if the American "totemic system" were geared toward witnessing, supporting, and systematically confirming a *naturalization of society*—endowing people and human groups with a natural, universal, and irrefutable essence, as occurs with the identification of the national state with the eagle, political parties with the elephant and the donkey, automobiles with horses, sports teams and certain associations with bears, tigers, and lions—instead of a *humanization of nature,* when animals come to be endowed with divergent feelings and singular intentions that the players strive to translate and decipher, as seems to be the case with the animal game in Brazil.

The reduction to a natural essence is the final and definitive point of many arguments and situations in American culture in which the expression "natural" can be associated with any dimension of the system, especially when the ideal of equality also touches the realm of nature. From this stems the proliferation of animal protection societies, which in the Anglo world in general and the United States in particular has prevented mistreatment, averting the death of certain animals and creating singular contradictions, for in America there are horse races and greyhound races, but cockfighting is banned. There is an extensive citizenship, as Philippe Descola (1998) reveals, that is applied hierarchically to certain animals.[45] In this context, I must note that there are probably more than 120 million pet cats and dogs in the United States.

In addition, it is part of American culture to believe in the existence of certain ways of being, doing, thinking, eating, legislating, monitoring, reproducing, and relating as "more natural" than others. It is therefore good to insist once again on the point made earlier: centered on individualism and equality, American society leveled the organizational references that for centuries had ordered social relationships. Besides age, sex, and money—classificatory categories always in constant debate and redefinition—it is suggested that the best rules would be those in greater harmony with that "natural essence" behind the customs and the laws, which masks, hoodwinks, and deforms them. By manifestly rejecting, criticizing, or redefining home, family, clan, caste, name, and hereditary titles, American society tends to take nature as its behavioral matrix. A point, be it said, made by Ernst Troeltsch when he says, comparing and contrasting "Western" naturalist and essentialist universalism with German romanticism: "American democracy, in its political and social aspects, tends to issue in the strictest conservatism; it regards its principles [based on individualism, atomism, and the idea of progress] as eternal and divine commandments of morality and of law" (Troeltsch, 1950:204). This dimension—as Dumont shows (1980: appendix A)—appears clearly in American racism, when physical attributes are isolated, reified, and taken as symptoms of natural (and essential) tendencies, which would justify the establishing of inequalities in the bosom of a system founded on egalitarianism and also justify its very opposite: the hoax of a hierarchy imposed by differences of class, through the intermediary of an array of dualisms perceived as "natural." In this way, hierarchical questions of class are reduced or transformed into questions of race or gender in American society. In the United States there is less talk about rich and poor, about the powerful and the weak, than about "straight," "natural" differences between "black" and "white" and between "man" and "woman."[46]

As a consequence, the best customs—the laws and institutions capable of producing virtue and impelling society in the direction of progress and civilization—would be the most "natural." As the sociologist William Graham Summer would say: "The truth is that the social order is fixed by laws of nature precisely analogous to those of the physical order" (Sahlins, 1976a:103). Individualism and competition are natural tendencies, adopted through the customs of the society, which, from this perspective, merely replicates nature. This ideology is so deep-rooted that there is in American cultural anthropology a unique current, exclusive and successful, paradoxically called "cultural materialism," whose promise is to explain cultural facts by reducing them to their minimal natural (or material) components, obviously hidden and basic to any precise sociological understanding. From this perspective, the postpartum taboos of some South American indigenous societies, Aztec cannibalism, and the scared cows of India are institutions determined by the absence of protein and the need for fertilizer, as argue, respectively, John Whiting (1964) and Marvin Harris (1974, 1978).[47] In the field of "biopsychology," not to mention the "sociobiology" synthesized by Edward O. Wilson of Harvard, there are almost weekly announcements of the discovery of genes that explain, at their root, behaviors such as aggressiveness, selfishness, the logic of institutional "choice" culturally viewed as most appropriate, chemical dependency, certain mental disturbances, and even sexual tendencies (or, as it's put nowadays, preferences), all "mediated," as Sahlins (1995:8, and especially 1976a: chapter 4) says, "by the corporeal sense of pleasure or pain."

In contrast, "Brazilian totemism" does not deal with exemplary characters—protohuman and paranatural beings like Mickey, Donald Duck, or Bugs Bunny—who emerge in the expressive field of cinema, television, literature, the newspapers, and sports, those intermediate zones very appropriately called entertainment—but with singular subjects relatively distant from society: "bichos" such as "tiger," "stag," "donkey," "butterfly," "monkey," and "lion." These beings operate as a symbolic bridge to society but remain strange, possessing reasons unknown to mankind. Because of this, these "bichos" do not arise in the rational limpidity of cinema, in the context of a colorful spectacle, public and charging admission, with a preset time to begin and end, and encompassed by a contract: they appear mysteriously and unbidden, in dreams and coincidences. It is precisely in these zones beyond our control that the "bichos"—merging with numbers and with the dead—manifest themselves, which leads us to the evocation of old adages and almost forgotten knowledge, bringing to the surface the opaque side of our social history.

In Brazil, the system of the animal game is not destined only to glorify, caricature, confirm, or legitimate behavior but has as its objective offering passage to "another world," a threshold capable perhaps of sidestepping fate and providing a hoped-for change in social position. In so doing, it establishes the practice of wagers that, as occurs with rites of sacrifice, demands a concrete action—an "offering" of money—with consequences for the "sacrificer-bettor," who may become poorer or richer.

The animal game carries us beyond observation, by making us speak and attempt to hear the bicho-beings and their numbers, the objects of our hunches. Instead of doing like the Americans and amusing ourselves with the exaggeration, the clear and inescapable vanity, stupidity, or wisdom of the animals, in Brazil we convoke a certain array of animals chosen according to the contingencies of history, transforming the "bichos" into privileged interlocutors in the human task of producing meaning in life. That is to say, in Brazilian society, the animals listed in the game undergo a fundamental change and are submitted to a veritable rite of passage. Once initiated, they lose their biozoological domain to become one with numbers and thereby take on the profile of active, enchanted beings. So enchanted that they can change the course of our lives.

X

For all these reasons, we studied the animal game as a total institution.

It is not a matter of denouncing its organization but of revealing how that organization is coherent with the design of the activity: a modality of a game of chance driven by "bichos." These entities focus attention because they engender a double logic: they encompass numbers, naturalizing them, and they "numeralize" the animals, allowing their "culturalization." If lotteries depend on numbers only, the animal game rests, as Mauss (1990: 43–46) would say, on the "force" of the 25 totemic animals capable of embracing a whole universe of meaning. It is this force (and the "spirit" behind it) that promotes the circulation of wealth and, in an urban context that theories of the city declare to be devoid of humanity, evokes sympathy, loyalty, and honor—basic ingredients of gift-giving and receiving, sacrifice, vows, and reciprocity.[48]

For us, it is this encompassing system that molds the social and political organization of the animal game, not vice versa. In other words, without the idea of "bicho" and without the system formed by the animals that Brazilian ideology constructed and dramatized, it is impossible to understand an institution like the animal game. It is in fact the cosmology and the impeccable organizational system legitimated by it that guarantee and recognize the hierarchy among the bookies and link animals to numbers, numbers to numbers, and bookies to bettors. By modernizing social practices rooted in relationships of magical "force" between animals and numbers, this cosmology engenders immense confidence among bettors, imparting to the small slip of paper that proves the bet more value and more respect than an identity card or some new law that, after all, may or may not "catch on" as we say in Brazil. It is the belief in the bichos, and in the numbers with which they totemically associate, that incorporates all the activities of the game, from bettors to bookies and bankers.

If it is a dream that produces the hunch, guaranteeing the hope of winning and shaping the style of the wager, it is the belief in the honesty of the bookie that assures the actualization of the bets, which sets in motion the entire symbolic system. One dimension does not exist without the other, for what is the network of the animal game (an illegal but not illegitimated gambling system) if not a scheme of receiving and paying out of money with the same volatility and social invisibility of dreams and other sources of hunches? If the links between the player and the bichos are permeated by feelings of intimacy, they become concrete at the moment of the bet, when they are mediated by a system based on the honesty of the bookies.[49] These are accessible and popular "bankers" of the everyday world, who maintain with the gambler a relatively transitory link but one defined by deep loyalty and total confidence, because both share the same belief system and the same risk of playing an illegal lottery.

Between bookie and bettor a tie of some moral density is forged, similar to that which the player has with his intimate, domestic, or favorite bicho— the bicho that is the object of his hopes. It could be said, always inspired by Mauss, that it is the "spirit of the bicho" that, like a talisman, promotes the reincarnation of honor and reciprocity. In this sense, the "bichos" are the *hau*—the spirit—that, like ancient contracts, incarnate the relationship and the tie of reciprocity of the "productive virtue" between the bettor and the banker who centralizes wealth but, like Tlingit and Kwakiutl chieftains, is forced to destroy it through "charitable" redistribution. This is, in my view, the ideological base that produces acceptance of the banker as a "Maecenas."

As occurs in the art of hunting and in the rite of sacrifice, the act of playing the animal game opens the doors of a symbolism that reactivates mutual respect, interdependency, reciprocity, sympathy, and confidence as a critical fact of the world. From the moment one has the hunch till the moment of the bet, the gambler has the sensation of social distinction and the hope of gain, sentiments that the bet-taker sustains and confirms, treating everyone with "due respect," calmly listening to their hunches, suggesting with consideration and friendship the best method of "surrounding" the animal on which one is betting, and, in case there are winners, paying off religiously and honorably that to which they are entitled.[50]

Without this cosmology that links numbers and bichos, the bankers—modeled after the aristocratic values of Baron Drummond as rich people and therefore honest and charitable—would be culturally naked.[51] For what they really bank is a set of beliefs essential to the construction of Brazilian morality, which despite the supposed impersonality of the urban world, is widely reiterated in the intimacies and confidences that constitute an important part of Brazilian sociability. This is especially true in relationship to the construction of the person, that entity who, as I have shown throughout my work and have emphasized before, seeks both individual political rights as well as the respect, consideration, and moral dignity that are relational values. It is not a matter, therefore, of a defective society prone to easy gain, as some critics claim, but of a system that discerns the value of money as a privileged instrument for the construction of the "person." So the problem is not one of easy money, as Vianna Moog argues, but of an overly demanding conception of "person," which confirms the aristocratic ethos of the entire system.

Forbidding instead of domesticating the animal game is, therefore, an attempt to inhibit one of the rare mechanisms capable of linking house to street in Brazilian society. On the other hand, the animal game helps us better understand totemism itself. Which is paradoxical, because this comprehension is achieved through a modern, urban, national experience—a transformed lottery system—engendered by social change.

In truth, the totemism of the animal game is neither a tribal phenomenon, associated with an ingenuous projection of society onto nature, nor animism, nor a proof of mental confusion. On the contrary, what these identities of the animal game irrefutably reveal is that social institutions arise without asking the permission of sociological theories. What we have here is an authentic totemic system, but a totemism linked to a modern activity: a mass-directed lottery, a game that incorporates into its institutional whole a modern ideology of risk, of social mobility, and of making money. Endowed with an elaborate divination system and with a corresponding set of sacrificial practices, the game lets one win money that will effect a change in position in a highly hierarchized system. Now, gambling and risk are "modern" elements associated with the ideal of social mobility that is part of paid labor and of a system encompassed by the market and by equality of all in the eyes of the law. Furthermore, this totemism does not operate through the sustaining and legitimating of social groups in a cyclical, repetitive, anti-historical order, as occurs in tribal totemic systems, but expresses an ideal of rapid social change, by means of an activity that negates manual labor and reaffirms individual good fortune and mystical sagacity, having emerged in a historical setting marked by radical sociopolitical transformation.

From all this, it can be said that the totemism of the animal game is a "trans-" or "antihistorical" operator in the form of an ideology of hunches and predictive bets, without, however, ceasing to be a lever destined to create social mobility in the midst of a social organization relatively closed to vertical movement for most of its members, since it is mindlessly rooted in "superiors" (the "rich" or "those on top," those who have everything and don't need to play the animal game) and "inferiors": the "poor" or those on the bottom (who have nothing) and find themselves obliged to "chance it."

The presence of the animal game thus shapes a singular structure, demonstrating that in Brazilian society we have both a system of hierarchized, self-contained social categories—"pseudocastes" that, as Lévi-Strauss suggested, "represent themselves as natural species"—and "totemic pseudogroups": the bichos and numbers that reshape and redefine reality and "represent natural species as castes" (see Lévi-Strauss, 1966: chapter 4).[52] But we shall make a critical addendum surely unforeseen by Lévi-Strauss, for the animal game has as its objective precisely the "declassification" of people, potentially resulting in the disarranging of the framework of social categories set by laws of private property and by money, through its incessant creation of "new rich" and "new poor." In this deeper sense, it is an instrument for promoting transit between social categories whose position in the system is probably more rigid than our futile sociology supposes. And it is also an original code, able to integrate pseudototems, pseudocastes, or social sectors with the market by means of the random dance of numbers, the clever running of the bichos, and the ever rekindled hopes of sacrifices or wagers.

In any case, this essay attempts to disclose these symbolic components without ignoring their historical and social roots. Thus our effort at integrating the historical reconstruction of the emergence of the animal game with the structural elements of Brazilian society that, studied from a comparative angle and from a perspective that contemplates its universalism and singularity, allow discussing it as a popular invention of rare brilliance and provocative originality.

The animal game does justice to the immense creativity of the Brazilian people through what it distills of utopia and generosity, factors that probably explain why, like the cat it so admires, it has nine lives, despite police persecution, stupid, gross, and corrupt administrations, and a predatory elite that has always been more scoundrel than noble.

Roberto DaMatta
Jardim Ubá, Campos dos Goytacazes
and Notre Dame, July 1998

Behold, his lance held high, the knight errant,
Dom Aurelino Leal, the Javert of Gamboa,
Rather than do battle with exciting gambling,
He makes roasts of the bichos... He leads the "good wheel."

Brazilian newspaper *D. Quixote* (September 26, 1917)

(*A satire of Aurelino Leal, chief of police at the time.*)

CHAPTER 1

History and Sociology
of the Animal Game

The animal game is a modality of lottery very popular in Brazil, and it is known that currently close to 10 million Brazilians bet on a regular basis.[1] This lottery has the peculiarity of offering the bettor the possibility of wagering simultaneously on animals (bichos) or numbers. More precisely, the game establishes a link between a list of 25 bichos and a numerical series that is manipulated in order to form tenths, hundredths, and thousandths as well as a series of other objects—social and historical facts that, as we will see in greater detail later in this book, shape and inspire multiple betting possibilities.

The objective of this chapter is to offer a historical reconstruction of the animal game, seeking to clarify its origin and the sociopolitical context that gives it form, fame, and strength. In approaching the history of this modality of gambling, it is, however, worth noting a critical point to which we will return often in this book. The animal game, like many other popular Brazilian institutions, enjoys a dual root. On one hand, it has a clearly dated origin—a formal or "official" point of origin—and a recognized inventor. On the other, however, it is a game based on a system of hunches that is lost in time, founded as it is in dreams and other popular, relational, totemic elements that invoke an omnipresent, but seldom discussed, symbology of Brazilian society.

An examination of what has been researched and written about the "bicho" shows that the historical dimension has been the most investigated, probably because it revealed the most easily criticized aspects of the social order. The other side of the animal game, however, its expressive, symbolic, or dramatic dimension, has never been taken seriously by the majority of those interested in reflecting on this institution. As our objective is to explore the links between these dimensions, this chapter sets out to clarify the interrelationship between the history and the social meaning of the animal game.

The Creation of a Modern Zoo Looses the Animals

The animal game was created in 1882 by João Baptista Vianna Drummond (1825–1897), the future Baron de Drummond, who was at the time owner of the first zoo in Rio de Janeiro. Born in Itabira do Mato Dentro, in the state of Minas Gerais, João Baptista Vianna Drummond came to Rio de Janeiro while quite young, with the 3 *contos de réis* (a small fortune) that his father— a traditional "colonel" of Minas Gerais—had given to each of his fourteen children. Upon arriving at the royal court, he became active in business, dedicating himself, as the conventional wisdom of the time dictated, to importing cashmere and wines from Europe, in an office on Rua Primeiro de Março in the downtown area. His first success in the world of finance was, significantly, the fruit of speculation in the Rio stock market, an institution undergoing expansion and modernization at that time.[2]

After satisfying the ritual of being received at court, Drummond became part of the city's elite with his marriage to the daughter of the banker Gomes, an eminent figure of the period.[3] Drummond then went into public affairs. Friend and sometimes partner of the Baron of Mauá,[4] he became president of the company that founded the D. Pedro II railroad.

In 1872, when he bought a vast country estate at the edge of the Engenho Novo mountain range, Drummond began the project that was to bring him immortality. The piece of land had been part of the Fazenda do Macaco, belonging to Her Majesty the Empress Duchess of Bragança, who had received it as dowry upon marrying D. Pedro I, who by then was deceased. One year after acquiring the property—he was one of the first to invest in the real estate business—he founded the Companhia Arquitetônica, an enterprise whose objective was creation of the city's first planned residential area: the Vila Isabel district.

Challenging and redefining the traditional Portuguese architectural concept by which streets should be narrow so that two-story houses could provide shade, Drummond—with the help of the engineer Bittencourt da Silva—planned a residential space based on opposite principles. Vila Isabel would be a residential zone of wide avenues, obviously inspired by the Parisian boulevards that Drummond had just visited.[5]

As if to signal formally its modernity, the new district would be born marked by the abolitionist militancy of which Drummond was part; from this came the name Vila Isabel and the names of its thirteen streets, all identified with personalities engaged in the struggle for liberation of the slaves.

The Vila Isabel project was unquestionably modern and ambitious. It was intended that the district would offer a complete infrastructure of urban and leisure accommodations. To connect the new area to downtown, Drummond planned the Vila Isabel Railroad Company. Also in the original plan of the district was the construction of a mother church, a central square, and a sizable park for the leisure of residents.

The first auction for public sale of lots in Vila Isabel took place in 1874, but the great attraction of the district would come only in 1888, with the founding of the Zoological Park of Vila Isabel, an undertaking in planning since 1884, with the drawing up of an agreement between the Rio de Janeiro city council and the firm led by Baron de Drummond.[6] In fact, of the total area owned by Drummond, three hundred thousand square meters was set aside for the installation of the zoo, which, according to the ambitious initial plan, in addition to exhibiting rare and exotic animals, would also bring together Brazilian scholars to research and offer courses about the native flora and fauna.

When the zoo was inaugurated, Drummond—like a typical Brazilian promoter—brought into play his strategic relationship with the crown in an effort to mobilize state resources to ensure the financial viability of his undertaking, aware of the high costs of maintaining a zoological garden (Pereira de Mello, 1989:56). At that time (1888), the Chamber of Deputies was beginning to draft the budget for 1889, and Drummond requested a subsidy, for in the initial years the zoo was struggling to maintain itself. Like a story that would be repeated often in Brazil, the saga of the baron's zoo shows how it is easier to found and inaugurate ambitious institutions like museums, parks, libraries, cultural centers, art galleries, and universities than to support their expensive, demanding routines.

As Renato Pacheco, author of a pioneering anthology of the animal game, said:

The Zoo, in their words, had been inaugurated shortly before, but was threatened with closing its doors because of lack of resources. They requested "a modest subsidy." They declared, as basis for the request, that the Zoo society had enriched the Museum "with samples of all the animals that die in the establishment, that it attempted to import thoroughbred domestic animals to promote the improvement of the country's several species, and that it would construct a building devoted to periodic exhibits of domestic animals, horticulture, floriculture, and agriculture" (Pacheco, 1957:82).[7]

Just two months later, on August 14, another petition, this time bearing only Drummond's signature, took the liberty of reminding the Chamber where to find resources for his zoo without burdening the public coffers, by suggesting the use of moneys generated by games of chance to finance economically important or noble causes, as was (and continues to be) a common practice in Brazil and other countries.[8]

This was the most important part of the baron's petition:

> There are at present in the city several racing tracks at which the movement of wagers rises to thousands of *contos de réis* annually, returning ten percent of the gross revenue to the associations. Would it not be possible to establish that, of that ten percent, one or two percent be earmarked for religious establishments or those of recognized public service, like the Zoological Garden? A not insignificant amount would thus be obtained without burdening the taxpayer, for only gambling, which it is in our interest to repress, would be taxed (Pacheco, 1957:82).

Despite the imagination, the "modernity," and the political timing of the proposal, the budget committee of the Chamber of Deputies did not fully accept the suggestion, but it softened its refusal with the sum of 10 *contos de réis* annually, under the rubric of expenditures on agriculture. The year 1888 was, therefore, positive for Drummond's undertaking, for besides having obtained a subsidy, he ceased to be the citizen João Baptista Vianna Drummond and entered the world of nobility with the title of the Baron of Drummond, granted by royal decree.

This fact obviously attests to his prestige vis-à-vis the crown. Thus, in the month of October 1889, Baron de Drummond was celebrated and lionized in newspapers by José do Patrocínio, who wrote a celebratory note in his newspaper, the famous *Jornal da Cidade do Rio*. In the note, in unquestionable poetic-laudatory rhetoric, José do Patrocínio revealed unconditional admiration for the baron and also expressed the thinking of his time when he depicted Drummond as a successful agent—a true example—of the modernization to which all the Rio elite aspired.

It is worth reproducing in its entirety:

> The baron of Drummond, young and slender, loved by both men and women, arrived in Minas one day, saw, and conquered the square.
>
> He took it by storm, like any battleground.
>
> In alliance with the then king of the square, the banker Gomes—the baron of Drummond conquered the Stock Market with the same ease with which he won hearts. He prevailed.
>
> As banker, let all the sick who took him prescriptions from Dr. Valladão speak of his affability. There was never a more amiable pharmacist, nor one quicker to fill prescriptions.
>
> Finally, he left the square, leaving behind an unalterable nostalgia for his honesty and friendliness.
>
> He left the square, ready to rest.
>
> But the baron of Drummond admits no rest. To him, everything is possible in this world. Rest? Never!
>
> So he founded the Vila Isabel Company.
>
> What the Vila Isabel Company has been, everyone knows: a lovely, prosperous enterprise, whose soul is the baron of Drummond.
>
> But Vila Isabel was not enough for his active life.
>
> He founded the Zoological Park.
>
> Tired of dealing with men, he began, still in the service of men, to deal with animals. He gathered them, classified and caged them and—the Zoological Park was born, one of the greatest services to the city of Rio de Janeiro in recent times.
>
> He now lives for it.
>
> For it, and for the Avenue.
>
> For 4th Avenue, his great dream. An enormous dream, an admirable dream: to open in Rio de Janeiro's monotony and irregularity a wide street, open to the sun, healthy, a street to which to take the civilized foreigners who visit us, a street that attests to our love of hygiene.
>
> It is no surprise that this is his favorite dream and his sole objective today.
>
> Well may he dedicate himself to opening an avenue in the city, this man who has done no less than open in the nation the broad avenue of the progress of civilization.[9]

The period in which the baron and the zoo enjoyed official subsidy was, however, short-lived. With the proclamation of the republic in 1889, such aid came to be seen as monarchical favoritism and was summarily suspended as part of the efforts at consolidation of the new regime, whose agenda was transformative and authoritarian.

Curiously, and perhaps as a quintessentially Brazilian means of compensation, in 1890 the city council of Rio de Janeiro signed a new agreement with the Zoological Park Enterprise. In general terms, the new contract was similar to the earlier one, except for one crucial item. This clause was to change the history of gambling in Brazil, for the new contract gave the baron the right to establish and exploit, within the confines of the Zoological Park, "licit public games," subject obviously to fiscal oversight.[10]

Soon after the dizzying proliferation of lotteries and other gaming that followed the proclamation of the republic, in July 1892 the baron instituted a kind of drawing involving his animals—it was the so-called "animal drawing," whose objective was to alleviate financial difficulties the zoo was experiencing. The fact was announced in several Rio newspapers. Thus, the *Jornal do Brasil* commented in its edition for July 4, 1892:

> As a means of encouraging attendance by the public, rendering more frequented and well known this establishment that honors its founder, the firm has organized a daily prize that consists of drawing from among 25 animals in the Zoological Park one name, which will be sealed in a wooden box at 7 a.m. and opened at 5 p.m. and announced to the public. Each person whose admission ticket depicts the selected animal wins a 20$ prize. . . . The first drawing was held yesterday, with the prize going to the Ostrich, which yielded a total pool of 460$000.[11]

The newspaper *O Tempo,* in its edition for July 6 of the same year, stated:

> Besides this, the firm has decided to establish a 20$ prize by means of an original drawing. Upon entering the zoo, each person will receive, for 1$, a ticket indicating one of the 25 animals in the zoo. Atop a post 5 meters high, in a sealed box, will be placed a picture representing one of the animals, and whoever has the ticket will receive the prize.

And, as if to boast of the institution's modernity, the newspaper added:

The firm deposits, as a guarantee of payment of the prizes, 10$500 in a bank. Streetcar service is going to be increased, thus affording more comfort to the public.

On the 5th, the same newspaper stated, more descriptively:

Several amusements were inaugurated yesterday at the Zoological Park, among them the animal drawing, which has as its goal to stimulate attendance at the establishment. The drawing consists of the following: from among 25 animals chosen by the Firm, one is drawn each day and put into a box when the sale of tickets begins. At five p.m., at a given signal, the box is opened and the person with the ticket bearing the name and picture of the animal wins it as prize.

With this drawing, the baron achieved two basic results. First, he made use of official permission to establish games in his zoo, an item that the second agreement with the government had granted him. Second, he followed the suggestion of the Mexican Manuel Ismael Zevada, who banked a certain "flower game" from a house in downtown Rio de Janeiro (at the corner of Ouvidor and Gonçalves Dias), sagely adapting it to his undertaking.[12]

But of what did this failed "flower game" consist? In it there were also 25 flowers, arranged in alphabetic order, to which corresponded 25 numbers, drawn daily.[13] One could play the hibiscus (*aurora*), the pansy (*amor-perfeito*), the rosemary (*alecrim*), the moonflower (*boa-noite*), the camellia (*camélia*), the carnation (*cravo*), the hydrangea (*hortênsia*), the jasmine (*jasmim*), the lily (*lírio*), the magnolia (*magnólia*), the daisy (*margarida*), the violet (*violeta*), the rose (*rosa*), and the strawflower (*sempre-viva*), to cite the more popular ones. As would happen in the future animal game, bets were made on the flowers or on numbers corresponding to them. But the flower game never enjoyed the success hoped for by its creator.

Manuel Ismael Zevada then proposed an adaptation of the flower game: an "animal game" to be held at the Zoological Park as a way of attracting the public and generating income for the maintenance of the animals. To Baron de Drummond this suggestion was the encouragement he needed to put in motion a type of game that was to profoundly affect life in Brazil. This supports our contention that the animal game is the direct descendant of the flower game.

The novelty introduced by the baron, however inspired, was a mere transposition of the relatively static, contemplative kingdom of flowers to the fleet, motional universe of animals. Because animals are, among other things, more dynamic than flowers, whose existence in the social world is docile and passive,[14] the baron related two series that were opposite but symbolically very rich in evocative and symbolic power: numbers and animals, which, conjoined, formed the matrix for our animal game.

The adaptation of the collection of flowers to the collection of animals gave rise to the list of 25 bichos so well known throughout Brazil to this very day:

1 = ostrich (*avestruz*); 2 = eagle (*águia*); 3 = donkey (*burro*); 4 = butterfly (*borboleta*); 5 = dog (*cachorro*); 6 = goat (*cabra*); 7 = sheep (*carneiro*); 8 = camel (*camelo*); 9 = snake (*cobra*); 10 = rabbit (*coelho*); 11 = horse (*cavalo*); 12 = elephant (*elefante*); 13 = rooster (*galo*); 14 = cat (*gato*); 15 = crocodile (*jacaré*); 16 = lion (*leão*); 17 = monkey (*macaco*); 18 = pig (*porco*); 19 = peacock (*pavão*); 20 = turkey (*peru*); 21 = bull (*touro*); 22 = tiger (*tigre*); 23 = bear (*urso*); 24 = stag (*veado*); 25 = cow (*vaca*).

Everything indicates that this list brought together animals from the baron's zoo and others that peopled the Western and Brazilian social imagination, like the dog, the cat, the horse, the donkey, the cow, the rooster, the pig, and the butterfly. These, although endowed with great relational or symbolic value, permeating dreams and sacred texts, would hardly be an attraction in any zoo. The final result, surely based on an implicit or unconscious selection process, was a very rich set that goes from well-known animals totally dependent on us (the domesticated) to those that, enjoying autonomy from human society and being "ferocious" or "wild," can only be seen in books or abroad. If the former, as Sir Edmund Leach (1983) has discerned, are close at hand, precisely because of that they enjoy exemplary ambiguity and formidable evocative power; the latter, because they are far away, are marked by the no less allusive idea of the exotic and constitute the principal actors of the spaces reserved for their display, admiration, and, nowadays, conservation—zoos.

It is impossible to know how the baron drew up the definitive list of "his" bichos, but we do know that in the zoo he founded, the animals were housed in cages of different sizes. There were large cages for the lions, the tigers, the leopards, and the hyenas, as well as ample aviaries with toucans, hummingbirds, parrots, eagles, and other birds. Obeying the paradoxical modern technique of manufacturing artificial "natural environments," in the vicinity of the cages was constructed the supposed ecological niche of the animals' origins. The crocodiles had their lake, the tapir its pond with sugar-cane plume-grass, and the swans their royal water lily. There were also flower-boxes and fruit trees from the most diverse regions for the other animals. The attractions were many. The public could watch the distribution of meat to the lions and tigers, see the dance of the trained elephant, and amuse itself with the acrobatics of the monkeys and macaques—which in a Rio flourish featured the then famous monkey Sofia.[15] On Sundays there was music, a carrousel, and stands with sweets (Paraguassu, 1954:28).

To all these attractions was added the novelty of the "animal drawing." In the vivid description of Camilo Paraguassu, one of the rare memoirists of the animal game, confirming the newspaper articles of the time:

One day, the admission tickets to the Zoological Park appeared with the figure of a bicho and the following words (approximately): "If the figure of the bicho contained on this ticket matches that on the blackboard to be found in the interior of the Park, the bearer will receive twenty times the cost of his ticket." I saw, and held in my hand many times, those tickets.[16]

There were 25 bichos and the blackboard atop a wooden post standing in a tree-lined walk, to the left just past the entrance to the Park, under lock and key, was opened at five in the afternoon.

The baron himself put the figure of the bicho on the board. He would arrive at six a.m. and with the help of servants bring down the board, amid the greatest secrecy place the figure of the day's bicho on it, lock up the board, and order it hoisted again, after which he would withdraw. In the afternoon, around five o'clock, he would return, have the board brought down, and open it so the selected bicho would appear. The board was raised once again and the onlookers, the visitors to the Park, applauded and commented warmly, as is common among our people. Many inspected their tickets to see if the figure stamped on them was identical to that appearing on the board; but there were some who paid not the slightest attention to the tickets (Paraguassu, 1954:37).

After a certain initial indifference, the game at the zoo began to attract real crowds. So many people showed up that the streetcar companies created by the baron were inadequate to the task of transporting the visitors. Little by little, the promotion born as a means of attracting the public became an end in itself, and many of those who flocked to the Zoological Park's ticket offices had scant interest in the spectacle offered by the animals; their objective was to risk some money on the "animal drawing."

Within a short time after its creation, the animal game was already a phenomenal success:

> After three months in existence, the game was already yielding an extremely reasonable profit. *What botany had not profited Zevada, zoology was beginning to give,* for in a single Sunday close to eighty *contos* of tickets were sold, as admissions! At that time several men were working in the box offices and the number of gatekeepers was quadrupled (Costa, 1938, vol. 3:892–894; italics added).

The popularity of the game and the workmanlike way of executing the drawing of the bicho, done personally by Baron de Drummond himself, gave rise to buttonholing visitors hoping for a revelatory "tip."

A popular column of the time notes that he would respond to the insistent visitors in a mocking tone that evinced an intelligence in tune not only with the "savage mind" but with the ambiguity of Brazilian symbology. So when people asked, half seriously and half derisively, "What bicho is it going to be today, Baron?" he replied provocatively, "It's going to be the bicho that's most like a woman." Everyone bought the butterfly and it was the snake (Paraguassu, 1954:39).

From Drawing to Betting: From Visitor to Gambler

Historical research shows that the institutionalization of the drawing of bichos at the zoo went through two stages. At first, the game was a simple, innocent drawing. Visitors would arrive at the zoo and did not select the bichos that appeared on their tickets, for the bicho-admission relationship did not depend on the buyer's choice but on the order in which the tickets were sold. For example, suppose that each day a booklet of six hundred admissions was sold. In that booklet there would be 25 bichos representing the possibilities of winning the prize. Thus, each bicho would appear twenty-four times in the booklet.[17]

Each ticket conferred the right to compete for a prize at the end of the afternoon. The role of bettor-gambler was subordinated to that of visitor to the zoo, for visiting it led to the drawing, which consequently made the visitor a residual gambler when he acquired a ticket. At this stage of the evolution of the animal game there was no choice, and no such thing as a winner-bettor. There was only a visitor with an admission ticket, and a drawing.

Quickly, however, the spirit of the drawing was transformed, giving rise to the possibility of choosing the bicho at the time of purchasing admission. This is shown in an official correspondence of July 1892 sent to the chief of police by his second in command, in which, initiating the long and futile persecution of the lottery, he argues:

> In an effort to attract visitors to the Zoological Park, he [the baron] asked the director of public recreation for a permit, which was granted by the police, in view of the misleadingly innocent nature that could be deduced from the simple original description of the amusement. Nevertheless, once put into practice, this diversion has been verified to have the scope of true gambling, manifestly forbidden. The tickets sold contain the purely random hope of a prize in money, and the bearer of the ticket only wins the prize if he is lucky enough to guess the species of animal that is raised to the top of a pole. This diversion, prejudicial to the interests of the unwary, who in the deceptive hope of an uncertain gain naively let themselves be led astray, is precisely a true game of chance because wins and losses depend exclusively on fortuity and luck. As such an amusement cannot be long tolerated, and because many complaints have been lodged by persons adversely affected, I shall thus order the head of the Zoological Park to immediately suspend operation of said game, on pain of prosecution under Articles 369 and 370 of the penal code (see *O Tempo* for July 23, 1892).

In this second phase, the role of visitor became subordinated to that of gambler. As a consequence, a trip to the zoo became separate from the pleasure of the drawing, for an individual could now go to the zoo not to visit an educational site or one of leisure but simply to try his luck at the game. This change in focus allows characterization of the activity presided over by the baron as a game of chance and no longer a simple drawing, for what characterizes it is, among other things, the intervention of choice and the consequent linking of the bettor-gambler to a number (or, in this case, to a bicho) of his free choosing. This possibility of choice marks the activity as "gambling": an institution dominated by "luck" and/or by "chance."

As several authors have shown (Costa, 1938; Pacheco, 1957; Cavalcanti, 1940; Paraguassu, 1954; and Pereira de Mello, 1989), the possibility of choosing a ticket (and a bicho) denotes a stage in which visitors come to take part in the game in more active form. In this stage, therefore, the visitors-bettors arrive at the zoo's box office and immediately request: "Give me a cow, five crocodiles, three rabbits, two cats, etc.," indicating the motivation of the bettor fed by the excitement of the wager and of possible gain. This transformation can be seen in the innumerable requests for "tips" from the baron.

Between 1892 and 1894 the animal game went through what we might call its infancy or "amateur phase." Relevant features of this phase are the fact of the game being restricted to the confines of the zoo; the fact of the running of the game being in the hands of the baron, who was solely responsible for choosing the "bicho of the day"; and, finally, the fact of this type of lottery being legal.

It is worth reemphasizing that in this period there was an intense proliferation of lotteries and drawings that came to be a veritable craze in the city of Rio de Janeiro.[18] Among these multiple forms there would once again appear a modality similar to the animal game and its ancestor, the flower game. It was the game of foods (see Cabral, n.d.).

As the name indicates, the game of foods equated numbers to items found at the grocer's. Such a lottery was associated with the fact that the grocers were the first to distribute the animal tickets outside the zoo. With a sharp commercial sense and having observed the popularity of that lottery, they tried to take advantage of the rage and invented a game that they themselves could bank.

In the game of foodstuffs, a person could bet on "birdseed" (*alpiste*), "garlic" (*alho*), "olive oil" (*azeite*), "rice" (*arroz*), "sugar" (*açúcar*), "lard" (*banha*), "cinnamon" (*canela*), "coffee" (*café*), "beans" (*feijão*), "tobacco" (*fumo*), "flour" (*farinha*), "corn" (*milho*), "tapioca powder" (*polvilho*), "bacon" (*toucinho*), "candle" (*vela*), and "vinegar" (*vinagre*), to mention the best-known items.

Like the flower game, however, the game of foodstuffs—perhaps because it was not truly a "game of food"[19]—did not have the same popularity as the animal game and gradually disappeared. But it is interesting to note that these modalities of gambling—the flower game, the food game, and the animal game—all had exactly the same format: 25 elements in alphabetical order, associated with 25 numbers laid out in a continuum starting with zero.

In this context it is worth citing what Oswaldo Cabral said about this modality of gambling, explaining its lack of popularity:

> Several variants were tried or launched, without any great success . . . the public did not accept them—for "the animal game" must have bichos...
>
> It is indeed true that among such "nourishing genres" are some that clearly do not belong on the list because no one feeds on tobacco, soap, or candles... the attempt was ridiculed—and made no headway.

With his customary perspicacity, Cabral puts his finger on the critical point:

> It is probable, however, that as a factor of success such variants may have lacked the possibility of the "hunch," which as we shall see below has always constituted the greatest spur to attraction to the animal game. Who would have a hunch about the jasmine or tapioca powder?
>
> It is hard to dream about such things; it is impossible to discover them in the sky or link them to any accidental factor. Not so with bichos. We dream about them and about facts connected to them. In the sky, clouds take the form of sheep, lions, and camels—but never of tapioca, peanuts, garlic, camellias, or touch-me-nots... It would be as difficult to get a hunch about a flower or some type of staple goods as it is easy to obtain one about a mammal or bird.

Because of all this, the "food game" perished during this feverish phase of gambling in Rio, when, upon finding themselves formally free and equal, the people of Rio de Janeiro seem to have used the game as yet another expression of their new political status.

After this first stage, however, the nature of the animal game began to change. In fact, in the period from 1894 to 1895 the baron's game became so popular that many started visiting the zoo with the sole objective of speculating on the prize. The game now began to constitute an end in itself, as in this phase the public visited the zoo's cages with the ambiguous goal of seeing the captive animals and of "hitting." Paradoxically, bichos began running free in the imagination of urban Rio.

Without doubt, the most important fact of this period is the rise of middlemen, who, taking advantage of the popularity of the baron's game, begin to "bank"—i.e., finance—the animal game on their own initiative, creating a primary organizational network for the game and its fans. It is not known whether such middlemen were or were not working for the baron. But it can be stated that they formed a small legion that led the animal game to compete directly with the system of federal lotteries then being transformed into an activity coordinated by the national treasury. Thus, doubtlessly, the official prohibition of the animal game as early as 1895, while still in its infancy, by Decree No. 133 (the snake).

But, as occurs with everything that is forbidden, the animal game had already taken hold of the city. In the words of one columnist:

> The animal game caught on with the public, but the business of going to the Zoological Park every day was tiring.
>
> One day a sundries merchant (ah! The good old days!... today, all the grocery stores are "bars"...) decided to bank the game with his own money! There were sales records such as: "Butter, half a kilo; soap, one bar; vinegar, one bottle; broom, one; toothpicks, one box and ten *tostões* on the turkey, five hundred *réis* on the snake, and three hundred *réis* on the monkey." But it wasn't just one merchant, it was many!... From the Pharoux docks to Copacabana; from Ponte dos Marinheiros to Santa Cruz; from Santa Teresa to Pedregulho; barber shops, bars, notions stores—all had their agents; there were printed tickets and, in the afternoon, telephones transmitted the results of the drawing at the Zoological Park, which were also printed in the morning newspapers (Paraguassu, 1954:40).

But, as the site of the drawing was still the baron's zoo, many spectators bought large numbers of tickets at the park and waited outside for the announcement of "what bicho hit," thereby intermediating gambling. On the other hand, because the tickets could be resold anywhere in the city, the game began to demand an organization of its own. Thereby was created the figure of the go-between or bookmaker,[20] who bought large quantities of admissions and banked the game on his own, by forming a private clientele (Cavalcanti, 1940:65).

The innovation promoted by bookmakers made betting easier and allowed people to play without leaving their neighborhoods and residences, which all but eliminated the baron's spatial monopoly, for it was no longer necessary to journey to the zoo. Such a possibility also gave rise to another typical characteristic of the animal game, namely that of the middle class playing from the comfort of their homes, without venturing outside or putting themselves at risk. It was no longer necessary to get dressed or wait till nightfall, as was the case when they wanted to go to a casino or to the Jockey Club. If they desired, they could hire a boy who, among other things, would pick up the goods at the grocery and place his patrons' wagers on the animal game.

Another important piece of information from this phase is the reputed renting of space at the zoo to a well-known gambling promoter, Sr. Luiz Galvez. This leasing was apparently done without the prior knowledge of the Chamber or of the mayor's office, taking place in the period when the games at the zoo were becoming more noticeable, in 1894 and 1895 (Pereira de Mello, 1989:62).

The "Bichos" Organize

But we must not forget that, like any good promoter, the baron remained active, banking his agents who sold tickets in the city (Cavalcanti, 1940:65). Perceiving the irreversible success of the game, he opened offices in several places in Rio de Janeiro and, through his agents, expanded the game into various commercial locations, affording businessmen the opportunity to sell large numbers of tickets. In this franchise deal, the businessmen earned about 50 *mil-réis* per day, a good amount of money at the time. The idea probably originated with Sr. Galvez, who thereby contributed to the first "professionalization" of the animal game.

It is very likely that between 1894 and 1895 the animal game was exploited by three groups: (a) the "baron's agents," (b) the independent bookmakers (who possibly also sold other modalities of lottery), and (c) businessmen in general, who "banked" the wagers with their own money or received a commission on the sale of tickets. Thus various centers for the animal

game arose, and consequently the coexistence of several drawings. There
was, obviously, the drawing at the baron's zoo, but alongside it were many
other modalities for determining the "bicho of the day." This is confirmed by
the fact that variations of the baron's game came into being in other parts of
the country.

In the southern state of Rio Grande do Sul, for example, the game
adapted itself to local peculiarities, giving rise to a list of bichos which began
with the tiger and ended with the eagle and in which 24 was the number not
of the stag but of the rooster. This is the Rio Grande do Sul list:

> 1 = tiger; 2 = turkey; 3 = dog; 4 = ostrich; 5 = deer (*cervo*); 6 = stag; 7 =
> bull; 8 = horse; 9 = cat; 10 = ewe (*ovelha*); 11 = rat (*rato*); 12 = camel;
> 13 = pig; 14 = donkey; 15 = rabbit; 16 = monkey; 17 = armadillo (*tatu*);
> 18 = lion; 19 = dove (*pombo*); 20 = elephant; 21 = giraffe (*girafa*); 22 =
> bear; 23 = goat; 24 = rooster; 25 = eagle.

The deer, the ewe, the rat, the armadillo, the dove, and the giraffe are
not part of the definitive list that was accepted throughout the country. As
Oswaldo Cabral, who studied this southern variant of the game, demonstrates, dreaming about one of these animals would lead the player to check
the corresponding entry on the baron's list, which shows that the baron's list
of bichos was a point of reference as the official, oracular list.

There are records also that in the state of Espírito Santo, at the beginning of the century, there was not only an animal game but also games with
flowers, with fruit, with birds, and with tontines (a form of association in
which the capital of members who die passes to the surviving members).
And in Diamantina, in the interior of Minas Gerais, the animal game had already made inroads by 1895, as attested to by the acute observations of Helena Morley, anticipating contradictions between the role of the game and
the bookies, a political and moral hornets' nest that remains unsettled to the
present day:

> Yesterday Bibiana held a farewell piano dance for us. Besides her cous-
> ins, two bookmakers were there. João Antônio told us that we shouldn't
> pay much attention to them, as bookmakers in Rio de Janeiro are very
> discredited. But I told him: "What does that matter? They may be dis-
> credited there, but they have a lot of standing here and therefore we

can't treat them badly, because they're such nice young men. Besides that, only since they've been in Diamantina have we seen any movement of money. Before the animal game everybody was flat broke. What a fine invention that game is!" (Morley, 1971:262).

We also find mention of an animal game in the state of Pará in 1924 (see Pacheco, 1957). Another example of its rapid penetration is a prophetic and, in the atmosphere of power in Brazil which later would link bankers and politicians, not unexpected list arising in the state of Santa Catarina, as early as 1898, which equated the 25 bichos with politicians and public personalities. Columnists of the period indicate that in Santa Catarina, a setting crisscrossed by roads, bookies would go from house to house in long treks from early morning till late afternoon to take their customers' bets. Often, to hasten the process, they would travel by bicycle. As is typical of the animal game, the results would become known promptly by five o'clock, by telegram, perhaps directly from Rio de Janeiro, headquarters for a kind of high command of the game, which released the results along with those of the legal lotteries.

The notable fact about all these variants is, without doubt, the issue of confidence in the "bosses" of the game. This credibility allows people to bet without harboring the suspicion that if they win the bookies won't honor their obligation.

In a way, this intriguing "credibility equation" must be somehow related to the game's founder, the promoter João Baptista Vianna Drummond, who was a noble, a baron of the empire. But how to explain its permanence when the baron was replaced by a network of clandestine financiers?

After the outlawing of the animal game, the astuteness of the new leadership lay in linking the result of the game to legal numbers—whether the results of legal lotteries, the revenue of the customs house, also published daily, or any other trustworthy number in the public domain.

This was in flagrant opposition to the elementary system of the so-called "little box" game, which had certain characteristics in common with the baron's. In both cases, a single person determined the "bicho of the day" and the result was kept in a location under lock and key in view of the bettors. This was often a compartment behind a portrait of the baron, which guaranteed honesty through proximity to the sanctified founder of the game; or the box belonging to the owner of the establishment. In general, the result was displayed on a blackboard situated atop a pole or on the roof. Thus the result was in sight but out of everyone's reach, in a spot where it could be watched and protected.

Despite these precautions, there was always suspicion of "crookery" in the "little box" game. We will return to this point in the next section, in which we study the sociology of the game. For now, it is worth rementioning the plasticity demonstrated by the animal game, for neither its official interdiction nor the campaigns of repression that were to follow prevented its spreading to the farthest corners of the country.

Another curious example of inventive adaptation took place in Nova Trento (Santa Catarina). There, as Oswaldo Cabral again reveals, the animal in the little box was replaced by a stone drawn at random from a keno set.

All these data, especially the local variations, attest to the animal game's formidable vertical and horizontal penetration into Brazilian society and also help us to understand how it has incorporated itself into local habits, undergoing adaptations but always finding a place in the heart of the populace.

A frequent means of obtaining a trustworthy and satisfactory result for the bettors was linking the result of the animal game to official lotteries, a vivid example of the imaginative use of official institutions by the people.

At that juncture, however, the immense success of the animal game was beginning to predispose the authorities against it. In fact, since 1894 the proliferation of games of chance had begun to constitute a "problem" for the republican authorities, who planned to make use of the tendency to wager as a source of revenue through institutionalization of a federal lottery.

Gambling has always been present in society, but when the republic was proclaimed and the egalitarian creed and the ideal of individual freedom were adopted as the basis of citizenship the activity expanded considerably, coming to the awareness of the elites as a social problem meriting discussion, regulation, and control.

Of all the phenomena associated with the spread of gambling in the nation's capital, the bookmaking houses, probably because of their visibility, were the principal target of political repression. Thus, in mid-1894, the first assistant police chief of the Federal District investigated the activities of these houses with the intent of separating establishments that had authority to sell pools on horse- and footraces—which were classified as "leisure games"—from those that dealt with any type of raffle or lottery, including the animal game, by broadening their field of action without breaking the law.

This trickery would give rise to a typically elitist attitude, as was observed in our "Initial Hunch" (see note 28), causing chiefs of police to consider themselves morally obligated to "protect the people" against their own desires, in the form of what they called "the harmful effects of games of chance."

In the case of the animal game, whose popularity was overwhelming, the persecution was doubtlessly determined, as Pereira de Mello suggests, by the secret accord between the organs of repression and the Federal Lottery, which wanted a clear field for its future wagers as soon as the system was launched. Another factor that legitimated police action was the tumult provoked by the crowds that flocked to the entrance of the Zoological Park to obtain the result of the drawing (Cavalcanti, 1940:53).

From all this came the first legislation aimed at dismantling the structure of games of chance in the city. In January 1895, the municipal executive authority issued Decree No. 126 (corresponding to the sheep), which outlawed the lotteries and raffles run by the bookmakers and limited their operating the games and competitions in frontons and bowling alleys to one day a week (see Pereira de Mello, 1989).

The games held at the zoo did not escape this action by the police. But the animal game was so well established with the people that, already in 1895, there was the dodge of selling tickets under the guise of life insurance and investments.

Thus, in a short time the "animal game at the Zoological Park" had established itself and was competing with other forms of lottery for the bettors' patronage. Agents of the clandestine lotteries, worried about the unexpected strength of the baron's game, tried to combat it in Brazilian fashion, by means of legal action. To do so, they sent an anonymous letter to the mayor asking that measures be taken against the animal game. In other words, the other man's game . . . (Pereira de Mello, 1989:59).

Gambling and Repression: The Official Reaction

The result of this was the issuing of Decree No. 133 (the snake), on April 10, 1895, which authorized Mayor Cesário Alvim to rescind the contract with the promoter João Baptista Vianna Drummond, the individual in charge of the zoo. This is one of the best examples of what Weber called the unintended consequences of social actions, for instead of putting an end to the game, as intended, by positioning it as a clandestine activity and rendering it equal to other games of chance, the decree had the effect of legitimating and recognizing its strength.

The work of Pereira de Mello (1989) suggests that the campaigns against the animal game were marked by lack of coordination among the measures and, at times, among the interests of the municipal legislative authority, the executive, and the police themselves. But the fact is that, as we have seen, they produced some palpable effects,[21] like the totally complementary relationship between police and bookie.

As repression became nationwide and more sophisticated, the bookies began to organize in order to achieve the opposite effect. The result was that repression, as we have suggested, was the principal force responsible for organizing the game, uniting the bookies, and consequently provoking the expulsion of "amateurs" or occasional bankers, because an extralegal activity becomes a serious thing, entailing risks and the possibility of severe social loss.

Perhaps because of ideological disdain for capital, esteeming instead land and titles, the monarchy had always looked upon gambling with indifference and even a measure of condescension. After all, from its point of view, money did not make the aristocrat or purchase blue blood. Therefore, until the advent of the republic, games of chance had been overlooked and to some extent ignored.

The so-called war on gambling had always been sporadic and, furthermore, spasmodic and local, driven entirely by the police. In 1899, the chief of police of the Federal District sent to Mayor Cesário Alvim a communication in which he asks for an end to the licenses for games of chance that were constantly being granted by the municipal executive. He argued that such licenses conflicted with the police effort against gambling. The chief of police used the occasion to inform the mayor that in a few days he would initiate a campaign against gambling in general and against the "animals game" in particular. The campaign did not take place, but the tone of the missive presages the attitude of the police in the following decades, especially the great police offensive of 1917, against the animal game.

A bit earlier, however, in 1913, a controversy with a very contemporary feel made the news. The chief of police at the time, Sr. Belisário Távora, was accused of conspiring with the game's promoters. These accusations, as Irineu Marinho's newspaper *A Noite* reported, caused a scandal and cost him his job. He was replaced by Sr. Manoel Edwiges, who promptly undertook a census of gambling houses in Rio de Janeiro. The survey listed 648 betting places in every area of the city. However, Sr. Edwiges would remain in office only five months; in December 1913 Sr. Francisco Valadares was named to replace him.

This instability in the post of chief of police reveals the beginning of a relationship between bookies and policemen fraught with ambiguities. But it would be necessary to wait till 1917 to witness a more ambitious action to combat gambling. To understand this repressive movement, however, we must not forget one important factor, already mentioned. We refer to the pressure exerted by the National Lottery Company to exterminate clandestine lotteries—and the animal game was the largest of these—and to halt the issuing of new licenses for lotteries in general, which the mayor's office declined to do.

Created in 1896 and unquestionably part of the liberal-republican modernization plan aimed at making ambition something positive by deriving financial and fiscal advantage from it, the National Lottery Company watched with interest and envy the success and expansion of the animal game throughout the country. From 1898 on, it began to take a more active stance, diverging from the lenient position of municipal authorities, who took a local view of the matter. Thus, beginning in 1917 it became a driving force in favor of repressive measures against games of chance.

In August of that year an unprecedented campaign began against the animal game, soon to be known by the significant name "Animal Killer." Spearheading the movement was the chief of police himself, Sr. Aurelino Leal, and the police captain of the 3rd District, Sr. Armando Vidal. For three months, the entire police force in the city was mobilized for the campaign, which effected hundreds of arrests and closed down 868 animal game betting houses.

Despite its furor, however, "Animal Killer" would be the target of countless criticisms that, in the most Brazilian of ways, brought into doubt its legality, dividing public opinion and setting a portion of the people in opposition to the jurists. This disagreement became a heated controversy, spilling over into sophisticated, erudite debates in the press and making its way to the Chamber of Deputies in the person of Maurício Lacerda. According to that deputy, the fierce campaign of repression of the animal game originated with the political pressure that the directors of the National Lottery Company put on the chief of police. The pressure extended to the directors' financing of the repressive operation by the police. This unmasking raised doubt about the legality of the campaign, leading the populace to protest against the brutality of the enforcement action and finally to suspicion of collusion between the police and the board of directors of the National Lottery Company. The result, as might be expected, was an end to the "Animal Killer" campaign, in December 1917 (see Pereira de Mello, 1989: chapter 3).

Thus, only in 1946, under President Eurico Gaspar Dutra, did the animal game suffer its hardest legal blow, when it was definitively outlawed along with other games of chance. So it was repression that, paradoxically, gave life to the animal game as a state-recognized institution, by creating the conditions for its unification. Without police intervention, it would have been difficult for the agents of the game, who till then were competitors, to unite against the agents of the state apparatus.

At this point another equally important door opened. Organized repression, acting systematically, increased the appeal of the activity and created a defensive, evaluative self-awareness that forced it to organize. If the game had been merely an inconsequential, hopeful pastime, now that decrees officially depicted it as a moral lapse on the part of the middle class, it was transformed into a tempting, interesting activity—precisely because it was forbidden.

Repression, therefore, initiated a new phase for the animal game: institutional self-awareness. There was also the structuring of a reliable network of agents to take bets and bear the weight of the voluminous hunches that increased the bankers' profits and produced standardization of the results, rendering them unmistakable, easily accessible, and reliable, a critical element in any game of chance.

From Repression to Professionalization

On a more concrete level, the first effect of the prohibition was to sever the link between the drawing of the bicho and the zoo. The game then developed into a multitude of variants. In the words of one observer of that period:

> At this time, the game has developed in such a way that within a single game there are almost six hundred! There is the Old, the Modern, the Rio, the Alternate, the Century Plant . . . And how many others? Popular, Elegant Company, Modern, Lotto, Brazilian Industrial, Flower Mu-

seum, Fluminense Guild, Sunrise, Sunset, Carioca, Guarantee, Light from Heaven, Hope, Star of Destiny, Security, Help from Our Lady, Talisman of Luck, and many others (Edmundo, 1938:904).

The second effect was to provide visibility and importance to those who, outside the park, sold the tickets. With time, though, the small vendors succumbed to the owners of the lottery agencies, whose greater capital and organizational resources allowed them to centralize the game. The great "captains" of the activity began to emerge, who, because they handled more wagers, could offer greater advantages to the bettors.

Everything indicates that the persecution of the game led to its unconditional public acceptance, which accorded it social legitimacy against an elitist and ill-intentioned legal prohibition that made the government seem a common enemy and made the police easy prey for enticement by the game's bankers.

But who were these first bankers, and how did they function?

If we accept Cavalcanti's opinion, the great majority of the first large bankers of the animal game were immigrants—Arabs, Spaniards, Portuguese, and others, who because they were foreigners could take the risk of participating in an illegal activity. Such people had no roots in the land and were not obligated to share the local codes of honor and shame. Without a family name, without relatives, and without acquaintances, this group had little to lose and could carry out a semi-criminal social existence, which surely facilitated the risk of challenging the law and compensated for its pacts with the agents of repression.

Another of the most notable difficulties in suppressing the animal game was the style of betting, which had no fixed location, could be done at home and with little money, and was totally founded on the mutual confidence between bettor and agent, a link that reproduced in practice the magical tie between bicho and gambler. This floating organizational system, based on confidence and loyalty, integrated bichos, bettors, and bookies and rendered superfluous any proof of the bet—a document that proved officially the relationship between buyer and seller of the bicho. Thus, when there was a raid, the bookies would hide their betting lists and the police would lack the proof to arrest them. Further, as bettors and bookies formed a true community of interest founded on honor and affinity, the betting public (then as today) protected its gambling agents, who were also the go-betweens to the universe of social ascent to which it so aspired. The well-known paradox of condemning the bookie but sympathizing with the animal game thus became established.

The Animal Game Hits the Newspapers

Thus far we have been studying the formation of the animal game. Now we will investigate the model by which the animal game established itself as the most popular clandestine lottery in the country. It is our hypothesis that such a process was facilitated by a group of daily newspapers dedicated exclusively to providing tips for the game. These papers, which began to emerge in the very first years of the twentieth century in every Brazilian city, constitute an excellent source for studying the impressive diffusion process undergone by the animal game. They also demonstrate how in Brazil newspapers, a modern invention linked to the circulation of political ideas, served paradoxically as an instrument for the sale and capture of slaves (see Freyre, 1979) and as a source of tips for the clandestine game.

These newspapers devoted exclusively to tips featured diverse sections. There are parts dedicated to cabbalistic calculations difficult to decode, alongside drawings in which one must discover figures of animals suggested by lace on skirts or feathers on hats. We also find columns of seers of the most varied magical and mystical types. There are *caboclos* (a social type resulting from the mixture of whites and indigenous peoples), fakirs, card readers, and numerous others linked to the enchanted universe of magic, each offering tips and substantiating them in the respective coded tongues corresponding to the external aspects of their cosmologies.

Along with these tips we also have "rational and modern" statistical analyses, which show the bichos that are "overdue," that is, those that have not hit for a long time and logically have a greater mathematical probability of being selected. These newspapers also offer the reading public statistics on their correct tips. As there are many columns providing tips, it is not difficult for some of them to be right, buttressing the system as a whole.

The publication of magazines and daily newspapers dedicated exclusively to the animal game is eloquent proof of its success and how deeply ingrained it is in the habits of the people of Rio de Janeiro, a "modern" people who know how to read and write and who are to some degree accustomed to means of calculation, with a special, paradoxical propensity for deciphering relatively complex cabbalistic codes. These data reveal beyond the shadow of a doubt how the animal game has penetrated the entire system, not as a simple, innocuous, spontaneous activity proving the innocence of ignorant "masses," as Lima Barreto and other "old" and "modern" intellectuals have said.

The tables, statistical charts, and all the calculations connected to the animal game constitute the educated—we almost said "erudite"—side of the hermeneutics aimed at predicting the winning bicho. The newspapers reveal the plasticity of the population of players, as well as of the animal game itself. This plasticity comes from its capacity to allow betting on any number, any bicho, any quantity desired, thus satisfying every taste and ambition. In the same way, the system of tips unites popular versions of the cabbala with black magic and with the array of dreams and particularistic beliefs of Brazilian society. All this without overlooking the belief in mathematically based calculation that modern scientism offered to the populace.

As one columnist of the time aptly said, the animal game began to constitute and be constitutive of the "soul of Rio de Janeiro," and to be part of it:

As is customary, and nowadays more than ever, business, in its advertising, always makes use of new ideas, of blatant events, of prominent facts . . . well then, several businesses have used the idea of the animal game to benefit their sales. Some cigarette factories have created and launched onto the market small packs containing figures of the 25 animals. The "tipster" cigarettes always bore an animal figure and awarded prizes to anyone with the entire set . . . consider that, in the majority of the brands offering prizes, a given figure would take weeks and even months to appear! . . . with the hopeful collectors always consuming that brand of cigarette!

What about news of the result of the drawings?! It spreads fast! . . . One hour after the drawing, which in general occurs in a place that no one knows about, in Santa Cruz, Jacarepaguá, Ipanema, São Cristóvão, Caxambi, Tijuca, all of Rio knows which bicho hit. Small strips of paper containing the numbers drawn are glued to lampposts, to walls of buildings, and often deposited in the iron gratings that protect trees along public walkways. And those who feel and know the "enchanting soul of the streets" (as a title it belongs to João do Rio, but as an expression, to all who reflect) see those who move quickly, withdraw a little piece of paper, and continue on their way; and those who stop by the lampposts or along the walls, some with pencil and paper, to copy the winning numbers. What is interesting is that ladies, policemen, office boys, students, priests—in short, people of every category—all stop (Paraguassu, 1954:43).

In Rio de Janeiro in 1903, we have *The Mascot, The Talisman, The Bicho, The Ronde, Naked Rio,* and *The Tip*—all dedicated exclusively to the animal game. Even the major newspapers like the *Jornal do Brasil* had their tips columns, in this case "Ladybug's Tips," soon imitated by other papers. Thus, *O Radical* had the column "Which Bicho Hit"; *A Manhã*—belonging to the federal government itself, the declared enemy of the game—had the column "Dreams of Rivers." In the state of Espírito Santo, the *Folha do Povo* carried the column "Noah's Ark." And in São Paulo, because the game was prohibited, columns appeared disguised as "numerology" or "astrology" in the *A Hora* and *O Dia,* respectively.

In fact, as Luiz Edmundo informs us in his celebrated *O Rio de Janeiro do meu tempo* (1938, vol. 3), by the year 1900 the animal game was already the most important nongovernmental lottery in the country. Since then, the game has been noteworthy for its ability to maintain itself as a private business in a public area that is traditionally a state monopoly—despite prohibitions and all the campaigns of repression directed against it.

Through the newspapers, the animal game took control of the entire country.

Triumph of the Animal Game

Another important consequence of police persecution was the creation of a formula for awarding of prizes. As there were 25 bichos, each came to comprise a group, and each of these groups, as mentioned earlier in "Initial Hunch," corresponded to four tenths up to the numbers 100, 1,000, or 10,000. The bicho whose group included the last two numbers drawn in the Federal Lottery would be the winner—an activity, thanks to Brazilian institutionalized paradoxes, perfectly legal. Thus, the bichos were associated definitively with numbers in an unusual equation that would prove to be extremely rich in possibilities.

But the linking of the animal game to the lottery raised other questions as well. Till then, the "result," that is, the prize for the animal game, went to whoever had the last numbers of the first prize, or sometimes the grand prize, in the lottery. But the lotteries offered five grand prizes daily. This led to the invention of the following modes of play: "old" play, which consisted of betting only on the bicho corresponding to the first prize; "modern" play, which meant betting on the bicho that resulted from the sum of the three first prizes in the lottery; the "alternate," in which players tested their luck on the bicho resulting from the sum of the first, third, and fifth prizes; the "Rio," which significantly meant total betting by playing the sum of the five grand prizes.

These gambling modalities, however, fell out of favor. Nowadays, more practical modalities are at the disposal of players, who can bet on all the lottery prizes. The bettor can thus play the first prize—"the head"—or the "second," "third," "fourth," or "fifth," which equates to playing the bicho corresponding to the last two digits of the second, third, fourth, and fifth prizes of the Federal Lottery.

The bettor is likewise allowed to play the variations. In this case, he says he "played the race," "from first to fifth." He can win, therefore, once, twice, or more often—even every time, which is quite rare. It is also possible to bet on two bichos simultaneously, making the so-called "deuce." In this way, if the bichos are drawn in any of the five places, the bettor will receive the award corresponding to the bet made. When the game is played with three bichos, in any two positions, it's called "playing the trio." Clearly, in order to win it's necessary for the three bichos to be drawn in any of the positions. Finally, if someone bets on four bichos, he is said to "play the quartet."

The game of tenths obeys the same conditions, as do those of the hundredths and thousandths. But it is even possible to play "inverted" hundredths and thousandths. By betting on a number of three or four digits, the gambler wins if the hundredth or thousandth containing them, in any order, is drawn.

The association of the animal game with other lotteries had its origin, as we have seen, in the banishing of the game from the zoo. If it was no longer possible to open the blackboard on which the bicho appeared at day's end, it would be necessary to invent a new procedure. Once the correspondence between the 25 bichos and their respective tenths, hundredths, and thousandths was established, the outcome of the animal game could be coupled to any number of public record. It was in this manner that the animal game could be linked to the drawing of the Federal Lottery, the amount of revenue from customs, or any other number in the public domain. In other words, it was systematic police repression that propelled the animal game from a local pastime to one of citywide and national scope. The price of illegality was the sophistication of options as well as profits.

The animal game survived repression. Today it extends throughout the country and is under the control of a single command made up of lottery bankers in Rio de Janeiro. This command meets in an office located in a sophisticated commercial building in downtown Rio. It is this exalted command that resolves the problems of the animal game and drafts its well-designed and realistic national policy, which among other things includes: agreements with politicians and the police; payment of employees; reassignment of betting sites; punishment of turncoats; etc. The drawing, the basis of the game's trustworthiness and the heart of its nationwide legitimacy, is also within its purview, being maintained in confidentiality and occurring in alternating locales to avoid police raids. Thus, each state sends representatives who monitor the drawing of the numbers, which is effected by means of a metal globe with an opening at one of its poles.

In a matter of minutes, news of the winning bicho spreads through the city, as from the beginning of the twentieth century there was an efficient communications network connecting every headquarters of the game, which in turn linked the betting sites under their control. Currently, the verification system uses an extremely modern network of computers that calculate the prizes to be paid in each betting site and area.

One interesting fact that must be mentioned is the permanence of the expediency of tying the result of the animal game to the outcome of official lotteries. The 6:00 p.m. results on Wednesdays and Saturdays are tied to the drawings of the Federal Lottery, the 6:00 p.m. results on Friday to the drawing of the Lottery of the State of Rio de Janeiro (the Loterj).

By the already-described process of successive concentration of control of the game in the hands of the large "bankers," the present-day configuration emerged, in which a single banker, like a true modern head of state, can have vast regions under his direct control. In Rio de Janeiro alone, for example, it is estimated that there are more than three thousand sites for betting on the animal game. On average, a well-located site yields 3,000 *reais* per day and a sidewalk bookie takes in 500 *reais* per day (values as of February 1999).

Though not an all-inclusive list, there are eight established ways of playing the animal game. Each bet of 1 *real* (approximately 34 cents in U.S. dollars) yields 18 *reais* in the group; 60 in the tenths; 600 in the hundredths;

4,000 in the thousandths; 18.75 in the group deuce; 300 in the deuce of tenths; 130 in the group trio; and 3,000 in the tenths trio.

According to one informant—the manager of a betting site in the Lapa district—the average of the total take awarded as prizes is on the order of 10 percent; the owners of the site get 15 percent of the gross, and the rest goes directly, with no taxes or discount, into the bankers' hands. These are extraordinary figures.

What is impressive after a century of existence is the animal game's capacity for overcoming obstacles. Agility and capillarity are its hallmark.

Some Sociology

We have seen that the animal game was invented in the 1890s, at the advent of the republic, and with it a generalized outbreak of speculation—a wave of liberal individualism—took hold of the country. This was a radical political transition, for in going from empire to republic, Brazil went formally from a consistently aristocratic, slave-based, hierarchical society to a nation that legally and politically represented itself as egalitarian and consisting of free citizens with equal rights. In this sense, the advent of the republic led Brazilian society to experience something beyond a new political regime.

The new laws demanded a profound social transformation, a true revolution whose consequences are being felt even today. It was in this context, which culminated with a change of political regime, with the freeing of the slaves, and with a series of social movements, that the animal game emerged.

A Century of the Animal Game

October 1990 marked the centennial of the animal game. The celebration of the centennial took over the streets of Vila Isabel in the form of a carnival. There was a raised stage for the scheduled attractions, lavish distribution of beer, and crowds of people scattered in the bars and along the sidewalks in the vicinity. The observations of the celebration made by Elena Soárez allow us to draw a series of parallels between the animal game in its initial phase and today.

It was curious that, after a century, Vila Isabel continued as the territory where the animal game originated. Also, the type of festivity gave us the impression that no time had passed, for in the street carnival created for the celebration we noted the joyous and peaceful interaction of children and adults, young and old, men and women, rich and poor that creates an unequaled and traditional atmosphere of harmony seemingly so rare in the great modern city. The neighborhood opened itself to guests and many residents brought chairs onto the sidewalks to watch the movement, transforming the street into a tranquil and welcoming veranda.

The setting was that of a family party in a city of the interior. Speaking with people, we learned that such parties were common, for every year the birthday of the baron's grandson was commemorated in that same manner. Not only was the Vila Isabel district celebrated in that ritual, but also the figure of Baron de Drummond himself emerged during that anniversary of the animal game's origin.

Vila Isabel observes the date of October 3, 1890, when the baron obtained official permission to exploit games of chance. The public commemoration of that original date by the "firm" that today exploits the game in that area of the city operates like an instrument of social legitimation, for it accentuates the presence of an illegal activity. It is a kind of political ritual that assures a contradictory social legitimacy to an activity that juridical fiat has situated outside the law. Everything takes place as if the rite were seeking to establish a link between the public's taste and the antisociological desire of the elites to correct the customs of the people by laws and decisions whose reasons are unknown to a large portion of the populace.

The conflicting images suggested by comparison of two moments in the history of the animal game—its birth and its current structure—lead us to an array of paradoxes that will inspire the analysis that follows. What we observe is the transfer of control of the game from a nobleman, at the pinnacle of the social hierarchy, to a clandestine network of "captains" and agents composed of a plebeian group at the margins of the social universe.

The visibility of the celebration—for which invitations were printed and distributed beforehand—demonstrated a curious confrontation between the incredible penetration of the habit of playing the animal game and its clandestine, illegal status. In a profound sense, the ritual of commemorating its origin forged a link between the visibility and the invisibility of the animal game.

Another facet of the ritual was reflection about the transition from the baron to the contemporary "lawbreaker." The ritual allowed one to see how the game navigated socially from a promotion carried out by a nobleman with the specific objective of providing resources for the maintenance of the zoo's animals, to a clandestine lottery, consciously taken on and controlled by a network of lawbreakers.

Looking back, one can say that the decades from 1890 to 1920 marked the fundamental period in the structuring of the animal game. It was in this period that it embarked on the path of organizational growth. Further, control of the animal game became unified by the command in Rio de Janeiro, as methods of controlling bets and determining results grew more sophisticated. The culmination of the process was when the relationship between the command of the game and its agents acquired obvious stability; though interrupted at times, the agreement has always remained systematic.

The crucial point in the creation of the animal game was the advent of the republic and the cessation of state subsidy to the enterprise belonging to a member of the nobility. In exchange, the provisional government offered permission to hold "drawings in general" at the zoo. This cut, probably motivated by ideological considerations—after all, how could a government that represented the credo of liberty and equality continue to subsidize the enterprise of a baron of the empire?—accelerated Drummond's search for other resources. But it must be remembered that at this stage there was no animal game, only promotion and a drawing. And it was the baron who chose the "bicho of the day."

But the drawing was quickly transformed into conscious and deliberate betting. It is curious that this change corresponded on the popular level to an equally drastic transition on the political level. In fact, if in its initial phase everything was orderly—the drawing was entrusted to a nobleman—in its second, all was random. The lottery was handed over to probability, and consequently to conflict and equality. If in a hierarchical society such as imperial Brazil had been, social relationships were relatively foreseeable and everyone knew his place, under the republic the issue was one of trying to achieve the exact opposite. It was now an open system in which individuals could be classified more by what they did and less by who they were, more by their work and less by their family name. Everywhere, there should be fewer drawings and more betting and hunches.

This displacement closely corresponded to the dynamic of the animal game. If the order of society went from hierarchical to formally democratic, the animal game also underwent a sophistication of its wagering modalities. This sophistication was accomplished through the introduction of various numerical combinations, opening a growing probability for the hunch player and bringing the animal game closer to other types of lottery that operated solely with numbers.

Curiously, and concurrent with the process of numerical sophistication, there was a vigorous growth in divinatory practices focused on formulating hunches, which reinforced the traditional way of seeing. Constructing the hunch—a phenomenon of great importance that will be the topic of the next chapter—invoked the possibility of establishing a new correspondence between bichos, numbers, dreams, intuitions, sudden visions, and every type of accident, positive and negative.

In sum, in the original design of the game we have a nobleman who determined the result by choosing the "bicho of the day." With transfer of control to a network of lawbreakers with a marginal position in society, the game acquired a mechanism for obtaining the result—the drawing or the correspondence with official numbers—that was both impersonal, not subject to manipulation, and no longer the fruit of an arbitrary personal decision.

With the introduction of numerical series the game expanded its betting possibilities and assumed its more probabilistic, abstract character. Now one could win more and play more combinations. However, as if to compensate for this modern, impersonal aspect, gamblers invented a divinatory activity that reestablished communication between different levels of reality by reconstituting a lost sense of enchantment and continuity.

Thus, for every individualistic and egalitarian proposal to modernize the system we find a kind of hierarchical counterproposal that allows the synthetic recapture of aspects of the previous universe. Obviously, we are not speaking of two self-contained periods but of processes based on combinations, amalgams, syntheses, and incorporations that, in turn, generated a very special social dynamic.

New Times, Old Habits: The Animal Game and the Republic

"Which bicho hit?"
"Deodoro!"
(J. Carvalho, 1990:146)

It is worthwhile in this part to bring together some social and historical aspects that broaden our understanding of the animal game as a comprehensive social fact and not merely a datum in the history of lawbreaking and crime in the city of Rio de Janeiro and in Brazil. The historic-social context that engendered the animal game was marked by the following events:

1888—Abolition of slavery
1889—Proclamation of the republic
1890—Separation of church and state
1890—Invention of the animal game

Prudent as it may be to mistrust "official changes" that occur in Brazilian society, it seems no less prudent to recognize their social significance and, above all, their legal implications. The gradual elimination of a slave-based economy and the consequent development of urban centers, as well as the change of governmental framework and the legal system, formed an institutional order and an economy based on the market, individual rights, and paid labor. In sum, a bourgeois system, liberal, individualistic, and modern.

The transformation experienced by the animal game was a significant one. Instead of a drawing by a "noble"—a figure emblematic of a personally driven, patriarchal society—the game now acquired a certain impersonality and can be placed alongside insurance policies and lotteries in general, institutions that also proliferated with the implantation of a modern social ethic in which so-called "laws of the market" dictated the norms, "naturalizing" and impersonalizing society. Now those responsible for its dynamic were no longer the nobles but an array of universal processes and motivations—which for that very reason were impersonal and anonymous.

In this sense, the "animal game system" can be seen as a code that expresses both the values recently instituted by the triumph of the republican movement—such as equality and social mobility—and the underlying elements of the society, which valued social immobility, hierarchy, and the relationship of everything with everything else.

At the time the animal game was invented, in 1890 in the city of Rio de Janeiro, 29 percent of the population was composed of foreigners; those from other parts of the country made up 26 percent, and only 45 percent were natives of the city. In the first decade of the republican regime, however, a tremendous demographic reversal took place.

Manumission of the slaves and the heightened migratory flow exceeded the capacity for employment and housing. The result of this growth and rapid demographic diversification was an escalating impersonalization in social relations. From a community where everyone knew each other, given the funneling process imposed by hierarchy, Rio de Janeiro became a city where population flow and new rules of government made people equal before the law and consequently engendered impersonality as the ideal (albeit still formal) basis of behavior.

Add to this the specificity of the triumphant conclusion of the republican movement, paradoxically called a "proclamation." The minimal popular participation in the transition to republicanism gave it an aspect of fortuity and surprise—of what among us has come conventionally to be known by the significant term "coup," a name that emphasizes an unusual and unexpected event. In this sense, the republic was indeed more "proclaimed" than instituted.

The mass of the populace, as historians of the time emphasize, was taken by surprise by the "military parade" of army general Deodoro. There was no republican tradition to legitimate the new regime and position it as the decisive outcome of popular interests. The people, as we know, remained outside the process, watching "awestruck" the elites' maneuvers. But even the military and political elite directly involved in the event were far from achieving a consensus about the new national value system (see J. Carvalho, 1991). And in fact various models for the republic vied for legitimacy and official recognition. There was the liberal North American model, there was the model of direct popular participation inspired by French Jacobinism, and there were the more abstract and evolutionist positivist conceptions, not directly concerned with forms of government at all. A model for the republic was sought that would adapt to the Brazilian case, or more precisely, to the specific interests of the groups involved. This clash of rivals and ideological models spilled over into a veritable battle revolving around the symbols that would express the new government and synthetically manifest the new national creed.

In the cogent interpretation of José Murilo de Carvalho, what was sought was an "image of the new regime, whose purpose was to reach the popular imagination and reshape it in the framework of republican values" (1991:10). In this first phase of republicanism there was an important symbolic debate about heroes and national symbols that would affect specifically the nascent cosmology of the animal game, a system that emerged in that period.

But despite the symbols and the democratic ideology, the republican transition took place in a profoundly hierarchical and unequal society. In this context, the idea of a market as regulator of the interests of formally equal agents was something difficult to put into practice. It could be (and was) instituted to the letter of the law, but what in fact occurred was the sanction of the law of the strong, which was accepted in a society characterized by inequality.

In the early moments of the republic, juridical/political egalitarianism could only favor the socially superior, people who could use the new rules of the game, including a free market, for their own benefit. Furthermore, to aggravate this situation of cultural and/or moral uncertainty, well-established symbols of the old order, like the image of a distant but just and paternal emperor (as was Pedro II), were likewise swept from the scene and rendered suddenly inoperative.

These modifications began in the year before the proclamation, for as a consequence of the abolition of slavery in 1888 the imperial government resorted to the printing of currency as compensation for losses suffered by coffee growers, who were now obliged to pay wages. This expedient was maintained enthusiastically by the provisional government in its struggle to gain acceptance. As José Murilo de Carvalho explains:

> Once the right to issue currency was conceded to various banks, the streets of Rio de Janeiro were flooded with money without any gold reserve, followed by the well-known speculative fever, the *encilhamento,* described so well in Taunay's novel. According to one newspaper of the time, "everyone gambled, the businessman, the doctor, the jurist, the civil servant, the broker, the salesman; with little capital of their own, with the difference in interest rates, and almost all with the very collateral of the game itself" (J. Carvalho, 1991:19–20).

In this social atmosphere in which speculation was encouraged and was born associated with a new sociopolitical creed, nothing was more reasonable than having the animal game and the lotteries as one more option for getting rich and changing one's position in society, becoming more equal than the mixed-race and former slave population marked by centuries of servitude and by inequality as a moral value.

The magnitude of this appears in accounts of the era, like that of Luís Edmundo Costa in *O Rio de Janeiro do meu tempo,* which speaks of a "frenzy awakened by the animal game never before seen in any other modality of gambling" (1938:888).

The same Luís Edmundo Costa observes that, until the advent of the animal game, gambling was moderate in Rio de Janeiro. There were horse races, jai alai, and a few members-only clubs where roulette was played. The other games of the time were family affairs and took place in homes as social entertainment. This was the case of *jaburu* (which used a small roulette wheel with figures of animals), baccarat, lotto, and various card games known as *campista, bisca,* and *burro-em-pé.* Lotteries had existed in Brazil since the beginning of the nineteenth century but seem to have enjoyed little popularity. Around 1840 raffles were common, and in 1847 the Federal Lottery had begun its drawings. There was still a large number of gambling houses, but the type of gambling then in vogue was the casino or cabaret variety, which brought together public figures of the time. But this type of social gathering was restricted to the elite.

In contrast to casino gambling, the animal game spread through the streets of Rio and reached the entire population. It was a game of the street, a game that could be carried out at home, a game that did not oblige the player to don a tuxedo and go to a social club or some haunt of the high-society crowd. For that reason, the animal game was described as the "vice of the people" as opposed to the "vice of the rich" occurring behind the closed doors of casinos and private clubs (see Pereira de Mello, 1989).

There is, therefore, a profound connection between the social changes taking place at the turn of the century and the spread of gambling. If the new credo of the national state was freedom and equality, we cannot forget that it was introduced legally in the bosom of an aristocratic society dominated by barons. In the institutionally hybrid setting, gambling, and especially the animal game, emerged as a mechanism that would come to signal the possibility of vertical mobility for the masses. Put another way, the institutionalization of the ideal of political equality and the formal dismantling of the imperial order, in a society in which work was marked by slavery, brought speculative fever to the surface and consolidated a cheap, easy, and unpretentious game. This game was marked by a familiar mythological and totemic appeal that mapped out and established relationships between animals, numbers, and money and in so doing symbolically linked the poor to the rich and the weak to the powerful.

All of this helps us to understand the often-noted association, in the transition to republicanism, between the new political regime and a speculative wave in which luck and not the market (or work) was the arbiter. The new capitalist order, precariously assimilated, was an open invitation to speculation, creating and destroying great fortunes overnight. The aristocratic and stable imperial order (in which the hierarchy of social practices did not contradict the order reigning on the political and legal planes) was replaced by a liberal and formally egalitarian structure. The tranquil calculus that typified the aristocratic code of gentility was replaced by frenetic jockeying for power and by the desire to get rich by playing the stock market.

Speculation in the stock market was in fact frankly encouraged by the provisional government, for as newspapers of the time pointed out, expressing a generalized climate of optimism: "The Republic is wealth!" (J. Carvalho, 1990:26).

If the majority of the populace was far from the "invisible hand" that governed the market, conferring wealth upon the richest and transforming barons into capitalists and capitalists into liberal "barons," it was close to the invisible hand of luck. This luck, conceived in a personalized manner, was like an "invisible hand" that acted through dreams, hunches, and affinities with the bichos.

Because of all this, it is our thesis that, on a fundamentally sociopolitical plane, the animal game constituted a return to the old and good universe of personalness in a context marked by brutal official impersonality, when the government pitilessly dismantled the system of symbols in force in the society.

With the retaining of existing hierarchies and interest groups alongside the multiplying of the demographic contingent at the margins of the law and the labor force, the underworld of gambling and criminality swelled. Nevertheless, criminal expedients were not limited to the underworld. Municipal representation became uncontrolled because there was no authentic electorate to demand accountability; in the political field the immediate consequence of this was recurrent private deals and personal horse trading, with the emergence of collusion and corruption.

The circle was now closed: concern with limiting participation and with controlling the world of disorder opened by the republican era had ended up leading to the perverse absorption of that world by politics. With this, Rio de Janeiro witnessed the emergence of a corrupt civil service and systematically fraudulent elections dominated by criminal gangs and lawbreakers in the style of Totonho and Lucrécio Barba de Bode (the name means "goat-beard"). Described by the early-twentieth-century novelist Lima Barreto, they were the owners of brothels and gambling houses. Crooks such as these were the kingpins of politics, the makers of elections, the promoters of demonstrations, even at the federal level. The formal egalitarian order blended with the existing social hierarchies, making—as Carvalho says—the lawbreaker a citizen and the citizen a lawbreaker (J. Carvalho, 1991:37ff.).

This, in general terms, was the social environment in which the animal game arose.

While the elites struck at Brazilian society with the proclamation of the republic, the people interpreted the outcome in their own way, joking: "What bicho hit?" someone asks. Another replies roguishly, "Deodoro!"

Civilly and politically powerless, the masses dealt with the new republic the only way they could: as the outcome of the animal game. If powerless from a legal, intellectual, and political standpoint, they reveal a notable imaginative capacity in reacting ironically to that random event so removed from the daily course of their lives. In a certain way, however, they put aside their notorious "stupefaction" to propose an extremely sagacious interpretation of what was happening around them. Under the guise of passivity, then, the people read what came from above as a theater of "bichos." In that tragicomedy, a king (represented by the lion) leaves, and in his place enters a ravenous, authoritarian, factious military elite, whose totem and commander can only be, as President João Baptista Figueiredo would confirm some ninety years later, the horse.

Anticipating briefly what will constitute the heart of the present study—an interpretation of the classificatory system that drives the animal game and helps characterize Brazilian modernity—we see that already at the beginning of the twentieth century, events and personalities were associated with the "bichos," the target of an active and intelligent popular reinterpretation. Thus, the statesman Rui Barbosa was associated with the eagle, the one who is at a higher level—the only one who actually flies and sees everything around him and who through intellectual strength positions himself above the rest. Rui Barbosa was, then, the "eagle of the Hague." The eagle, as our informants say, identifies "the one who conquers through his arguments" (since Rui Barbosa was the cleverest delegate at the Hague international conference) or has the "gift of gab," using his talents to persuade or seduce. And the governmental palace, the Catete, at that time the presidential residence, came to be known as the "Palace of Eagles" because it was crowned by five sculpted eagles, each looking in a different direction as if seeking—and seeking haphazardly, as the people said—paths for the republic. Similarly, and by the same logic, the bankers of the animal game are called "eagles," in contrast to the players, designated "donkeys."

In this sense, old Baron de Drummond, creator and first banker of the animal game, gave rise to both an original interpretive code, forever used by the people as an instrument of participation in the events happening around them, and a lineage of eagles (or vultures) still "at a higher level" a century later, soaring haughtily and voraciously over the urban Brazilian jungle.

Massive confusion in the city and Court of St. Sebastian of Rio de Janeiro, midway through the Year of Our Lord 1896, with the frightening animals game that was spreading everywhere. Fortunately, the authorities and sensible people seem determined to run this menagerie off, and it's about time. Onward.

Pereira Neto, *Revista Ilustrada* (June 1896)

CHAPTER 2

The Animal Game as Totem
and Sacrificial Rite

It is surprising to find that the animal game does not appear as a subject of investigation in any of the classic interpretations of Brazil, which confirms the ideological schism that, among Brazilians, separates those institutions constituted and nurtured by the people from the facts and ideas the elites assume to be serious and worthy of intellectual consideration. Certainly because it is a marginal institution, the animal game remained outside the studies devoted to an overall understanding of Brazil. But it did not escape the encompassing eye of Gilberto Freyre, or the subtle comparative considerations of Vianna Moog. Thus, in both Freyre's *Casa grande & senzala* (*The Masters and the Slaves*) and Moog's *Bandeirantes e Pioneiros* (*Bandeirantes and Pioneers*), the animal game appears as an institution that adds fuel to the interpretive fires the authors developed in these works.

For Moog, inspired by Max Weber, the animal game emerged at the core of a recurring question: "Is not the extremely Brazilian animal game the authentic expression of subconscious terror, as well as of the very Brazilian desire for quick riches?" (Moog, 1955:337). This question brings us back to Moog's thesis that the Brazilian formative process was motivated by the idea of obtaining the maximum of wealth with the minimum of effort, whether by the predatory exploiting of nature (through an unending pushing back of borders, or "bandeirantism") or by the aristocratizing of the colonizer that transformed our first inhabitants into mere imitators of the hierarchized social life of Portugal.

Moog's thesis makes sense. This is not the place to discuss Moog's ideas but rather to call attention to one basic point: the fact that, to him, the animal game is nothing more than a secondary actor, a marginal proof of a larger and more inclusive tendency—"bandeirantism" as a social value embodied in the drive for rapid enrichment.

Freyre gave more attention to the animal game. Within a culturalist and romantic interpretive framework, Freyre saw the animal game as the mark of a system of primitive beliefs, in this case one of the more obvious contributions of the "Indian" to our cultural hybridism, read positively for the first time. In his words:

> Of the indigenous tradition, there remained in Brazil the taste for games and children's toys imitating animals: the very game of chance called the animal game, so popular in Brazil, finds the basis for such popularity in the animistic and totemistic residual of Amerindian culture later reinforced by that of the African (Freyre, 1984:135).

It is clear that for the Freyre of *Casa grande & senzala* (*The Masters and the Slaves*) the animal game complex is located in a "cultural unconscious," an area in which he finds "survivals" or "residuals" of three ethnic groups— "Portuguese," "indigenous," and "black"—at the root of our identity.[1]

For Freyre, this "animistic and totemistic residual" is a testimony to our indigenous side, a magic-archaic dimension characterized by identification between men and animals, typical of backward cultures, whose logic is based on a deceptive contiguity between nature and society. Proof of this is in their toys imitating animals, the very idea of "bicho" as a broad and general category of understanding in Brazil, and the habit of bettors in the animal game having affinities with certain animals in the same way that in some Amerindian societies the neophytes take certain animals as their protectors or tutelary entities, in an association that anthropology terms "totemic."[2]

Freyre's thesis has the virtue of calling attention to a profound aspect of the animal game, advancing our understanding of how that institution attracts the masses precisely because through it one can postulate a link of intimacy between nature and culture. But he falls short in two critical aspects.

Freyre employs a traditional conception of totemism, seeing it through its more explicit side as merely a mechanism of identification between a cultural element (an individual or a social group) and a natural element (a plant, a meteorological phenomenon, or an animal). In so doing, he loses sight of the differentiating aspects of totemic thought, for according to the classic demonstration by Lévi-Strauss (1966), what totemism actually postulates is an identity between systems of differences, one operating at the level of nature and the other at the level of culture or society. Interpreted this way, totemism is much more a means of separating and discriminating than a proof of the confusion or the logical indigence of so-called "savages."

The second aspect is even more telling and important, for it reveals how Freyre sees the idea of "culture" as an entity situated outside of history.[3] By proceeding in this manner, he fails to perceive that in the case of the animal game the animals with which the player may identify are those arbitrarily "chosen" by Baron de Drummond from a set in a Zoological Park, in a formally modern urban environment and a context in full transformation. To put it another way, the list of "tutelary animals" at the disposal of a player in the animal game has a clear historical determination, being marked—as if that were not enough—by the founding of a "Zoological Park."

Such a historical context compels a better characterizing of this animal game totemism. Really, if the game has a relationship to a totemic complex, this does not happen because it is a displaced representative of some indigenous trait that has miraculously survived, as an evolutionist Victorian anthropologist of the stripe of Sir James Frazer or E. B. Tylor would say in the interpretive line set in motion by Freyre. This happened because he reinvented, in a context of accelerated "modernization," a logic of identities and differences between natural and social beings that particularizes these implicit, undomesticated systems of classification.

In other words, the totemism exhibited by the animal game has nothing to do with the antihistorical attitude embedded in Franz Boas's romantic culturalism, so splendidly articulated by Freyre, but is related to an ingenious and supremely original capacity for relating series of objects that the bourgeois culture categorizes as discontinuous: animals and people, nature and culture, social facts and numerical series. Such a synthesis was achieved in Brazil, and it is fitting to reconstruct it, an analytical effort that leads simultaneously to ideological elements and to social values dynamized by the animal game, keeping in mind that the process takes place in a specific historical context.

But in dealing with the animal game, one must not overlook one critical fact. In this case, it is not only a matter of forming a bridge between "nature" and "culture," as occurs in classical totemisms, but also of relating *numbers* to animals and persons, which permits linking the totemism of this lottery to the idea of the game and of wagering, provoking and promising new associations.

It is in fact in this linkage between animals and numbers—those entities that since the time of the Pythagoreans have enjoyed a special position in our cosmology, being treated as pure beings governed by their own dynamic—that the originality of the animal game lies. This originality permits its inclusion in the framework of totemic phenomena but, at the same time, qualifies it as a historically marked totemism and for that very reason "modern" or special.

This totemism, by linking animals, human beings, and social events to numbers, allows them to be interpreted from a triple perspective: from a stochastic, probabilistic angle in which what matters is the random force of accident and chance (or luck); from a singular position of a hermeneutic both personal and biographical (in which numbers and animals are viewed in function of the peculiarities of the players seen in their singularities); and finally, from a cosmological, structural perspective, when an appeal is made to the guidelines of a collective belief system able to coordinate an overall view of men and animals, of nature and culture, of this and the other world. From this angle, the animal game would not be a mere "primitive residual" of an indigenous system that has miraculously survived among us but a peculiar institution and a curious, intriguing, finished expression of "modernity" (or, if you prefer, of "transmodernity"), just as it is manifested and exists in the case of Brazil.

In this sense, the totemism of the animal game does not reject the framework of the "great narratives" of the capitalist universe, those myths embedded in the greater promise of making a lot of money and changing social position, in what is called "success," nor does it lose sight of the Brazilian logic, "savage" and uncultured, of alliances with nature. This logic reintroduces into the modern historical drama its dissolution, by revealing that everything can equally well take place within a framework of synchronies between animals, numbers, and men. Furthermore, and as if all of that were not enough, the animal game captures a numerical array that references the scientistic dimension of calculation and rationality.

It is, however, unlike classic totemisms, which postulate an association with an animal so that the group adopting it can forever differentiate itself from the other. Brazilian totemism of the animal game is carried out in order to facilitate probabilistic calculation within the framework of a game of chance, with the explicit intent of promoting dislocations in a structure of social differentiations perceived as hard to overcome by individual effort and, consequently, by work alone. Thus it permits an animal series to be the target of calculation, which "culturalizes" numbers, humanizing them and situating them within reach of social facts. Also, it extends the possibility of quantifying and transferring an animal series into the target of probability, "numeralizing" a limited set of bichos and an infinite series of events in the society.

In order to be able to explain the link between totemism and the animal game, it is necessary to bring to light the logical axes by which the 25 bichos of the series invented by the baron combine to generate an infinite number of messages that will be employed in popular hermeneutics under the name of "hunches."

But this relationship must be qualified. We have to keep in mind from the outset that the "totemism of the animal game" is not intended to construct relatively unequivocal social identities, being above all else part of a game. It is not a matter of equating a clan to an animal, a bear, say, in order to separate it unequivocally from a neighboring clan of, say, the eagle, by the oppositions between a land animal (the bear) and one that flies (the eagle). For what is important in the game is the use of animals to better penetrate into society and, further, to humanize a set of numbers in order to make them easy (and useful) for gambling. An animalized number is a figure endowed with a new reality: with a concreteness capable of arousing emotion, thus making it useful for being dreamed, imagined, and found in the setbacks of life—and transformed into wagers.

Unlike tribal totemisms that prevent the sacrifice of the eponymous animals, the totemism of the animal game postulates its permanent sacrifice, for it is a stage in a complex process that culminates in a hunch and a bet on the animal with which one sympathizes and/or feels an affinity.

There is no doubt, then, that the animal game initially permits a "totemic reading," but only, in a second stage, in order to transform that reading into a magical rite: the betting or "playing," by acting upon a "hunch," which in turn, in a final phase, beckons with the possibility of a "change of condition" for its practitioners. In this zeal to obtain practical results it resembles sacrifice, an institution that in some way complements the purely interpretive act of contemplating (or praising) the order of nature, transforming it into a propitiatory, relational practice. It becomes a "bet," significantly called "a leap of faith," without defined limits, which allows it to be compared to communion and even more to donation, renunciation, and oblation—acts that to Émile Durkheim were perhaps more permanent than the communion postulated by the seminal theories of Robertson Smith (see Durkheim, 1996: chapter 2, part 4; Lévi-Strauss, 1966; and for a critical review of the theories, Valeri, 1985:62ff.).

In other words, the animal game is simultaneously gambling and a scheme of interpretation intended to institute the hope of gain and of social mobility. As such, it offers a link between natural discontinuities and social inequalities—its aim is obviously to surmount them. Doing so, it establishes a cosmology that mixes (up) with the set of internalized values in practitioners' souls, as a constituent part of Brazilian ideology.

But the animal game does not end with the establishment of this homology between two systems of differences—one "natural," the other "social." It also, as we have said, implies an action: the act of betting. The totemic scheme serves as a divinatory and propitiatory framework aimed at leading to a result for the player, who deep down wants, in the words of one informant, "to hit the bicho and become a winner."

A Cosmological Game

All of this raises the question of whether the animal game is really a game. Inspired by Lévi-Strauss, we understand as a game a situation in which the contenders start out from an equal footing—since all are subject to the same set of rules. As the result of their actions, this initial symmetry is transformed into inequality, for the "game"—just like the market to which it is analogous in the so-called "real world" of the economy—engenders winners and losers. But in the case of the animal game, wagers are not made directly, free of mediation. In an ordinary game of chance, such as poker or roulette, there are hunches but no preexisting fixed, well-structured system of divination integrated into the cultural system in which the gambler lives.

In other games of chance, the player may have strong intuitions but the situation and his performance are basic, in the sense of changing his strategy and his movements, which adapt according to the actions and tactics of the other players.[4] In the animal game, however, bets are prized in terms of specific knowledge, a knowing based on a cosmology that allows the unveiling of an immense array of messages that give rise to the so-called "hunch." And because the animal game is characteristically elastic, permitting bets to be made in keeping with the pocketbook (and wishes) of the players, it creates an ambiguous area because its players can claim they're not "gambling" but merely following "hunches" given them in dreams or transmitted through happenstance or by the spirits of their ancestors.

In this sense, it is essential to point out that in the animal game it is not the player who chases the hunch but the hunch may very well pursue and torment the player, who "receives" it unwillingly like a spirit or uninvited guest, in his dream and in his bed. This intrusive, intimate, or domestic character of the hunch is important, for it allows the player to evade his public, bourgeois responsibilities (the so-called "collective obligations," *soi-disant* altruistic), for he plays because he "has hunches" and not the other way around.

As the animal game takes place through the mediation of a collective network in every area of the city, from the "bankers' fortress" to the home, porch, and bedroom of each hunch player, any gambler can make his bet without leaving the house—and even without money[5]—since the bookie can come by the house to take the bet.[6] So everything happens as if it were the dream, the animal, or the chance occurrence that engendered the need to play and not the contrary, as happens with gamblers who are obliged to go to a casino or other special locations to make their bets.

This absence of the frame typical of other forms of games of chance takes the animal game out of special settings where attendance requires previous preparation such as attitude or special attire. Thus, the animal game assumes an aura of innocence and associates itself with the religious sphere, with popular symbols, and with daily life. This set of attitudes helps us understand why many players of the animal game don't think of themselves as gamblers and don't read their obsession as a vice. To them, the bet is not just a loss of money but a sacrifice, a gesture of hope in life and, above all, in the system. It is an act of faith: a "small leap of faith." Helena Morley—a young adolescent who lived in Diamantina, Minas Gerais, at the end of the nineteenth century and who around 1895 (see also note 5) mentioned the animal game—had an aversion to any type of gambling, which "immediately made her sick" and which she considered a "vice," but she loved playing the animal game, which seemed to her like a pastime, an amusement, and an innocent daily ritual parallel to the cruelties of life (Morley, 1971:150).

All of this places the animal game in an ambiguous spot between "true gambling," which is a "vice" and leads to misfortune and moral alienation, and an "innocent game" linked to the good soul of the people, like a technique of divination that, informed by benevolent spirits or by irresistible hunches conveyed in intriguing dreams, allows people to play systematically without considering themselves inveterate gamblers.

This absence of a locus and the use of common symbols frees the animal game from the moral burden linked to the idea of gambling, which motivates the characteristically Brazilian practice by which one does something while professing to do its opposite.

People play the animal game but say they are merely innocently and religiously "chancing it." Money is lost, but the emphasis is on the infallible hunch. In the same way that in Brazil it's said there is no racial prejudice but no one wants their daughter to marry a black man, people can bet heavily in the animal game while still declaring that it's not gambling but the realization of a hunch or the symbolic hunt for some favorite bicho. This doubtlessly explains the popularity of a game tied to daily life and to age-old beliefs.

Another difference is that the result of the animal game does not depend on any specific knowledge, the "know-how" typical of roulette and card games, in which the gambler maximizes his chances by means of a set of techniques that range from passionate involvement to bluffing. The outcome of the animal game is independent of any action on the part of the player, although it may depend on faith and magical beliefs.

Such conditions probably explain the necessity for controlling the outcome by magical means, which affords popularity to this modality of gambling. In fact, unable to modify the results by physical or technical performance during the course of the game—a game, be it noted, without an "opponent," competition, encounter, or situation of direct confrontation to personalize and create an adversarial relationship between the "bank" (or establishment) and the player—the players in the animal game evoke magical means designed to help them "hit" the bicho of the day. These magical means, among other factors, help categorize the animal game as a special modality of lottery.

To find out which animal is going to "hit" (or "show"), the player carries out certain operations whose core consists of decoding messages and formulating strategies to guarantee his victory. This transforms the wager into a rite and the determining of the hunch into hermeneutics, an interpretive system that aids in coordinating the desire for gain with the goal of "chancing it."

So true is this that in case of error the blame is not attributed to the system but to the player's inability to read correctly the identifying signs that would lead to the right choice and to gain. Thus, if a player dreams about a cat falling off a roof, bets on the cat, and the donkey comes up, he concludes, validating the system: "Well, if cats don't fall off roofs, the donkey was me for not knowing how to interpret the dream." From this emerges the following "totemic syllogism":

1.   Cats don't fall off roofs.
2.   If a cat does fall off a roof, he's a wrong cat, a "donkey-cat."
3.   Therefore, if a player bets on a cat that fell off a roof, he's a donkey.
     By taking the medium for the message, he proves himself as much of a donkey as a cat that falls off a roof.

In the same way and by the same logic, Simone Soares in her book about the animal game mentions the case of the player who dreamed of pigs licking his hand but who should bet on the dog (because, after all, pigs don't lick their owner's hand, dogs do), and of the bettor who, having dreamed of a group of slapstick comedians known as the Trapalhões, bet on the monkey (the Trapalhões do crazy things, like monkeys), but the butterfly won because, as the bettor himself explained, there are four Trapalhões, and 4 in the animal game is the number of the butterfly, not the monkey (Soares, 1993:98–99)!

These cases confirm that the player in the animal game knows well that which many scholars have failed to perceive and is implicit in the logic of totemism: the fact demonstrated by Lévi-Strauss that every system of identification acts through differences, and that there are no continuities without discontinuities. If on one hand cats are linked explicitly to rooftops, pigs to their owner, and the Trapalhões to monkeyshines, they are also related to an implicit system of differences capable of revealing other dimensions attributed to those same entities, revelatory of other "truths" associated with them, namely: cats that fall are donkeys; pigs that lick their owner's hand are dogs; and the Trapalhões herald the butterfly because they are a group of four (the number denoting that "bicho").

A good dreamer/bettor, like a good savage thinker, must know how to operate the system in all its dimensions, understanding the logic of its explicit and direct identities as well as its implicit and indirect differences, as the above examples reveal. So much so that many players state that "you shouldn't bet on the bicho you dreamed about" (Soares, 1993:99). This principle, however, is invalidated by the very practice of the game, when players reveal their affinities with certain numbers, persons, objects, or animals as infallible hunches.

Here are some examples from a list of infallible dreams, gathered by Soares (1993:100ff.), transcribed and summarized with some modifications: dreaming about a penknife or a wedding ring equals the ostrich (because the ostrich eats anything); cotton or beans equals the eagle (Soares doesn't opine about the reason for this identification, but we might suggest that both cotton and beans float, or "fly" in the air or in water); clogs or a plow equals the donkey (because of the noise and the association of the plow with poverty and work); a girlfriend or pretty woman equals the butterfly; a fight equals the dog; the desert or old people equals the camel (because of the setting and the hump); a mother-in-law or a train equals the snake (mothers-in-law are treacherous and arrive by train); a child or a kiss equals the rabbit (because of its delicacy and softness); a pan or theft equals the cat (because of its agileness and the fear cats have of cold water); an automobile or rifle equals the lion (the weapon used to face a lion, the automobile because of its power?); dirt or fat equals the pig; Indian ornaments equals the peacock; soccer equals the bull (because of the spectacle, as in a bullfight?); adultery or the forest equals the stag (heightened sensuality? horns? mysterious locale?) . . . Additionally, certain affinities provoke dreams. Among them are tying one's legs before sleeping (one dreams about a four-legged animal), and eating something unusual, like bananas, raw kale, or boiled eggs, before going to sleep. An article in the magazine *Realidade* (June 1966) says that two elderly ladies in the state of Goiás even charged for their infallible dreams.

Let us take a look, however, at these operations that demonstrate how the animal game shapes both a structure and an original hermeneutic that allow the linking of ideology to specific social practices.

The Wager as Ritual

Let us examine the act of betting as a dramatic gesture that links the animal game to the ritual of sacrifice. When one places a bet in the animal game, he undertakes a metaphorical hunt, for the bichos must first be "stalked," "watched," "cornered," and "pursued." When the player is successful, "hitting" (just as a hunter would) the animal "first on the list," there occurs a concrete junction between the poor world of men and the infinitely rich world of fortune (of dreams and the imagination) where the bichos reside.

In the act of betting, the chosen bicho is transformed into a mediator between the planes of nature and culture, but now it abandons its place in a mythic-cosmological series to become the agency for a practice and the focus of a rite of social ascension that is the justification and final objective of the system.

If the system represented by the series to which the animal belongs rests on homology among three parallel sets—those of natural species, of groups and social categories, and of numbers—at the instant of the bet metaphor becomes metonymy, shaping itself into a structure designed to link container and contents, just as happens in sacrifice.

In this structure, as Durkheim taught us long ago, there are two fundamental positions: the sacrificer-gambler and the divinity (the bicho targeted by the bet). These are polar positions, for the divinity, being sacred, is all-powerful and lives apart on a plane superior to that of the sacrificer. The object of the sacrifice is precisely to construct a link between these two planes by means of an offering to be sacrificed. Theoretically, as is known, the more valuable the offering, the more successful the sacrifice, because, in keeping with Durkheim, men need the gods, but the latter would not have their divinity assured without men.

The gesture that corresponds to this attempt to link gods and men by means of a "sacrificial contract" is, in the case of the animal game, the wager. This act attempts to break down the wall separating the world of need, in which the gambler lives, from the mythic universe of abundance contained, supposedly retained, and obviously kept under lock and key by good fortune or luck. The cosmic plane in itself does not guarantee luck, for it is necessary to choose and bet, running a risk and performing a "sacrifice," to become a winner. Now, the focus of this search is the animal chosen for the "sacrifice of the hunch," which will be "pursued" and "cornered" by the gambler-sacrificer, who will intercede with "his" bicho so he can propitiate positively through his bet and his sacrifice.

Sources of the Hunch

In the animal game bets are filtered through a preexisting system of hunches, of choices that are effected based on events that make up part of the player's daily routines. It is this sphere that activates the cosmological system of the game, for it is hunches that allow separating the animal from a totemic series, in which it rests in a splendid cradle, in order to place it as a sacrificial offering to the great god of fortune.

Hunches have as their privileged source dreams and extraordinary events, such as accidents or misfortunes either positive or negative, coincidences and catastrophes that occur not in the carpeted setting of the casino but in the opacity of everyday life. As one of Simone Soares's informants said, "the [animal] game exists because dreams exist" (Soares, 1993:20, 98). In other words, it exists because human beings construct their lives around fantasies that necessarily are beyond the control of routine and consequently place at risk (and at the same time reinforce) everyday interpretive frameworks, threaten the established classificatory order, and upset the prevailing morality.

One fine expression of these fantasies is the samba "Acertei no milhar" ("I Hit the Thousandths"), by Geraldo Pereira and Wilson Batista, composed in 1940 and used as one of the epigraphs of this book, in which the subject of the drama, a totally anonymous "individual" married to one Etelvina, sings about one of the most Brazilian of dreams. Winning big in the animal game, the "thousandths," and suddenly becoming rich, he takes a series of steps that correspond to highly precise symbols appropriate to his new social position, namely: (a) he quits his job—for, in Brazil, despite "the workers' movement" and the "labor party," work continues to be associated with poverty, punishment, and certain other unsuitable forms of social invisibility and exclusion. Despite all the changes, the people don't forget (DaMatta, 1989:31) that the Portuguese *trabalho* (work) comes from the Latin *tripaliare*—to martyr with an instrument of torture—and is still a punishment; (b) he does a makeover of his appearance, changing his wardrobe (giving his old clothes to the poor) and his furnishings (the old furniture must be duly burned); (c) he changes residences, transferring to a luxury hotel, a "Palace Hotel"; (d) he provides his wife, crushed by her domestic duties, with every sensuality in the world, promising her a second "honeymoon," a phase emblematic of all the pleasure that a "person" can enjoy; (e) he changes his name and becomes a noble, transforming himself in his dream into a marquis, nobleman, and viscount and his wife into "Madame"; (f) he commits the supreme and glorious act of aristocratizing: making himself a foreigner in his own country, becoming Frenchified (he should learn French and proposes changing his wife's name from Etelvina to Mme. Pompadour!); (g) he puts his children in a boarding school (where they will be recycled, making useful friendships with members of the elite); (h) he pays all his debts (for one who suddenly changes social class pays his bills and breaks with the chains of reciprocity that tie him to the owner of the grocery store, where selling on credit expresses the longstanding social debt); and finally, (i) he tours Europe, "South America" (a name more palatable for our continent than "Latin America," the designation of a problematic social area), and Paris in a poetic "blue airplane" (symbol of extravagant taste, independence, and the radical mobility of the very rich). "But suddenly," the song says, "sudden-like," his wife wakes up the fantasist, who without great disappointment discovers—for, as a good Brazilian he's a realist at heart—that it "was time to go to work" and that it "was all a dream, my friend!"[7]

It is this set of experiences, decoded in reference to the set of 25 bichos, which serves as the focal point of an original and creative popular hermeneutics and constitutes the basis for a system of hunches. Received as raw or elementary messages, such experiences are the point of departure for formation of the hunch and the elaboration of betting strategies.

It is possible to recognize in the practice of the animal game two distinct moments. In the first, the player receives the "message" from those sources and interprets it in a way to translate it into a bicho and a number. In the second, after having identified and chosen the bicho, he executes the bet.

This procedure recalls an old and revolutionary formulation by Marcel Mauss and Henri Hubert (1972), according to which magic is an act of change. In fact, where previously there was a theoretical and formal relationship, surely a static one, between two sets of differences, there now exists a practical-dynamic one. It is a bridge between symbolic universes, for, once identified, it is a certain bicho (with its respective number) that will represent the player in the uncertain world of fortune.

At this point it is fitting to follow more closely the course of a typical player in the animal game, from the instant he gets the hunch to the moment when he interprets it. Such a course begins with the practitioner going into a special state. Sleep is the most common inductive agent of this state, for it links us to a sovereign source of hunches: dreams and their messages. It must not be forgotten that states of alert, though secondary, can also be potential sources of the hunch. When all is said and done, the player should constantly be "open" for the "hunch" to miraculously or freely appear, to insinuate itself subtly and subliminally into his awareness so that it can be duly captured.

The state of "openness" requires a suspension of interest in relation to the overwhelming, ordinary flow of daily routine. It demands changing lenses so that the rational, practical, and linear reading of the world is replaced by a view aimed at discovering the real text contained in the accidental, the fortuitous, the virtual, and the seemingly random. In this mode of perception what is prized is the extraordinary, the occult, and the unforeseen. If in daily life we pay more attention to the consistency that lends plausibility to routines, transforming them into realities that guarantee order and sense, in the state of "openness" to hunches everything may be a sign. A car accident, the sudden sight of an animal, a number that appears unexpectedly on the side of a truck, a figure suggested by clouds, the presence of a person or object can be read as signs, presages, or messages to be perceived and decoded by the player.

Intrinsically, it is a technique of reading the world opposed to that emphasized in school and in the newspapers—those heralds of rationality and linearity—that allows perception to be directed to areas collectively demarcated as useful for the generating of hunches. If in school we learn to situate events along a spectrum that runs from indifference to attention, in accord with their relation to our agendas, intentions, and programs, for the player in the animal game everything comes to be, if not important, at least suggestive, for all events near or far, hot or cold, domestic or foreign, natural or social, are potential sources of the hunch.

Nevertheless, paradoxically, the less effort the player makes to receive these signals, the better. In this subliminal and marginal territory in which utilitarian reason is placed in quarantine, what is valued is passivity, the latent state that camouflages intentions, the oblique glance. Reason, intent, and a plan of action, which demand rationality and an adjustment of means and ends, get in the way of receiving the signals that help capture the bicho.

In this field, dreams emerge as the favored source of hunches.[8] In dreams we visit unknown places; we establish unsuspected relationships; we change the appearance of people, landscapes, and objects; we compose music; we speak languages we do not know; we talk with the dead, fly, and live underwater; we kill and we die. Often we awake, like E. B. Tylor's "animism"-inventing primitives, perplexed and intrigued by the reason for all these apparently meaningless texts.

From a sociological point of view, it can be said that sleep characterizes a temporary and positive "social death," planned and paradoxical because it is necessary. This loss of consciousness is contrary to the commonplace and one from which we always return, which frees us from mortal ties and the social roles we normally play.

In the abandoned dream-state we are subjected to unusual and even forbidden images, such as seeing the future and speaking with the dead. This last virtuality is in fact doubly valued from the point of view of the hunch, for aficionados almost always interpret dreams as messages from the other world. First, because dreams lead to the loss of control of the oneiric images produced by an unconscious in touch with itself. Second, because dreams induce experience in a universe ruled by a different set of norms. And finally, by the fact equally crucial for our arguments that every dream, as Freud taught, actualizes a peculiar combination of power and impotence, of absurdity and rationality.

For all these reasons, players pay great attention to dreams, especially dreams about disappeared or deceased people. Dreaming about the dead is an excellent presage, whether the dead person indicates the number to be played or because, through his presence, associations can be sought that result in good hunches—such as an animal that resembles him or the date of his birth, marriage, graduation, or death, or even the number of his sepulcher.

The dead, transformed into noble and powerful ancestors or into benevolent guardian angels, or protecting spirits, live on by executing pacts with the living. Thus, they appear in dreams, insinuating infallible hunches in behalf of those who are struggling with the trials and necessities of this life.

The role attributed to the dead should not occur by chance in a society in which the home, the family, and friends constitute basic institutions. What this privilege attributed to dreams about the deceased members of the home and family indicates is, on one hand, a veritable ancestor cult within the framework of a game that renews hopes of bettering one's position in society; on the other, it is one more proof that in Brazil death kills, but the dead do not die (DaMatta, 1987b:173).[9]

Another basic source of hunches is extraordinary events. License plates of cars involved in accidents; the sudden sight of an animal in an unusual place (a horse in the heart of the city, a cat in a bank, a rat in a movie theater, a dog run over in the middle of the street); any number that comes up in recurring or unexpected fashion; the shape of clouds and other phenomena of the same order fall into this category. Alongside this there are many atypical situations that become transformed into sources of hunches.

One of us (Elena Soárez) discovered, when she visited a certain animal game betting site as part of her research, that she was approached by an inveterate player who displayed curiosity about her presence there, making notes and asking questions. After she clarified her presence, the player asked her student number in the master's program at the National Museum, for in his mind such a number surely contained a good hunch. Faced with the impossibility of remembering the number, Elena Soárez was then asked about other numbers that figured in her identity, like her license plate, which was 5721—the "she-goat" thousandths—whose association with the feminine pole was, however, not the most flattering, as we will see later.

Such procedures reveal that almost anything, even the indicative marks of identity (date of birth, ID card number, license plate, etc.), can be read as sources of a hunch, which forms an alternative to its serious, official, legal, and, naturally, sterile register in terms of magic and money.

Another source of hunches and intuition are those beings considered special or privileged, such as pregnant women, the handicapped (especially the crippled), children, the old, and people at the edge of the social world.[10] The case of the dead, which obviously belongs to this series, constitutes an extreme example.

One of Elena Soárez's informants, a lady who has been playing the animal game daily for over twenty years, states that, of the people around her, the best "hunch" always comes from her elderly maid and the worst, from her husband. The maid is a woman in her seventies who was born and raised in the countryside and doesn't know how to read or write. The husband, in contrast, is an active and cultured attorney. For that very reason, the informant listens attentively to all her maid's dreams and tries to interpret them in terms of the bichos, but she ignores her husband's dreams, considering them sterile in terms of the game. Sophistication, cosmopolitanism, total insertion into bourgeois life and rationality make people disenchanted and occasion the loss of the capacity to suggest interesting hunches.

In their previously cited classic essay on magic, Marcel Mauss and Henri Hubert state that the exercise of any magic rite presupposes that the practitioner distance himself from his "normal" or routine state, as this distancing provokes a new vision of the world. Later in the same text, Mauss and Hubert list a set of beings to whom magical virtues are attributed. On the list are women, children, gravediggers, and foreigners—special types because of their marginal or oblique position in relation to the routines and official or central powers of society, since they are people *between* social positions and/or existential states.

Distant from and even opposed to "official power," these categories of people are a source of mystical or magical strength. If they lack the capacity to command through rational means, by using the law or their position in the system, as is typical of routine political or civic power, they can nevertheless afflict people through the evil eye, sorcery, or any other peripheral and unofficial attribute—called "magic"—duly equated with it.

Especially in the critical phases of the life cycle, such as menstruation, pregnancy, and childbirth, powerful natural or supernatural processes are attributed—in many societies and/or historical periods—to women. They are, therefore, a common source of ambiguity, which enhances, for many, their capacity for exercising magical powers. The same thing happens with children, a good vehicle for hunches because they are uncontaminated by the interests and selfishness that rule the world of adults, to which they belong only marginally. Thus their innocence and simplicity, strong sources of magical intuition. (Roberto DaMatta, for example—it is worth rementioning what was already said in the prologue of this book—had his first conscious experience with the animal game when he was a child and gave his maternal grandmother a winning tip, confirming this capacity of children as good sources for hunches.)

Another way of getting good hunches is related to divinatory practices, such as dropping olive oil into a glass of water and hoping that an image will form that resembles a bicho, or throwing water onto the wall and observing the shape of the stain, etc. In all these instances, we should note, a random manifestation is called forth from that temporal fact at the edges of daily routine.

Another expedient used to obtain a hunch is prayer specifically "to hit the bicho," when one tries to enter into direct contact with the other world. A good example is the following prayer:

My little gambling boy, who bought a deck of cards, who played seven cards, and all seven times won, show me the animal that will come up today. Now, now, now! I did this in the name of Almighty God, Holy Jesus Christ and my mother the Most Holy Mary, and the divine Holy Spirit. I petition the spirit of F. so he may come to my presence and show me the animal and tell me the hundredth in tomorrow morning's lottery. . . . God, I ask you, Lord, send me in your holy name the soul of F. through the power of omnipotent God . . . in the name of Jesus, Joseph, and Mary show me the animal and the hundredth for tomorrow's lottery because of St. Ubaldo, St. Francis, because of these saints and words and because of the twelve apostles, because of all God's saints and Abraham and Jacob because of the angels St. Raphael all the virtues of heaven and the blessed St. John the Baptist, St. Thomas, St. Philip, St. Mark, St. Matthew, St. Simon, St. Judas, St. Martin. Because of the martyrdom of St. Sebastian, Sts. Cosmas and Damian, St. Dionysius with all their companions of God, by the heart of King Daniel with the four Gospels I ask you to tell the soul of F. to show me the animal and tell me the hundredth for tomorrow, I beseech by the four pillars of heaven that my request not be ignored, I ask you creature of God, I ask by the two tongues that are repeated. By these powers (Ramos, 1942:263).[11]

This prayer embraces, democratically and inclusively, basic figures from the Catholic pantheon, along with Jewish prophets and even kings and a certain St. Dionysius. Note also the significant fact that the prayer is directed to a boy.

Besides the codified techniques such as dreams, special events, and prayers, there are methods oriented specifically toward numbers, demonstrating their importance and their concreteness in the system. Thus, there are some who specialize in manipulating numbers, adding, dividing, subtracting, or multiplying the results of the animal game for the last three days, or doing combinations starting from certain days of the months, or even using special tables in which are recorded the winning numbers from the latest lotteries.

All of this shows that the sources of hunches follow a path from the highly structured and cosmologically oriented—dreams and accidents, filtered through hunches given by powerful categories—to divinatory actions closer to singular practices, explainable by personal preferences. Just as there are bichos (and numbers) for every taste, there are also divinatory techniques for every preference.

Marcelino Perdigão, a brother of Roberto DaMatta's mother, was convinced that he had found an infallible system for winning at the animal game. The system depended on watching the results of the various lotteries that he researched in minute detail, searching for the most diverse numerical combinations and, later on, adding them and dividing them. Furthermore, Marcelino was equally on the alert for the messages of dreams—especially those from the dead—and always bet on the sepulcher number of his mother, Emerentina. Along with these, shall we say, mystical-empirical measures, Marcelino maximized his possibilities of winning by "surrounding" the bicho "on all seven sides"—i.e., by playing its numbers and their various combinations. Having won some times, Marcelino would repeat euphorically that he had invented a way of "clubbing the bicho." In his youth, Roberto DaMatta witnessed proof of the method, which consisted of a sheet of paper with various numbers diligently complied in lists, which gave them a certain air of order and "science."

The Bichos Are Good for Gambling

If at the end of the nineteenth century the animal game was treated with a certain degree of indifference, what were the factors that awoke the passion that soon came to dominate the people of Rio de Janeiro, to the point that police were called in to control the tumult caused by players gathered at the gates of Baron de Drummond's Zoological Park?

One of the elements that made the animal game popular was the fact that the "bicho of the day" could not be predicted. The fact of our dealing with a structure characterized by randomness, probability, and by what we call "luck" (or "chance"), helps us understand this unusual interest in the animal game. For though the bicho could be chosen, it wasn't possible to determine its appearance at the end of the day. Speculative activity focusing on formulation of the hunch is, without doubt, one of the greatest attractions of the animal game and, at the same time, that which confers its singularity amid the panoply of other modalities of lottery. In fact, in the words of Cabral, one of the few who have taken this institution seriously: "getting a hunch means believing in and trusting that such and such a bicho will 'hit,' that is, will be drawn, on the day the player makes his bet. To chance = gamble. Having faith = playing the game" (Cabral, n.d.:15). Formulation of the hunch changes everything because it transforms the position of the recipient of the hunch (who is in a state of passivity) into a sacrificer (and a player), which constitutes an active position.

From an empirical and "objective" point of view, it is obvious that the chance of hitting continues to be a question of mathematical probability.

However, once there's a hunch, the player experiences his chance as luck in its double and contradictory meaning. On one hand, he struggles with probability; on the other, he finds himself dealing with the idea that deep down (who knows?) it is possible to transcend the random and indifferent, giving it a structure, capturing the probable and the fortuitous in a net of determinations. On the intellectual plane this belief is equivalent to a passing from chance to necessity, and on the plane of social meaning to the possibility of unveiling the future and fate, overcoming the indifference of the world and of "life."

When Animals Become Bichos

But there can only be an established system of hunches because such a system is based on a rich but established array of 25 animals—the "bichos"—who propitiate all sorts of symbolic ties to other dimensions of social life. It is beyond a doubt because of the bichos that this form of lottery became a local and national passion, surpassing the flower game and the foodstuffs game created in the same period.

But just who are these "bichos"?

It is worth noting, initially, that the list of 25 animals that make up the animal game is not homogeneous but composed significantly of a majority of peaceful animals. It is an artificially constructed system by means of multiple criteria that if not for the alphabetical constraint would be very much closer to an implicit or unconscious design than to rational and objective rules or motives. It is a set created not to achieve a specific task, or to demonstrate a previously established point in relation to the human or animal kingdom, but one engendered by what can be called a "dynamic of cultural or ideological tendencies" that operate at the heart of Brazilian society. It is a self-sufficient totality: its constituent elements are brought together by symbolic motives, alien to the objectives—and, without doubt, to the explicit judgment—of its creators.

In general terms, the uniqueness of the list lies in its being composed of "bichos," not "animals." To understand this, however, it is necessary to study what in Brazil is classified (and understood) as a "bicho."

In Brazilian society, the category "bicho," because it is broader, encompasses that of "animal" and allows for distinguishing between the two classes.

If the animal is an inhabitant that belongs to nature, the bicho is a typically social being, a marginal and aberrant entity that belongs to the social imagination. An animal has to be a hippopotamus, a giraffe, or a tapir. But a bicho can be anything: animal, spirit, apparition, even a person. What qualifies something as a bicho is its ambiguity, its exoticism, its appearance, or its lack of definition.

When we say "So-and-So is a bicho," or "He looks like a bicho!" we are emphasizing exceptional qualities or certain aberrant and unclassifiable dimensions of his physical or social person. The great Brazilian folklorist Luís da Câmara Cascudo perceived this aspect well when he stated in his *Dicionário do folclore brasileiro*: "Bicho is any animal that is neither man, bird, or fish." Further, "bicho" would be any animal that, if man, bird, or fish, had a look strange or colossal in the species and therefore very ugly (Câmara Cascudo, 1988:124).

"Bicho," as Câmara Cascudo stresses, can also be used to designate a vision, apparition, or spirit from the other world, in clear association with everything that transcends ordinary experience. On the other hand, the word is equally used to designate free or uninhibited behavior—as in the expression "let the bicho loose"—when emphasis is placed on the erotic side of each one. There is obviously a hierarchical relationship between "animal" and "bicho," for if every animal is a bicho, not all bichos are animals. Once these basic differences are established, we must ask: what makes the 25 animals on the animal game list "bichos," and why do they constitute special cases?

The answer is contained in the question itself. It is not their intrinsic or individual qualifications that cause the animals to be considered bichos but the fact of their being part of a list that addresses itself both to empirical reality and to the world of dreams: to the universe of hunches and gambling.

This exceptionality transforms the 25 animals into bichos and sets them apart from the "natural world" in which they originated. Such marginality vis-à-vis nature allows them to be equated to certain typical events, themselves exceptional, in the world of culture.

In the same way that the sources of the hunch lie outside the control of reason and human intervention, the animals on the list are distinguished from others by their exceptionality and, obviously, by their marginality in relation to the control exercised over them by society. If the dog, the cow, and the cat are controlled animals in real life, it cannot be forgotten that they represent numbers whose appearance eludes conscious rational control. That is why they are bichos. That is why they are good for thinking about, for dreaming, and for gambling.

Everything takes place as if a set of social experiences difficult to explain and interpret—accidents and dreams—found a welcome when correlated to a set of animals that are bichos and therefore enjoy remarkable symbolic power, as well as a position of exceptionality and extravagance. Now, it is precisely this charge of social meanings that permits the integration of the bichos into daily experience, making the 25 animals powerful sources of hunches. For they are not merely a set of nonhuman entities but beings that in Brazilian society act as much inside the world as outside it, setting in motion the link between known and unknown, familiar and exotic, banal and extraordinary. Furthermore, the bichos enjoy exceptional intimacy with and distance from human beings, which makes them ideal for being pursued as sources of the hunch. These hunches make it possible to go from poverty to wealth by means of a complex process in which the dead are equated to the bichos and the latter to certain numbers, forming a closed, dynamic system.

We can now respond more completely to the question of the motives that brought the animal game to achieve such popular acceptance, while the flower game and the foodstuffs game did not enjoy the same degree of success.

How can you dream about objects that don't lend themselves to symbolic representation? Dreaming about flowers and foods is much more complicated than dreaming about animals that, like bichos, are more than natural beings: they are metaphors for human society.

In fact, if we compare the three series—bichos, foods, flowers—we see immediately that only the first of these occupies an intermediate spot between nature and culture. The "foodstuffs" series appears as nearest the pole of culture, while the "flowers" series is completely within the pole of nature.

Further, the "foodstuffs" series is also the most irregular, for besides "foods" it contains supplementary products like soap, candles, and tobacco. If we look at this series in greater detail, we perceive that it is actually a shopping list of items sold in groceries. However, despite these formal inconveniences, the list of foodstuffs has classificatory potential. We stress this possibility because in Brazilian society there is an abundance of metaphors originating in the universe of foods and eating. In this sense, there is nothing more significant than recalling that the verb "to eat" (*comer*) serves us as a symbol of the hierarchical encompassing of one person by another, as a metaphor for the sex act, in which in an idealized, revelatory, and exemplary fashion, the man "eats" the woman.

We also know that food acts as an index of identity and social position, as seen in the expressions "flour is food to the Northeasterner," "to be on top of the beef jerky," or "to be treated like sponge cake," as opposed to "eating the bread that the devil kneaded." From these expressions one can deduce the potential of foods as instruments of social classification (see Da-Matta, 1989).

Besides this, it is hard to see in the collection of 25 "foodstuffs" a metaphor for human society, for foods are an intrinsic part of human beings' world, invented by them, chosen, produced, consumed, and digested, suggesting in their totality a metonymic relationship instead of a metaphorical link. Foods are rarely paradigms or models of action, for their part in the world of men is instrumental, as means to an end. In fact, in the majority of human societies, foods are charged with utility.

When we think about the flower series, we see that, contrariwise, they are too close to nature. In reality, it is difficult to conceive of a set of flowers as metaphor for human society. Popular wisdom suggests just the opposite when it declares that "In life not everything is flowers!" Flowers would, however, be associated with the positive and aesthetic side of existence, such as the feminine dimension of social life, representing fragility and delicateness.

On the other hand, flowers, like foods, are highly instrumentalized, for we give flowers, cultivate flowers, buy flowers. The relationship they establish with humans is not one of independence but of subservience or subordination. As we have indicated, flowers are a medium of exchange and of communication; they color and perfume our lives, as instruments for beautifying existence.

However, like any collection, flowers have the potential to provide human thinking with a model of differences. We bring flowers to women and friends, and use them to cover our dead, which reveals the possibility of ritualizing fertility and sterility, juncture and disjuncture, or loss. If we remember the flowers that made up the Mexican Manuel Zevada's flower game, we will see that they too offered a model of differences. There we find flowers with rather suggestive names such as monsignor, martyr, nostalgia, forget-me-not, evergreen, dawn, good night, angelic, perfect love, etc. In addition, we find the immediate connotations of the carnation and the rose and the social uses made of flowers—flowers for funerals, weddings, and birthdays, for young women, mature women, amorous conquests, rejection, boutonnieres, living room vases, decoration, etc. It is a very rich set that allows the ritualization of fundamental opposites such as masculine/feminine, fertility/sterility, sacred/profane, life/death, happiness/sadness—oppositions more than sufficient for the establishment of a model of differences applicable to any domain.

The disadvantage of flowers as compared to bichos, however, is that they participate in human life as objects. To have flowers it is necessary to admire them, cultivate them, and consume them. In relation to this point, it is recounted that the flower game attracted attention and caused a clamor because when the number was drawn, Zevada would shout the name of the corresponding flower. If the flower was the daisy and the winner was a man, the crowd was unforgiving and would break into guffaws. As a result, many would withdraw and not claim the prize to which they were entitled, fearful of being the target of mockery from those present. This shows that, despite flowers being useful for typifying certain social situations and dimensions, they do not offer a frame of reference for a broad variety of social experiences.

From all this, it can be stated that of the three series in question, it is the bichos series that occupies the clearly intermediate position between nature and culture. Perhaps because there is no doubt that, in the domain of society animals are the beings that best represent certain moral and/or aesthetic qualities, having, like their counterparts, emotions and singular ways of life that vary according to species.

It is precisely this that we will see in the next chapter, when we discuss in detail the characteristics of the set of bichos in the animal game.

CHAPTER 3

Who Are the Bichos?

As we saw in the previous chapter, from the emergence of the drawing of bichos at the Zoological Park in 1892 until the moment when this mechanism for fundraising achieved autonomy as a game, there occurred the birth of a true classificatory science that, by bringing together numbers, animals, and social "things," re-created a refined and paradoxical "modern totemism" whose principles are systematically used by gamblers.

But such "symbolic superstructure," providing a popular hermeneutic, could only have prospered by virtue of the 25 animals "arbitrarily" called upon to make up the list of the animal game. It is these "bichos" that serve as reference to orient the strategies of the hunch and the practice of wagering, when the gambler materializes his hunch on the altar of hope through a pecuniary sacrifice.

It is obvious that the symbolic richness of these bichos impedes the formulation of a rigid interpretive code for the animal game. What they admit is a disparate set of sources for hunches, ranging from dreams and personal information exchanged at home and in the street between persons known and unknown, based on age-old wisdom or modern observation, to written information codified in manuals by specialists in numerology, the interpretation of dreams, and the cabbala, books that can be acquired at newsstands or bookstores.

This omnivorous character of the animal game, able to cannibalize—despite the statistics, universal laws, and the apparent subjection of the people to the means of mass communication—the literate and the illiterate, the written word and orality, follows a well-known and paradoxical "complementary competition" much to the taste of the Brazilian system.[1] This competition uses both modern means and traditional sources of the hunch, imputing value to both (we almost said, inspired by Jorge Amado's novel *Dona Flor and Her Two Husbands*, "choosing" both), as if for the gambler everything merited respect.

But if we wish to penetrate the heart of the system, we have to understand the classificatory principles by which these 25 bichos are categorized and ordered, distinguishing each from the other and among themselves as special entities in terms of multiple criteria. For it is surely these attributes that explain the richness of the scheme invented and maintained by the animal game.

The study of interviews conducted with players, an examination of *Antologia do jogo do bicho,* the pioneering book compiled by Renato José Costa Pacheco (published in 1951), and analysis of the voluminous oral literature gathered by various students of Brazilian folklore in the states of Espírito Santo, Minas Gerais, São Paulo, Alagoas, and Amazonas between 1910 and 1955, in addition to observations made during field research, will serve as the basis for this attempt to explain the list of attributes or distinctive characteristics of the animals in the animal game, with the goal of specifying their most expressive qualities.

The examples below represent a sample of this type of material, which allows us to verify how the animals on the animal game list as "bichos" are "read," classified, and interpreted in Brazil.

Example 1: From a folk song collected in 1951 by Sr. Wilson Balbino in São Lourenço, in the upper Rio Novo, county of Colatina, state of Espírito Santo (Pacheco, 1957:99):

Number one is the OSTRICH
Which begins the count

Number two is the EAGLE
Which has a curved beak

Number three is the DONKEY
Which won't move unless shod

Number four is the BUTTERFLY
Which flies in the mist

Number five is the DOG
Which fetches without being asked

Number six is the GOAT
Which gives milk to the poor

Number seven is the SHEEP
Which is a blessed beast

Number eight is the CAMEL
Which carries twice the weight

Number nine is the SNAKE
Which never misses its pounce

Number ten is the RABBIT
Which is a wary beast

Number eleven is the HORSE
Which is of the saddle

Number twelve is the ELEPHANT
Which sleeps leaning back

Number thirteen is the ROOSTER
Which sings at dawn

Number fourteen is the CAT
Which has caught lots of rats

Number fifteen is the CROCODILE
Which leaves the dry for the damp

Number sixteen is the LION
Which is a respected beast

Number seventeen is the MONKEY
Which is an ill-behaved beast

Number eighteen is the PIG
Which gives the market lard

Number nineteen is the PEACOCK
Which has golden feathers

Number twenty is the TURKEY
Which circles the house

Number twenty-one is the BULL
Which has broken many carts

Number twenty-two is the TIGER
Which is black and spotted

Number twenty-three is the BEAR
Which cavorts to win coins

Number twenty-four is the STAG
Which has outrun many a dog

Number twenty-five is the COW
And the numbering is done.

Example 2: A dream related by Cícero Dantas dos Santos and heard by Sgt. Luís Loureiro, found in the same anthology:

I dreamed I was in a very large field. Suddenly, an OSTRICH appeared. I quickly ran after the animal, which fled from me. Tiring of the effort to overtake it, I sat down, but at that instant I spotted an EAGLE flying toward me at a low altitude. I tried to hide under a large tree beside me. When I plunged into the leaves, a DONKEY that was hiding there, maybe to get out of working, ran off at full speed, frightening a bunch of BUTTERFLIES resting on the flowers. That was when I noticed that the donkey was galloping away. It was because, when it came out of the leaves, a DOG, which was chasing a GOAT, came by in a mad dash in search of refuge. So I decided to find out where the dog and goat came from. I climbed a hill, some distance away, and saw at once a flock of grazing SHEEP and, some thirty meters farther, a man riding a CAMEL. He was probably the owner of the sheep, and his animal was loaded down with an enormous amount of baggage. The man was playing a flute, and, poor thing, didn't see that while he played, a huge SNAKE was coming out of a box, amusing itself with the sound of the music. At that instant, the snake discovered that, besides the music, to his relief there was inside the wire cage a pair of RABBITS from India, which within a few moments would be deceased. Having nothing to do with that, I tried to get away, continuing my journey. When I climbed a rise, I heard moaning. I tried to see where it was coming from and soon saw a HORSE lying down, covered in blood, and near it a man with a broken leg. When he saw me, the unfortunate man asked for help and showed me what had caused it all. It was an ELEPHANT that had attacked him. I picked the man up in my arms and went looking for help. We had been going for some minutes when I heard a ROOSTER crow. Then the injured man told me that where the rooster was crowing there was a house. I headed there. As soon as we arrived at the side of the house, we saw two CATS fighting over a CROCODILE hide that was still fresh. At that moment we heard a roar that made my hair stand on end. In a cage, a LION was savoring the crocodile meat. To the side, in small cages, were dozens of MONKEYS cavorting happily. Further on, a large sty full of wild PIGS. I thought: it must be the house of some wild-animal hunter. When I turned to the other side of the house, I saw a tremendous fight going on between animals. It was the PEACOCK and the TURKEY, tearing each other apart over a female turkey, who was watching it all with a satisfied expression. That was when the owner of the house appeared, a strong, tall, dark guy who came up to me and the injured man to offer assistance. He quickly tried to treat the injured man and made him comfortable, then invited me to see all the animals he had caught in traps to sell to the circus. Up ahead was the animal cage; I saw an enormous Bengal TIGER. In another cage was a very large BEAR, and further on a pair of STAGS, well tended to and the owner's plaything. At that moment, a lady showed up carrying two buckets and told the owner of the house to invite me to have some milk that she had just taken from a fine-looking COW in the corral. When I started to drink the milk, the vessel fell from my hand and spilled on my clothes. That was when I felt two strong pinches and heard some insults, for the spilled milk wet the bedcovers and my old lady.

There you have it, buddy; that was the dream; you can bet on any one of the animals. Now that's what I call a real dream!

Example 3: The set of correspondences in equation form listed in the manual *O jogo do bicho: Como jogar e ganhar* (*The Animal Game: How to Play and Win*), written by Gehisa Saldanha, in which each bicho is associated with a distinctive or predominant trait (for example, the ostrich is gluttonous, the eagle is intelligent, the donkey is stupid, the tiger is aggressive, the bear is treacherous, the stag is delicate, the cow is fat).

Example 4: List of correspondences, taken from the manual by Gehisa Saldanha:

A black bird indicates the OSTRICH; shrewd people suggest the EAGLE; a pretty woman is the BUTTERFLY; if you dream about flight or persecution, you should bet on the DOG; a mountain climber recalls the GOAT; a dream about becoming rich demands betting on the SHEEP; a desert is the sign of the CAMEL; a dancer is the SNAKE; a brood of offspring is the RABBIT; a ride is good for the HORSE; brute strength is the ELEPHANT; a moonlit night or a dawn is a hint for the ROOSTER; a thief is associated with the CAT; water is home to the CROCODILE; a wild beast is represented by the LION; acrobatics symbolize the MONKEY; a good chunk of roast brings to mind the PIG; vain is the PEACOCK; parties and banquets serve TURKEY; if you dream about a barbecue, play the BULL; if you're being attacked, that indicates the TIGER; a false friend is the BEAR; a delicate man is the STAG; and prostitution, the COW (Saldanha, 1986:60).

Example 5: In this set we have some terms associated with each bicho. These equivalences were found in the personal notes of one of Elena Soárez's informants:

Ostrich = elderly people, home; eagle = Rui Barbosa, white paper, a courting couple, a cardboard box catching fire in the air; bear = deceased person, marital infidelity, ungrateful friend, religious type; stag = horns; cow = woman giving birth, maternity.

Example 6: In this list, from the same source as the last, we find the following emblematic equivalences:

Dreaming that you're eating indigestible objects or meals = ostrich (no. 1); dreaming that you're flying = eagle (no. 2); cold, caverns, skin, friend, snow = bear (no. 23); adultery, homosexual, impotence, member, vagina = stag (no. 24); son, pacifier, child nursing = cow (no. 25).

Example 7: This final document, in verse form, was also collected from personal notes of informants:

Dreaming of a feathered animal, so black that it shines, is sure to be
the OSTRICH;
Dreaming of a crafty person, a smooth talker, you can bet on the
EAGLE;
Dreams or thoughts about loops in the air, I know the BUTTERFLY
will hit;
A chase on a hillside hints at the DOG;
Climbing a mountain till it crumbles under you is a sign of the GOAT;
Doing business to make good money
is the hunch for the SHEEP;
Dreaming about the desert, riding through the dunes,
is the CAMEL and the beginning of fortune;
Dreaming about belly-dancing, with a dancer who sways,
is a hunch for the SNAKE;
If you're pushing forty, to check the tool bet on the RABBIT;
Dreaming about riding and other amusements,
it's the HORSE for sure;
Dreaming of pile drivers, or a steamroller, the bettor should remember
the ELEPHANT;
Dreaming about a moonlit night, beautiful and silvery, the ROOSTER
has to hit;
Dreaming of leapers that come through the roof, bet on the CAT to
make some change;
Dreaming about waters in a swamp is a sign of the CROCODILE;
If you dream about wild beasts and groups of animals, play the LION
with unequal hundredths;
Dreaming of great leaps between a nest and a hole means the
MONKEY is coming up;
Dreaming of a hind leg or a ham is a matter of the PIG;

Dreaming about a vain and ostentatious young man is sure to be the
PEACOCK;
If you dream of celebrations, or Christmas things, then know that your
bicho is the TURKEY;
Dreaming about barbecue, with drinks and a blast, be sure to play the
BULL;
If you're choosing beasts and don't know which to keep, it's the TIGER
that will head the list;
Dreaming about false friends, about people giving a speech, can only
be a sign of the BEAR;
Dreaming of gays, or idle talkers, is a good hint to play the STAG;
Dreaming of the ill, conveyed on a stretcher,
is a sure sign of the COW.

Principles of Classification

The animals in the animal game series can be separated according to the following criteria: wild or domesticated—or closer to or further from society;
by the role they play in the system; by the way in which they live and move
about; by the types of movements they make; by their physical dimensions
and characteristics and by the way in which they carry out their collective
life, whether in "bands," gregariously, or in isolation; whether they are passive or active in the struggle or clash of life; by their social potential; by the
types of social relationships or ties that they are capable of establishing; by
their sexual potentialities; and by their capacity for invoking the sacred and/
or profane planes. Besides this, the bichos can also be read as vehicles of
prosperity or setbacks; life or death; or even as references to prevailing racial
perceptions in Brazil.

Of all these distinctive attributes or dimensions, the most important,
most obvious, and most traditional is that dividing animals into the "wild,"
"fierce," and hard-to-domesticate (such as the tiger, lion, crocodile, eagle,
and snake), and the "domesticated," tame, harmless, or familiar (such as the
donkey, butterfly, dog, goat, sheep, camel, rabbit, horse, elephant, rooster,
cat, pig, peacock, turkey, bull, and cow). The latter, incidentally, comprise
a significant and overwhelming majority, displaying a tendency contrary
to that of Western bestiaries, which prefer wild predators (Salisbury,

1994:133).[2] It goes without saying that certain bichos, like the ostrich and the monkey, fall somewhere in between.[3]

The other dimensions that allow contrasting and thus distinguishing among animals help to qualify this central cleavage, which, according to the suggestion of Sir Edmund Leach, goes from the nearest to the most distant in society, having equivalents as much in what is considered food (or not) as in relation to the categories of people with whom one may (or may not) have sexual relations (see Leach, 1983).

Situated along this first dimension of contrast we have the following schema:

[More Savage
Lion "king of the beasts"
   Tiger "the wild animal"
      Crocodile "lives in swamp waters"
         Elephant "lives in circuses or zoos"
            Eagle—Snake—Crocodile—Bear "tamed animal, circus"
               Butterfly "lives free in the grass"
                  Monkey "leaped out of the jungle"
                   Stag
                     Ostrich "lives in the fields"
                       Bull—Camel - Peacock
                    Rabbit
                     Pig "in the sty, mud"
                        Rooster "in the house and street, on the roof. Thief"
                     Dog "man's best friend
                         Cow—Horse—Donkey—Sheep—Goat
                       Rooster—Turkey
                           More Domestic]

Observe that in example 1 the lion is seen as a "respected beast"; in example 2, the same animal devours a crocodile and the bear is represented as large; in example 3, the tiger is aggressive; in example 4, the tiger is an attacker and the lion is represented as a wild beast; and in example 7, the tiger and the lion are seen as wild beasts. The contrast between "wild" and "domestic" establishes a gradation—in other words, from animals distant from society, which attack human beings, to animals that live in permanent contact with men, serving as mascots, guards, companions, means of transportation, objects of aesthetic contemplation, moral examples, sources of food, and as food itself, as is the case of the cow.

However, each of these groupings admits many other differentiations.

One such is that which the public makes between the lion and the tiger, situating the former as "king of the beasts" and the latter as merely a "large cat." Thus, if the lion emerges as a symbol of kingship, courage, pride, and valor, the tiger appears "felinely" as the animal that "slaps you and hides its hand" and "only shows up at the wrong time."[4] It is, thus, no accident that in Brazil the lion symbolizes the income tax, that basic organ of state revenue collecting, which gives that institution a double identity. On one hand, it has the efficient modernity of impersonal collectors of taxes—which, after all, everyone must pay. But on the other, its leonine being harks back to a sovereignty that shapes social superiority, political evenhandedness, and, at the extreme, the fact that this lion can be tame with the rich and fierce with the poor, as the Brazilian experience proves.

This same distinction operates in the great field of domesticated animals, serving to distinguish the cat from the dog. The cat, as a tiger on a smaller scale, also "only catches rats by treachery" and, even domesticated, is an animal that remains by the "stove" (where it sleeps), preferring the marginal and ambiguous areas of the house such as the kitchen (a zone where foodstuffs are transformed into meals), the porch, the thresholds of doorways, windowsills, and, naturally, rooftops (all of these situated between the internal and external dimensions of the residence). Furthermore, when the cat is in the street, it wanders about with other cats, forming bands that, roaming through the night, are a perfect metaphor for the bands of criminals infesting the streets of large Brazilian cities.[5]

Through this same logic of physical reduction, common to nondomesticated thought, the dog approaches the lion as "king of the household," being friend to man and protector of the house. The dog is to the inside of the house (sacred, "human," intimate, fragile, secret, and feminine) as the cat is to the outside, which is public, visible, and masculine. As one informant explained: the lion, a noble predator, "roars in the brush," while the dog—friend to man—"barks at home."[6] The tiger, however, "meows in the woods, like the cat." As opposed to roar and bark, which would be virile "voices," the meow connotes a behavior read as dissimulated, human, and close to something that in Brazil is seen as a negative side of the feminine condition. Barking expresses masculinity, univocalness, and social superiority. Contrariwise, meowing denotes a traditional and feminine multivocalness, for it can be confused with petition, pain, and, at the extreme, social inferiority, pusillanimity, dissimulation, and—perhaps this is the key—sexual pleasure.

Cats are linked to the feminine universe metaphorically and metonymically. It is worth remembering that, in Brazil, women can be referred to as "she-cats" (*gatas*); cats are related to the sexual power attributed to women, and, as Robert Darnton points out, in French *chat, chatte,* and *minet* have the same meaning as *pussy* in English, denoting the female genitals (Darnton, 1985:95). It is also known that in certain societies the cat cannot be sold, only lent (see Mauss, 1990: chapter 4, note 4).

The crocodile completes the trio of the most savage, for, besides being untamable, it is a fearsome predator that as a reptile lives between the water and the land. From this, surely, comes the popular view of the crocodile as a bicho symbolic of treachery and dissimulated, lethal attack. "Fool around and the crocodile will get you," goes the popular saying. In its condition as reptile, the crocodile—creeping and living in muddy, viscous areas between the wet and the dry, the solid and the liquid—is similar to the snake and also to the pig, another animal that lives in a hybrid environment and is considered equally "dirty." In this way, crocodile and snake form another subcategory, close to the domesticated but disgusting pig, as bichos associated with the inferior, the crawling, the dirty, and the ambiguous—difficult to classify. In addition, the crocodile is known as a bicho that "cries in the river sand," shedding its copious and well-known "crocodile tears," in other words, a weeping without meaning, an instrumental crying intended to deceive a victim.[7] Further, as we saw in our "Initial Hunch," the decree outlawing gambling in Brazil bore the number 6,259—"falling" into the group of the crocodile— and thus confirming its stigma as a deceptive bicho.

It is clear that the richest area of the "wild" vs. "domesticated" dichotomy lies in the border zone, where the poles approach each other, mixing and fusing the distinctive characteristics attributed to the bichos. Thus, the monkey, an extremely rich animal in the Brazilian symbolic universe, occupies precisely this gateway zone, halfway between the close and the distant. It's said that the monkey "leaped out of the jungle," caught up as it is in that magical sphere between animals and human beings. Suspended between the arbitrary but explicit and positive rules of the culture and the implacable, inescapable laws of nature—sometimes more here, sometimes more there—the monkey appears as an intelligent animal that the public considers capable of understanding both sides of this interesting equation.[8]

There are, then, those who have said that the monkey "looks like the boss," for in Brazil monkeys are the paradigmatic animal of wisdom and sexual misbehavior. In the sixth century, Pedro Damián, a pious priest worried about sins of a sexual nature, recapitulated a legend of Arabic origin that speaks of the seduction of a monkey (the pet of a count) by the countess. Seduced and in love with the perverse wife of his owner, the monkey finally kills the count out of jealousy (Salisbury, 1994:95).

When he was conducting ethnological research in the 1960s and 1970s among the Apinayé Indians of northern Goiás, Roberto DaMatta heard from backwoodsmen the story of a young woman kidnapped along the Araguaia River by a large monkey, with which she cohabited and bore a son. One day, the woman escaped by boarding a motorboat miraculously coming down the river where she washed clothes. Discovering the woman's flight, the monkey, disconsolate and enraged at losing his mate, beckoned from the shore alongside their small child, in a desperate attempt to make her return to their savage marriage. Seeing, however, the futility of his efforts, the monkey tore off the child's legs in a cruel, extraordinary gesture of revenge, provoking immense pain in the poor mother, who witnessed the scene from a distance. Such an "affair" was related as proof of the possibility of reproduction between human beings and monkeys and also as a perfect demonstration of the supreme intelligence and humanity of the simians.

The monkey arouses deep and intriguing reflections. As E. B. Tylor, one of the founders of modern anthropology, shows us, there is a myth that monkeys were once people just as we are. If the monkey doesn't speak today, it is in order not to be used as errand boy or vilely exploited as laborer, which from its point of view (and here we once again encounter perspectivism) would be a comedown (Câmara Cascudo, 1985:60).

The classic verse, still recited in many places where the art of small talk hasn't been replaced by the boob tube, put it this way, as Câmara Cascudo informs us in his *Dicionário do folclore brasileiro*:

> All the people admire
> The monkey walking upright;
> The monkey was once people
> And can walk however it likes.

In sum: in Brazil, and especially in a Brazil that depended on the labor of slaves, the monkey is a perfect "bicho," simultaneously included in and excluded from human society. There exists perhaps no animal more ambiguous in the Brazilian cosmology than this monkey that is a bicho, a first draft of man, constituting therefore a serious, as Mary Douglas puts it, classificatory challenge.[9]

In this same area of paradoxical beings we find the bear, which has the marked position of a "wild beast" capable of being domesticated. In the popular imagination the bear is a circus animal that "dances with the troupe for small change." In other words, the bear is a bicho that allows itself to be trained for a questionable reason: monetary gain. But, because of its size and temperament, it cannot dissociate itself from its condition as a dangerous beast. Another aspect that contributes to these attributions is the fact of the bear traveling with the circus, which brings it in contact with gypsies, criminals, and hirelings with no fixed address. As with these social categories, the bear has, as one informant put it, "a ring through its nose," which makes him a suspect animal, associated with cold climates, death, and treachery.

It is curious to observe, in this context, that such representations hark back to old images of the bear, from premodern Europe, as a man in disguise or a savage. This brings it closer to the monkey, for we know of the links between hunting bears and hunting savages, deliberately confusing one with the other (N. Davis, 1990:117). Furthermore, it was part of ancient beliefs that the bear did not mate in the manner of other quadrupeds but like human beings, with the partners facing each other. Because of this, many medieval thinkers supposed that the bear's semen was comparable with man's, thus making them capable of impregnating women (Salisbury, 1994:83–84).

The last bicho to be analyzed is the camel, which in popular belief is wild but, as occurs with the donkey, is actually a worker, for "it carries a double load." The camel, as one player said, "is a bicho that lives far away." "It's the Turkish horse," as one informant emphasized picturesquely, "the one that moves in the desert and the sand dunes." The classification as wild comes from the fact of its being a "foreign" animal, characterized by exoticism and spatial distance, as well as bizarre appearance: it's a large animal that has a "deformity on its back, a hump." This harks back to its prominent biblical lineage, for "it is easier for a camel to go through the eye of a needle, than for a rich man to enter the kingdom of God" (Matthew 19:24), and provides it with an enigmatic, positive air because it is known that hunchbacks bring luck.[10]

Having exhausted the list of wild animals, we can now enter the field of domesticated bichos. Let us see how this subset is presented in relation to its functionality or the role it plays in human society. In this sphere, they were separated into two domains: food and transportation. Let's begin with the alimentary representations. Here, the major division is between "meat" animals and "milk" animals.

In the latter sphere we have the cow and the goat, which are distinguished also by the final purpose of the milk they produce. Cow's milk goes "to the boss"—of the two it is the socially superior milk. Goat's milk, in the popular view, goes to the "poor and the pagans." From this it is possible to perceive how a nutriment transformed into a cultural thing—into food— helps to form opinion about two basic social types: the boss and the poor, also seen by the informant as pagans. Read as socially passive in addition to their being excluded from a positive religious identity, namely Christianity, pagans are doubly inferior. Thus the goat would be to the inferior as the cow is to the superior, a fact emphasized as early as 1936 by Gilberto Freyre (Freyre, [1936] 1961:139).

The word *cabra* (she-goat) also designates the hired gun, the follower, or the farmhand, people who live under the shadow of a "colonel," master, or boss. *Cabrita* is a woman ripe for approaching, loose in the "woods" like a person with whom erotic contact is open and free, without implying the establishing of any public commitment or matrimonial tie.

In the domain of "meat animals" we have, besides the cow, the turkey as the privileged supplier of festive meat at Christmas and other solemn, grandiose, and formal occasions. And if the meat of the cow is red, common, and heavy, turkey meat is white, light, and frugal, enjoyed by the more well-off and served with fruits such as peaches or plums to mark "refined" situations characterized by etiquette and special norms of behavior, for sweets reflect the superior, the aristocratic, the feminine, and the refined.

Next on the list is the pig, which provides a generous and fatty meat, always eaten in conjunction with some kind of celebration such as weddings and birthdays, in which the desire is to emphasize abundance and fertility. Finally, we come to the bull, whose meat is destined for the barbecue (a typical masculine activity) and also represents a celebratory situation in which many, generally one's friends, participate.

In another category of useful domestic bichos we find the peacock, of which only one part, the feathers, are used, as opposed to the other "meat animals," of which everything is used. In support of this reading is the con-

notation of the peacock's sexual ambiguity, being a bicho that symbolizes un-
abashed vanity, a trait seen as unmeritorious among the virtues of the social
world, especially insofar as the masculine domain is concerned. From this,
perhaps, comes the connotation pointed out by Freyre, for whom the peacock, "whose golden fan has become as symbolic of the house of nobles as
the crown of the royal palm," would bring (along with the dove) "bad luck to
homes" as a consequence of its transitory nature (Freyre, [1936] 1961:139).

In addition, milk and meat refer to two universes differentiated in Brazilian society, as milk invokes the feminine domain and meat the masculine.
Milk is ingested passively—is drunk—while meat is eaten, which further
implies the sacrifice of the animal. Besides this, milk is white, is associated
with children, and denotes purity and innocence; red meat, on the other
hand, is associated with sin, sex, and adult life, for it is linked to blood, glut-
tony, and destruction. Meat therefore seems something extraordinary, epi-
sodic, and ritual, in contrast to the routine and ongoing character of milk.
The feminine is linked to milk in a constant and passive way, while the masculine acts upon meat: by sacrificing the animal, cutting its body into pieces,
cooking its flesh, and, finally, offering it to society or, what amounts to the
same thing, to the gods. One domain denotes passivity; the other, activity.
One implies routine; the other, ritual. One is linked to life as stability; the
other, to death and sacrifice, which guarantee continuity and the renewing
of that life.

One negative aspect of the domain of alimentary potentials is made up
of bichos that eat what man does not. In this way, the ostrich eats indiscrimi-
nately, thereby associating itself with the vulture, a bird characterized by its
black color, which eats carrion and is considered a bad omen. Because of its
gray, opaque feathers the plumage of the ostrich recalls old age, while the
gigantic size of its eggs recalls accumulation and plenty. Another animal notable for the unusual type of food it consumes is the pig, which eats "slops"—
leftovers from meals, from which comes its link with all that is base and
dirty.

In this terrain of associations between bichos and nutriments, the pig
and the sheep occupy a special place, the pig because it "gives the market
lard," the sheep because it "gives wool to the mattress factory." By this candidly utilitarian criterion, they have much in common. But if we change the
classificatory parameter, they could not be further apart, for the pig is base,
filthy, and repugnant, a meat forbidden to Jews; the sheep is the biblical and
sacrificial animal par excellence. Christ is the lamb (that which is sacrificed

blamelessly) and, at the same time, is a good shepherd. The sheep, then, is a clean and superior animal, the purest of the 25 bichos on our list. Another marked difference is that the pig provides lard, another product that provokes the sacrifice of the animal. The death of a pig, as we know, is the cruelest and most violent possible, as no thought is given to alleviating the suffering of such a dirty and base animal.

Wool, the by-product obtained from sheep, can be removed without the death of the animal, which is "the kindest of them all." In sum, the sheep is "blessed among beasts," "the animal of our Lord." It is white and ritually pure, while the pig "wallows in mud." As we have suggested above, the sheep is widely used for sacrifices and its image was subsequently sacralized in Christian cosmology.[11]

In the domain of transport there reappears the cleavage between "the world of the boss" and "the world of the worker," for the horse is the animal that lends itself to recreational transport and privilege and characterizes the superiors, being also the "boss's mount" and "the puller of the lady's carriage"—unlike the donkey (and the mule), which "carries the farmhand" and cargo in general, a contrast also pointed out by Freyre (Freyre, [1936] 1961:139). The expression so often heard in Brazil, "to be a donkey of burden," is the best example of this reading, which, according to Freyre, would indicate the importance of equines as draft animals, which in Brazil would not replace slave labor until the second half of the nineteenth century (see Freyre, [1936] 1961:489ff., and especially 1959:328).

From this, undoubtedly, comes the association of the donkey with the humble and with manual laborers in general. But by way of compensation, one cannot forget that the donkey is a biblical animal, having carried Mary and Jesus on their flight to Egypt. In sum, it is an animal linked to hard work that brings neither fame nor riches, but whose humility places it as a sacred bicho, preferred and blessed by the Holy Family. A typical example of the "power of the weak," a hidden or implicit power that in certain situations encompasses the best-known signs of prestige and command.

At this point it is worthwhile to recall Bakhtin (1989:67) in his commentaries on the "festivals of the ass," so popular in the Middle Ages. In these carnivalesque gatherings the ass—a humble and blessed animal—was celebrated and people brayed like it and with it, provoking the regenerating laughter that is the heart of the carnival and popular festivals.

Along with the donkey, there is the bull as the bicho of brute force, pulling whatever is heaviest, like carts. The bull is associated with virility and physical strength. It is also linked to Portugal's King Sebastião the Hidden (Câmara Cascudo, 1988:758).

Rounding out these domains that informants tend to classify as "natural," we have the "gregarious" bichos. In this dimension, the rabbit is the symbol of procreation and usually appears in pairs. Monkeys come out, as one informant emphasized, using the language of the animal game, in "tens." The bichos considered feminine, outside the "band" class, are the snake and the cow, both seen as individualistic beings.

The snake is conceived as a metaphor for the "streetwalker" or the "fallen woman," who has gone her own way, with strategies and an agenda all her own. Its major point of reference is the biblical serpent that seduced Eve, who in turn tempted Adam and led to the original couple's expulsion from Paradise. According to the majority of the informants, no bicho (with the possible exception of the monkey) can be more Machiavellian or cunning than it.

The cow is the symbol of the "housewife" or the domestic woman, the perfect representation of the good wife controlled by her husband, after having first been a daughter and sister subject to patriarchal power. In its immanence and passivity as a "housewife," the cow has a specific place in the home. We will return to these distinctions when we analyze the feminine domain. For now, it is worthwhile emphasizing that the other bicho that is "found in a band" is the sheep, in a possible reference to "God's fold."

The great majority of bichos—17, in fact—appear in individualized form, as single beings, which doubtlessly increases their "symbolic power." If the most basic division has already been described as that which separates bichos into wild (untamable) and domesticated (trainable), it nevertheless undergoes the countless symbolic reformulations used in the construction of active and passive positions when these animals face one another or—even more suggestive—face the dangers of life in general, as in the following framework.

Table 1 comprises three contrastive dimensions: action, passivity, and exclusion. At the active pole we find, in the lead, the trio of wild beasts, that is, the trio of predators par excellence. In the second group of actives we have the bichos that still pose some threat to man—whether because of their physical size (the elephant), the vileness of their strike (the snake), or their skill (the eagle). Still in the terrain of the actives, a domain massively represented by the masculine element, and comprising eleven bichos, we have the "domesticated hunters" and the bichos of belligerent temperament.

Table 1. POSITIONS IN THE CONFLICT

ACTIVES	PASSIVES
WILD BEASTS	PREY, VICTIM:
(PREDATORS PAR EXCELLENCE):	RABBIT – "innocent"
LION – "king of the beasts"	PURSUED:
TIGER – "treacherous pounce"	DONKEY – "runs away from work"
CROCODILE – "reptile, cunning"	GOAT – "flees"
ATTACK MAN (POTENTIALLY)	
ELEPHANT – "crushing weight"	THE UNCATCHABLE PURSUED:
SNAKE – "planned strike"	STAG – "very fast"
EAGLE – "flies toward humans"	OSTRICH – "very fast"
DOMESTICATED HUNTERS:	"EXCLUDED"
CAT – "hunts rats, treacherous"	
DOG – "protects his owner, hunting	BUTTERFLY COW
companion"	SHEEP BEAR
FIGHTERS:	CAMEL PIG
ROOSTER – "fights with spurs"	MONKEY BULL
PEACOCK – "fights from vanity"	HORSE
TURKEY – "irritable"	

In this hierarchy the passives in the conflict are the victims, the pursued, and even the hard-to-catch quarry. The rabbit heads the list of the passive or victims, for although fast, it is an animal coveted by carnivores, and their habitual victim. The way of life of the rabbit—considered timorous, small, and white—contributes to this connotation of easy prey, despite the equally emphasized fact that it is clever and fast in flight. Nevertheless, what really counts in this attribution is the fact that the rabbit flees, eschewing confrontation. Under the second heading we find the "pursued bichos"—the donkey and the goat—animals that will appear also in the lower pole of the social hierarchy shown in table 2.

The final group of passives—animals that flee—is made up of the stag and the ostrich. Although extremely fast, and therefore uncatchable, they are nonetheless the target of the actives. In the case of the stag, in particular, this mode of classification is in keeping with its ambiguous position, situated between the feminine and the masculine domains. For the stag (a word that in Brazil denotes a male homosexual) is an animal that does not become prey but remains passive.

In this way, the category of "uncatchable pursued" holds an ambiguous connotation between actives and passives, whether in the conflict or on the plane of sexual potentialities.

The tables that follow categorize social and sexual potentialities, and also organize the domain of the other world, placing the animals in accordance with the fundamental poles of the sacred and the profane.

A Fantastical Brazilian Zoology

The attributes or social representations of the bichos address the sphere of culture and symbology. In the array of perceived differences in the series of 25 bichos we are able to equate the bichos to societal situations, categories, and values.

At the top of table 2 we have the eagle and the lion. The former embodies the power of deciding upon and formulating strategies: the true power, which comes with its sharp vision. The latter embodies the power acquired by right, legitimately: the lion, says an axiom of our culture, is king.

The most characteristic example of a public person designated by the eagle, as verified by the research, is Rui Barbosa, called "the eagle of the Hague." "Eagle" always refers to someone who occupies a superior social position by reason of his astuteness and intellectual capacity. If the lion is superior because of its strength or by unquestioned right, the eagle attains a position of superiority by its skill as strategist and orator. The eagle, male or female, is a good talker and has the gift of gab. Flying high, it takes in all of social reality, just as does a good speaker when he addresses an audience.

Besides this, the eagle is the only bicho listed in table 2 that flies. This singularity suggests the image of someone who has become individualized, who has surpassed the rest and is above rules. Someone who is free to decide his destiny and create his own norms. The eagle, as one informant said, "has a target and never misses."

It is curious to observe that popular taste, by placing the eagle/lion pair at the top of the social hierarchy, suggests a king and prime minister type of political system, or a president and political spokesman system, as if to indicate that official bureaucratic power is insufficient and that another kind is needed, the magical or visionary kind, a charismatic and connective power, in Weber's vision, capable of complementing bureaucratic or official domination through affinity and through emotion. Lion and eagle, therefore, are represented as the two legs of classic Western domination: the bureaucratic (or rational) and the charismatic (or spontaneous and magical).

Next in the scale of superior social types we have the elephant, represented as a noble and imposing figure, often associated with justice. Given its physical dimensions and its alleged sluggishness, some informants take it as a perfect embodiment of the legislative power. The elephant, therefore, like the parliament, represents something phenomenal and solid that nevertheless suffers from pachydermal slowness—curious in light of the fact that in the United States it is the symbol of the Republican Party (a party that represents itself as large and solid), as was mentioned in "Initial Hunch."

Significantly, indicative of the astuteness of popular thinking, such bichos exhaust important dimensions of public power. But the symbolization doesn't stop there, because economic power is symbolized by the tiger, which for some informants represents the successful businessman, who privileges ends at the cost of means. The tiger, as a wild beast and a feline, knows how to strike aggressively and suddenly, taking its victims by surprise. Thus, the social type it embodies is the businessman who ascends the social ladder through his ability to effect great coups.

The camel, as we have already seen, suggests the foreign element with talent for business. It is the bicho that designates the rich foreigner, the so-called "Turk" from the Middle East, associated with the three Wise Men who nobly offer "gifts" from afar to the Christ Child, thus revealing a profound respect for the Creator.

Last in the domain of the socially superior we find the peacock, which is seen as an "ostentatious young man," the "dandy" or "fop" type—a "happy young man, almost gay." Such a bicho represents the young heir, the young college graduate born to wealth. He is typically a "rich daddy's boy" who, because he is a parasite under his father's shadow, would remain at the threshold between the positive and the negative. This datum is in fact confirmed by the general belief in Brazil that the peacock and the dove are, as Freyre reminds us, "animals that 'bring bad luck to homes.'" This perhaps is explained, Freyre continues, "by the fact that they were animals symbolic of noble or rich houses: houses, in Brazil, normally ephemeral in their grandeur or their opulence" (Freyre, 1961:139).

Between the most cited superiors and inferiors we have the intermediate rooster and dog. The rooster, as herald whose commanding voice awakens us

Table 2. SOCIAL POTENTIALITIES (HEIRARCHY; MASCULINE)

EAGLE "in the heights; great decisions"	LION "the king; the strategist; respect; courage; the champion"	
ELEPHANT "nobility; justice; grandeur"		
TIGER "respect; knows how to make money" PEACOCK "heir; ostentatious; dandy" CAMEL "rich businessman; successful immigrant"		MONKEY "looks like the boss; imitation of man; caricature; – excluded from the classification; non-man"
ROOSTER "herald; voice; authority; indication of the master" HORSE "indication of the master"		
DOG "the intermediary; foreman; right arm; trustworthy man; link between superiors and inferiors"		
DONKEY "exploited" GOAT "inferior man; lower order; socially passive"		

Table 2A. TYPES OF RELATIONS

RESPECT lion; tiger; elephant; rooster	vs.	EXPLOITATION donkey; goat	SCORN monkey
SOLIDARITY dog; horse	vs.	TREACHERY cat; snake; bear; tiger; crocodile	

for another day of work, is replete with the authority of the superior. And the dog, which with its barking emerges, as we have noted, as the guardian of home and estate, represents the master and is seen as the "foreman's right arm." Both the dog and the rooster are indicative of the presence of a master or owner. Both are bichos with "commanding voices," serving in their way as metaphor for a boss or superior. The rooster, which summons us to the "struggle" and to "life," is a symbol of work, opposed to sleep and bed; the dog, which watches over the boss's employees—the "goats" and the "donkeys" —is constantly taking care to see that they meet their obligations, like a faithful and natural-born foreman.

In addition, the rooster and the dog also occupy an intermediate position between general domains of culture and nature: the former, in the transitional zone between night and day; the latter, by moving freely between house and street. These intermediate bichos represent the master's orders and are also the ones that come into contact with those actually condemned to work.

The view of work suggested by this table of social projections is not one in which the parties define their rights and duties in a negotiated, egalitarian fashion, but it reveals a universe of hierarchically structured social ties in which relationships have as their ordering source the boss, who is at the top and is seen as the basic reference point of the system.

In an oblique position to this "power structure" we find the monkey, which is "unclassified," for as representative of another perspective of human nature it is rather a model for social declassification. It cannot be included in the hierarchy of men, for it is not one of them, but—due to human similarity—neither can it be left out of this hierarchy.

Another possibility of classification suggested by the data analyzed speaks to the paradigms and social values associated with each bicho. Thus, respect is paid to the lion because it is the king and champion, to the tiger because it's a clever wild beast, to the elephant because it is powerful and believed to be gentle and reliable, and to the rooster because of the authority its voice imposes, the very word of the boss declaring the beginning of a day of struggle, toil, or work. These four are the only bichos related to the values of respect, but it is worth remembering that the rooster also appears as a metaphor for an active sexual life.

In opposition, however, to the idea of respect and distance, the donkey and the goat connote the absence of social protection and are seen as animals destined for exploitation. The horse and the dog are bichos of solidarity, while the cat, the bear, the tiger, the snake, and the crocodile are termed "the bichos of treachery."

One final observation about the domain of social hierarchy deals with a revealing and significant masculine hegemony. For all the superior positions are occupied by male bichos, with a quasi-exception in the figure of the goat, which, as we have mentioned, occupies an intermediate domain between masculine and feminine.

Let us now examine the "sexual potentialities" of these 25 bichos shown in table 3.

Under the denomination of "sexual potentialities" are the bichos associated with the masculine pole (the pole seen as "active"), with the feminine pole ("passivity"), and with the ambiguous terrain situated between them, which in Brazil has a very important role.

Heading this table we find an important "ideal minimal pair," the eagle and the butterfly. Thus, in various tables of hunches, people referred to the butterfly and the eagle as "a pair of sweethearts." We know that they are the only two bichos that fly, although they do so in radically different ways. The eagle is a solitary animal that flies high and decides on its path, precisely defining its targets, which it hits unerringly: it is, in sum, a hunter-predator that always comes from above.

But the butterfly—or rather, the flock of butterflies—floats, flying low, landing on flowers at will. The butterfly is construed as inconstant, scattered, beautiful, and merry. Its wings are "gilded," while the eagle "has a beak" that serves to seduce and capture. It is as if one offered itself to the other, for the butterfly flies freely, inciting the eagle that will seduce it with smooth talk. Further, the butterfly is seen as a "marriageable young woman." Deep down, the public sees the butterfly as "marriageable," unlike the goat, which is legitimate prey. The former would be "nice" girls (who have a home); the latter are women of the street.

In the masculine pole we have the bull and the lion as centers of reference. The bull's masculinity is based on his physical strength: he is the "macho" of the collection. The lion, it is worth repeating, is the brave one: the one that overcomes all with his majesty.

The elephant, rooster, and turkey suggest an immediate association with the masculine member. The elephant is the "bicho that trumpets," its "trunk drags on the ground," but by way of compensation it is slow moving. The rooster, in contrast, has a comb, is quarrelsome, and always erect and haughty.[12] It is also described as the "most authoritarian" of all.

Table 3. SEXUAL POTENTIALITIES

MASCULINE

FEMININE

EAGLE
"seducer; .
beaked; gift of
gab; promising
future"

HOUSE
BUTTERFLY
"marriageable
young woman;
pretty wings;
to be
captured"

STREET
GOAT*
"*cabrita*; 'coit-
able' young
woman;
woods; sexual
initiation; teats
and orifice"

BULL
"the mascu-
line; physical
strength; horns
(+)"

LION
"the brave; the
champion;
mane"

CAT*
"languid young
woman; leg
and breast"

ELEPHANT
"trunk; out-
sized member"

ROOSTER
"the member;
comb; erect;
quarrelsome"

TURKEY
"the male
member"

COW
"mother;
prostitute;
teats"

SNAKE
"experienced
woman;
Machiavellian
dancer;
profane sex;
vagina"

STAG
"homosexual;
horns (-)"

PEACOCK
"vain young
man;
effeminate"

OSTRICH
"large female
animal; buries
its head with
its tail sticking
out"

CAT*
"dissimulated;
sinuous;
languid"

GOAT*
"passive man;
teat and
orifice"

RABBIT
"procreation
couple"
(sacred/white)

MONKEY
"sexual hijink
group sex"
profane/black

In some lists of hunches we find a curious and amusing association with the rooster, as follows: rooster = "the thing itself," as if it were redundant to say "rooster = the masculine member." The turkey, in turn, it is worth repeating, is in Brazil another term to designate the male member. And we cannot fail to observe that the masculine bichos have, without exception, some physical attribute of virility: beak, horns, mane, trunk, and comb.

Turning to the feminine domain, we have the cow and the snake as important actors—the former as last stop in the trajectory of the "family girl," the butterfly, and the latter as the potentiality of the *cabrita*.

The cow, as we have seen, is the bicho symbolic of maternity and milk. It is wife, mother-in-law, and mother. The snake is the wise, experienced woman of the streets who dominates her customers with poisonous snares and Machiavellian schemes. The snake and the butterfly dance, but the former "does the belly dance," while the latter is an innocent and delicate "ballerina." Both, however, inspire sexual desire.

The butterfly—because of its beauty, innocence, and merriness—recalls chaste sex at the service of reproduction and the family, a union authorized and legitimated by a marriage ceremony. But the snake inspires the worldly, pleasurable, experienced sex of the streets. The snake sways in the belly dance and when it hunts squeezes its victim until it strangles it, images clearly allusive to the supposed wild sex of professionals.

The cow, like the mother, is asexual, living to nurse and feed the family. She is the fat matron who calmly watches over the children, takes care of her husband, and is not easily upset. Still, the cow is also associated with "prostitute," and the slovenly prostitute at that—as if the woman who fails to transform herself into a mother in the appropriate manner were running the risk of turning into a cow.

One last presence in the feminine domain is curiously enough the cat, which is associated, as one informant stressed, with "a languid young woman; with legs and breasts." We could conjecture that when physical attributes are explicitly emphasized, we are talking about women of the street; in addition, we have already seen that the cat is the "outside wall" animal, the animal situated between house and street, between domesticity and nocturnal savagery, of wandering bands and sexuality.

In conclusion, we note that the cleavage between house and street applies only to the feminine universe; what serves as internal ordering agent in the masculine universe is the bicho's potential for virility. Thus, the eagle is intellectual, the bull is virile; the lion is courageous, while the turkey and the rooster hark back to metonymic references, for in certain contexts they are the phallus itself.

Still on the mapping of sexual projections, we have a "middle column" made up of beings that offer a sexual connotation that cannot be reduced to the masculine or feminine poles. Heading the list of "threshold bichos" is the stag, which in Brazil designates the passive male homosexual. Another ambiguous bicho is the peacock, for its excessive vanity is seen as a feminine attribute. The case of the goat's ambiguity has already been explored, when we saw how it designates both a socially and politically passive man—a hired gun or *cabra*—and a young single woman. Also, the ostrich, a masculine bicho, is sometimes called *bicha,* a fact that perhaps is explained by its being a bicho passive in confrontation, which like the stag runs at great speed and cannot be overtaken. Combined with this disconcerting characteristic is the fact that both the ostrich and the peacock are flightless birds, which accentuates their paradoxical positions.

A final category in the domain of sexual connotations unites the rabbit and the monkey. The rabbit emphasizes the reproductive side of sexuality, while the monkey, like the snake, stresses sex as an instrument of pleasure, placing fecundity on a secondary plane. Such a dimension is accentuated in the case of the monkey, which is associated with the practice of sexual libertinism and of group sex (promiscuous), activities in which pleasure is maximized.

If all the dimensions of contrast studied thus far refer to things of society and "this world," the classificatory contrast between sacred and profane will bring us to address the "other world." This fact reveals that in the classificatory system of the animal game there exists a hierarchization of spheres that goes from nature to the other world, passing through a series of social spheres.

In this way, if the table that describes the masculine/feminine opposition has a paradigmatic pair in the eagle and the butterfly—and also a zone abounding with ambiguous beings—in the domain of the other world the model animals are the cat and the dog, as shown in table 4.

Of all the bichos, the best (and purest), as we have already commented, is the sheep. It is the "bicho of our Lord." Just below the sheep is the donkey, which "carried the Virgin," followed by the camel, in an obvious association with the Wise Men. In the terrain of the sacred, therefore, we verify the hegemony of Christian cosmology.

Table 4.

SACRED (high)	vs.	PROFANE (low)	4B. LIFE
	basic opposites		
SHEEP "the bicho of our Lord; blessed; the sacrificed one; the abused; hot"	———————	SNAKE "the bicho of evil; it swallows up the couple; the bicho of original sin; impure; cold, base"	RABBIT "child"
			BUTTERFLY "virgin"
DONKEY "carried the Virgin; the exploited one"	DOG "faithful friend vs. bicho of damnation; bicho of expiation"	MONKEY "a turncoat bicho; repudiated; devil; immoral; scorn; cunning black"	COW "mother"
CAMEL "carried the Wise Men"			OSTRICH, CAMEL "old"
	CAT "angel vs. thief"	BEAR "abominated bicho; nomadic; circus"	ELEPHANT, BEAR, PIG, TURKEY "deceased"
RABBIT "procreation of the species; white"		GOAT "gives milk to pagans"	SHEEP "sacrifice"

Table 4A.

PROSPERITY vs. (good omen)	MISFORTUNE (bad omen)	4C. WHITE vs.		BLACK
SHEEP "flock; fortune; good business"	CROCODILE "embarrassment; scandal"	SHEEP "blessed; sacrifice; soul"	basic opposites	MONKEY "devil; turncoat; immoral; body"
CAMEL "beginning of fortune	BEAR "death; false friend"	EAGLE "high"		OSTRICH "vulture"
RABBIT "luck; rabbit's foot (amulet); multiplication"	OSTRICH "black bird; vulture; eats everything"	RABBIT "procreation; child; purity"		BEAR "death; treachery"

DEATH

The rabbit also has a place in it, the bicho that carries out the chaste mission to "be fruitful and multiply."

In direct opposition to the sheep, "the blessed bicho," we have the snake—"the cursed bicho." In one piece of material analyzed, the snake appears ready to swallow up a pair of rabbits, which invokes the situation of Adam and Eve in Paradise when they meet the serpent. In addition, the snake crawls, has impure sex, and is treacherous and dangerous—all attributes consistent with its position in the profane domain.

Next comes the monkey "looking like a devil." Like a man seen in negative, the monkey is viewed as a "renegade" and "abjured" bicho, excluded from the official religion and the hierarchy of humans. Its proclivity for certain profane (and perverted) sexual practices contributes to this classification. The monkey also lends itself to embodying the instinctive side as opposed to the spiritual pole.

The bear is "the abominable bicho"—barbarous and dissimulated like gypsies, concealing its true nature as wild beast.

Finally, we have the goat, which gives milk to those excluded from the official rites and ideology.

The inclusion of the dog in the axis of "the other world" owes to its transformation—as "hound"—into a bicho associated with evil and the devil. This connotation leads to others of the "hound of hell" type, which imply closeness to the devil and "souls in torment," beings that, though dead, cannot enter the other world. The "damned" and those condemned to "damnation" are figures from Purgatory, the zone between Heaven and Hell. We could also speculate about the meanings of the terms "dog" and "hound." The dog is a loyal friend, a protector, and supportive, "man's best friend"; the hound is the demon and an apparition.

The same happens in relation to the cat, which was included in this axis because of its designation as angel. We might raise the argument that the cat has nine lives—it dies and rises again—and therefore enjoys an intimacy with the world of souls (and of border-beings). But this cannot be stated with certainty. In fact, ambiguity dominates the figure of the cat, which is simultaneously a bicho both domestic and roguish, lazy, dissimulated, and a thief.

There are also the bichos that signify "good omens"—luck, fortune, prosperity—and those that are symbols of "bad omens," adversity, and misfortune.

The bichos that propitiate material prosperity are the sacred ones. The sheep symbolizes fortune and good business, perhaps in allusion to the flock as a synonym for ownership and opulence or because of its attribute as a sacrificial animal, the vehicle of reparation that gives rise to blessed prosperity. The camel is the sign of the "beginning of fortune," and here, beyond doubt, is a reference to the Wise Men, who bore precious gifts.

The rabbit also figures in the list of symbols of prosperity. The rabbit's foot is commonly used as a good-luck charm. Simultaneously, the rabbit appears as the bicho of procreation, the one that reproduces rapidly and abundantly. Let us recall also that it is usually depicted as a couple.

There is also the possibility of reading the bichos by situating them along a continuum going from life to death—from the rabbit, the bicho of "a brood of offspring," of innocence and vitality; through the butterfly, read as virgin, beautiful, and sterile; not overlooking the cow, so pure in its motherhood; to the camel and ostrich, read as old and closer to death.

In the pole of death per se, we find the elephant dominated by its inertia and by being the only animal with the practice of creating its own cemetery, withdrawing to a place to die as if foreseeing the end of its days. The pig derives its presence at death's side because of its violent demise. And the turkey, as we all know, is the only animal in all of creation that "dies the night before."

The final paradigmatic set of opposites is that of ethnic categories, white/black, whose distinctive pair is the sheep and the monkey. The sheep excels by its immateriality as the sacrificed bicho, pure and good, in contrast to the dirty, immoral monkey, an acrobat whose existence takes the greatest advantage of its own body. It goes without saying that such a classification betrays the style of Brazilian racial prejudice: implicit, negotiable, disguised, unacknowledged, personalized, or, as Oracy Nogueira (1954) made explicit, "exterior," a "prejudice of mark": particularistic and contextual.

The drive by the police to put an end to baronial gambling burst like a bomb amid the 25 bichos in the drawin Great stampede by the animals and profound disappointment for the game's devotees.

A. Agostini, *D. Quixote* (Apr l 4, 1895)

CHAPTER 4

Final Reflections

Describing the World of the Bichos

Entering the world of the animal game is like following the White Rabbit in *Alice in Wonderland*. We tumbled down the rabbit hole and found there a parallel world where a gymkhana is under way—a gymkhana that began a long time ago and has no ending date. The events in this gymkhana consist of deciphering charades incomprehensible to the visitor, although simple for the inhabitants of that world.

Like the White Rabbit, all are in a hurry and are constantly consulting their watches: there's a game at two o'clock, four o'clock, and nine o'clock. Everyone runs all the time, looking for clues to the treasure hunt. Each one has a method and the clues may be in the most unexpected places.

Like poor Alice, we are perplexed at seeing them decipher intricate charades with such ease. As in Wonderland, the absurd is the rule: chance becomes determination, the arbitrary is read as destiny, and the improbable is transformed into an infallible hunch. The world of bichos is thus called because, wherever one looks, there are numbers and bichos. In it there is a formidable trick that consists of transforming any number into a bicho. However, the wisest and the most powerful would go beyond this, converting bichos into money.

In order to pass through the doors of this parallel world we must drink the Wonderland elixir, which—anthropologically—makes us see the bichos just as they are seen by the citizens of that universe.

We therefore adjust our gaze, and everything that appeared insignificant now becomes full of meaning. The side effect of the elixir causes some discomfort—we are immediately assailed by numbers that tempt us to chase after bichos in a frenetic pursuit. We must still put aside the moral premises that demand we take sides for or against gambling or, more difficult still, that we present an intelligent, studied, refined, and, naturally, definitive solution to this activity that is, beyond any doubt, an uninvited guest in a social universe that runs on money, investment, the market, and individual liberty. As if the desire to get rich with little effort, and the fascination with the challenging of chaos and the absurd, could be held in check by so many legal, enforcement, and disciplinary measures. It quickly becomes evident that it is a wearying and endless task.

The great difference between the world of bichos and our own is that in the former nothing is without meaning: all things go beyond themselves, and everything means something. Nothing happens by accident for those who have eyes to see, and, especially, to "read" the signs. As one player said, "Whoever has eyes to see, will see."

Although it is part of our society, the world of the bicho shapes a parallel social universe, implicit, relatively closed, and governed by its own laws. It is always present, but if we don't ask about it we will neither see nor hear it. Typical of its way of life is the characteristic style it uses to make sense of events that occur in the wider society of which it is part.

Let us take as an example one fact of national repercussion, the death of a celebrity, say—for example, the passing of the television host Abelardo Barbosa, known as "Chacrinha." The mass media will situate the event in the history of Brazilian television. They will recall the contribution of the "Old Warrior" to national culture, framing it with phrases such as "Chacrinha brought the figure of the clown into Brazilian television" and linking the biography of a common man named Abelardo Barbosa to the success of a famous character that he engendered, Chacrinha. The authorities will also frame the event in the same molds, emphasizing the notable creativity of Chacrinha for the community where he lived and which he enriched with the originality of his enormously imaginative work.

In the parallel, totemic, and hermetic world of the animal game, however, the death of Chacrinha is all that and also a lovely "hunch" for the next leap of faith. His flamboyant image can obviously be associated with the peacock; or with the monkey, for Chacrinha was a clown of the modern media; or even with the horse—wasn't he called "Old Warrior"?

What we have is an alternative reading whose basic characteristic is the rejection of a historicized, serialized, continuous, and endless perspective. The world of bichos proceeds by isolating the fact and ignoring the chain of accumulations typical of an interpretive bias founded in historical evolution-ism, which presupposes the rational interplay of individual interests, prog-ress, and accretion. Unlike this way of ordering the world, in which events form a whole and happen in accordance with certain patterns, orders, epis-temes, and internally consistent or supportive structures or paradigms, the world of bichos isolates them, taking them as "signs" or "messages" referring to a code of hunches—hidden sources of wealth and happiness.

In this type of interpretation, facts are read as references to a code situ-ated outside historically refined, sociologically wise, and politically correct bourgeois logic—a logic that sees everything in terms of included and ex-cluded, interests and disinterests, weak and strong, rich and poor, oppressor and oppressed. The world of bichos leaves the exemplary realm of history as progress and moral symptom to work the world from within. For it, facts are not to be weighed, measured, or evaluated, but unveiled. In the case of Cha-crinha, then, the gaudy appearance of a television host whose conduct on screen is driven by nonsense is linked (by unveiling) to its "true truth" con-tained, albeit implicit or hidden, in his being, which is to be simultaneously a clown—therefore, a monkey. We must immediately remind ourselves that this is a reality totally divergent from the monkey as zoologically defined and found in books on natural history. For it is a "monkey"—a model bicho or species—that is, at the same time, a hierarchized numerical set starting with the 17 tenths, the reference number that "clientelizes" and encompasses the tenths 65, 66, 67, and 68, all of which belong to the monkey.

Upon discovering the occult, hermetic, and for the player, profound link between form and content—gaudiness, nonsense, wisdom contrary or paral-lel to the system = monkeyshines—the event is transformed into a cabbalis-tic sign, the motor of possible structures for getting rich located in the inter-stices and thus invisible to the official interpretive system.

If for bourgeois, "official" Brazil a master of the media has disappeared, for the Brazil certain that it can by a totemic hermeneutic transform proba-bility into destiny and event into structure, the death of any celebrity is read isolatedly as a hunch, as a possible number and as a bicho to be stalked and duly sacrificed by the act of wager-and-sacrifice. This wager takes a hidden sign seriously and can spot it with clear eyes and free of the official interpre-tive system. Thus, instead of symptoms or examples, the animal game trans-forms the world's facts into signs and hunches.[1] The concrete fact becomes doubt and augury; the "real story" can come to be an invitation to wealth, confirming on this plane capitalism's "grand narrative" of striking it rich and achieving radical upward mobility.

Congruent with this type of deconstruction and unveiling, all the numbers related to the event will be "marked down" by the animal game bankers, who will pay less per unit wagered. For three days, Chacrinha's date of birth and date of death, the number of his tomb, the age at which he died, his automobile license plate, and other related numbers will have smaller payouts.

In the parallel world of the animal game, we find a different hermeneutic of contemporary events, an "interpretivity" that acts outside the parameters and logic that dominate official codes.

At the time of this research (1992) there were approximately three thousand places in Rio de Janeiro to bet on the animal game, as well as countless bet-takers scattered about the city. These places were part of the local scene. Placing a bet is easy for the player—all he needs is a number or bicho in mind—but not so for the inquirer.

For, because he is from outside, the inquirer shows up with an unanswerable question: how can an illegal activity be carried out in the heart of an urban area featuring every modern means of communication? Furthermore, how can the animal game be a violation of the law if everyone wants to and can play? And if everyone has access to the betting sites? How is it possible to put an end to the animal game by repressing only the "banker" and leaving the players alone? How, finally, to end a game that expresses so many important values of Brazilian society?

Just like the bichos that form it, the structure of the animal game has the shape of a pyramid. At the top is a high command formed by seven bankers with the power to decide the course of the game for the entire country, with the exception of the states of Ceará and Pernambuco. The command also names representatives for each area. In the case of Rio de Janeiro, the state is divided into five areas: Downtown, North Zone, South Zone, the Baixada Fluminense, and the Interior. Five representatives are named for each of these areas. These 25 men (who, it was said, were in fact 25 "wild beasts" or "bichos"), along with the seven in the high command, run the game.

The drawing was held in Rio de Janeiro at alternating locations, as a way of evading possible police raids. The other states sent representatives as monitors.

In Rio de Janeiro alone there were three hundred animal game bankers. Although a "big" banker is defined by the volume of bets that he banks (finances) rather than by the number of betting sites he owns, it is no exaggeration to say that a banker with the capacity to sustain and support (i.e., "bank") something in the neighborhood of four hundred sites is considered "big."

On a secondary plane are the managers of betting sites, who receive 10 percent of the total amount wagered. From this sum they take the daily payment for their employees and the famous and important "PP": "police payoff." The remaining 90 percent goes directly to the bankers, who are responsible for paying out winnings, which rarely exceed 10 percent of the amount sent them. Under the manager is the cashier, who receives the money from bets. At smaller sites, it is the cashier himself who handles the "closing"—that is, totals up the money coming in and conveys to the bankers' offices the numbers on which there is heavy betting. Finally, we have the "scribes," "annotators," or "spiders," who make notes of the players' bets.

The principal chain is that going from the banker to the annotator, but there are also those who work in totaling up the results, as well as the "transporters," who spend the day shuttling to the bankers' betting sites, picking up the moneys wagered, and delivering the prizes, already calculated, owed the winners. It is estimated that in Rio de Janeiro alone some sixty thousand people are directly employed by the animal game.

The ethics of the animal game, like any cosmological system, foresees only two situations: blind loyalty to the principles of the game, or betrayal. Disobedience is punished by death, and the authority of the high command is unappealable. The fate is sealed of anyone suspected of fraud.

Significantly for the thesis that we are defending here—that the animal game is an activity that shapes an alternative modernity, despite the game's incorporating the most modern capitalist calculus—distribution of betting sites obeys the aristocratic and traditional criterion of descent, by which the sites pass from father to son. And when the descendants prove themselves unworthy or unfaithful to the code of the animal game, they are eliminated and their sites go to the nearest banker who is also a friend.

When these laws are respected, everything runs in routine perfection.

The bettors are given a receipt for their wager, which reads, as with the most prestigious currencies, "pay to bearer"—and pay they will. Prizes are paid thirty minutes after notice of the result, in cash and hassle-free. And if some site manager reneges on paying the prizes, he is declared a traitor.

It should be further noted that the slips of paper on which bets are made are furnished by the bankers and are numbered, affording the banker rational control of his sites.

In the history of the animal game, cases of violent internal disputes degenerating into mass killings have not been infrequent. Nowadays, agreement in the high command is relatively stable, which brings a certain tranquility to the illegal activity and assures the smooth operation of its dealings.[2]

Given this, the bankers' immense fortune spills over generously into other activities. They are the recognized sponsors of samba schools, orphanages, nongovernmental organizations, policemen's groups, soccer teams, and politicians. Through these activities, following the traditional clientelist pattern, they form alliances with the community and gain social legitimacy. It is not unusual to see bankers who cooperate in the construction of schools and sports facilities in needy communities, where they become real authorities and enjoy immense popular prestige. So great is their power that they reach agreements with established political leaders, as well as with drug kingpins to assure safety in these communities.[3]

Many bankers have become owners of land, buildings, and commercial establishments as a front for their revenue. Currently, involvement of the bankers with organized crime and the drug traffic is suspected, given the investment potential. And now and then newspapers print information that would be the proof of such involvement. To list such facts would be, as they say in the animal game, to mistake a cat for a rabbit, for what matters here is distinguishing that which gives the game its power of enchantment and popularity: its system and the practices related to it.

Coming into contact with this world therefore requires that one act in accordance with its laws. It is necessary to be introduced by someone who enjoys its confidence. Although it can be found on any street corner, the animal game becomes elusive when we try to touch it.

Account of The Field Work of Elena Soárez
(July 1992)

To penetrate the world of the animal game, I proceeded like any other Brazilian: I looked for someone I knew personally who was acquainted with "someone from the animal game." There was an older man, who supplied Scotch whiskey to a relative of mine, who was "close friends with all the bankers and knew everything about the animal game."

Through my relative's intermediation I obtained his phone number and called him.

The voice that answered was exaggeratedly aged. As I introduced myself and mentioned the intermediaries, the voice got younger. I gave my telephone number and Sr. Gomes[4] called back. He inquired into my objectives and said little. We set up a complicated meeting in a public square, from which we went to my house, a place that he thought more suitable for our conversation.

I immediately perceived that Sr. Gomes's relationship to the animal game was an informal one. I imagined that perhaps he was a supplier of contraband to the bankers. In turn, he realized that I, at the time, knew little about the animal game, which gave him the opportunity to both suggest the paths I should follow to carry out the research and, simultaneously, to control the information afforded me. I presume that the fact of my being a young woman also contributed to the establishment of our relationship.

Sr. Gomes promised to take me to a meeting of the "biggest bankers" as soon as I was far enough along with the research and had submitted my findings to his experienced eyes.

It was not difficult to see that the interview was over for the time being. I stopped asking questions and taking notes and—of course—the conversation began to flow much more freely. Sr. Gomes told me that one of his great passions was the German army in World War II, along with their ideologies, generals, and strategies.

As he enjoyed talking about war, I listened to him tell of his best friend, deceased. The latter had been head of security for one of the biggest bankers in Rio. He was a man who stood over six and a half feet tall, weighed 330 pounds, and "killed a lot of people, but he had a good heart." Sr. Gomes had traveled frequently with this friend, always accompanied by a general who served as "cover," or official protection for his activities. When that friend was alive, Sr. Gomes made a lot of money. But, because of his size and weight, unfortunately, his friend died before reaching forty. After his death, however, the banker who was his boss and godfather to his children offered Gomes his friend's sites, as the latter's children were still very small. Gomes refused because he felt he had no claim.

Once, the two of them agreed to have lunch after meeting at the police station where his friend worked. Gomes was taken to a room where eleven policemen, among them his friend, were working over a guy. Feeling nauseated by that scene before lunch, Gomes made a gesture for him to "cool it."

Taking this as encouragement, he redoubled his blows. Sr. Gomes's friend was full of such "picturesque moves" and, although "good-hearted," was not very intelligent. One day, his car was broken into, and, furious, he killed the first "no-good" he ran into. A good-hearted guy . . .

After so much display of loyalty and black humor, I thanked him, and the encounter was over.

This initial interview demonstrated that the direction to take was a different one. If the intent was to investigate the "system of the animal game," I must look for players and not someone who was "close friends with the big bankers." I realized immediately that the higher in the animal game pecking order my informant, the greater the value of his revelations about methods of controlling the sites and the money, but the less the value of his information about beliefs and the cosmology of the bichos and their implications for the players.

In fact, the bankers opened the doors to a routinized criminality no different from other gambling centers. Like the players, at the level of hope and dreams I was facing the system of the animal game in all its concreteness and singularity.

From this first encounter, however, I took an interesting story: the fable-story of "the leap of Sr. Gomes's cat," a narrative that redounded tellingly on the interests of the research. Here it is.

When he was a young man, Gomes would bet on soccer in the interior of the state of Rio de Janeiro. When he stopped playing, he was "poverty-stricken." He lived in a rented room in a boardinghouse. The owner of the boardinghouse had a lovely cat, which she wanted to get rid of—"she was all the time saying she was going to kill the cat." Gomes, taking pity on the cat, took it to his room. The animal had the habit of eating spiders, and one day it leapt into its owner's lap with an enormous one in its mouth. Some days later, Gomes dreamed about spiders. He therefore decided to bet on the cat—the number 14, which comprises the tenths 53, 54, 55, 56—and the thousandth 0955. The thousandth came in "first on the list" and Gomes won a small fortune, allowing him to move to the city of Rio and begin his smuggling "business."

In the beginning he would buy liquor on credit from a smuggler and resell it. In time, he became more daring, his credit improved, and he began to make some money. He was then able to buy his first car, with the personalized license plate 3253, the thousandth of the cat. As his business prospered, he began looking for a house to buy. He found a residence that he liked and realized its number was 253! He decided to buy it, but the owner, noticing his enthusiasm, doubled the price. Gomes bought the house, even without knowing how he'd pay for it. On the day of closing, he bet on the thousandth 0253. He won and thus had enough money to pay off the house. Since then, he has played that same number every Friday, for the last thirty years . . .

Only once did Gomes resent his beloved cat thousandth. That was when he had a very loyal and efficient caretaker named João. One day João asked if he could have delivered to the house an iron door he had bought for his daughter, who was about to marry. The employer consented. It was a Friday and João handed the receipt, proof of the purchase, to his employer, who had agreed to receive it. The number of the receipt was 2207. That day, Gomes wavered between playing his usual cat thousandth or the eagle thousandth of his employee João. He ended up betting on the cat and João's thousandth hit "first on the list." As Gomes says: "Good Sr. João handed me a fortune and I didn't believe him!"

Accounts of this type constitute the bulk of my research material. They are stories of life, or rather, biographies interpreted using as their point of departure hunches, bets, and results of the animal game, which thus become transformed into "myths" or fables demonstrative of the crossroads that constitute the life of those who seek to win at the animal game. In them, existence is read by its financial and social "realities," as well as through an extra-official interpretive code made up of hidden signs revelatory of bichos and numbers. These signs act as levers in people's lives, transforming them into the subject of extraordinary events that for that very reason become central to their life stories. Thus is created between players and numbers (and bichos)—or vice versa, for this is the virtue of the system—a linkage of gratitude, loyalty, and patronage that is the raw material of a life marked by luck, fable, and the extraordinary. A luck that permits transcending the plane of a routine or banal existence, tied to the shortcomings of a system based on exploitation of labor and the reduction of people to mediocrity, by transforming anonymous individuals into persons "marked" by destiny, distinguished by hope, and pursued by faith.

Sr. Artur—an annotator of bets in Copacabana—tells a similar story in relation to the thousandth 2104 (4 is the "reference number" of the butterfly). In fact, 2104 was the first number that, in my role as researcher, I played.

At the beginning of the research I would spend hours unearthing biblio-graphical information, poring over newspapers, books, and magazines at the National Library. It was winter and a strong wind was blowing. For three straight days I had been sent to sit at table 21 (the bull). As it is the library workers who decide where a reader sits, I would go resignedly to this table situated next to the window through which a draft of cold air entered. I began to get a sore throat and to curse the woman who insisted on putting me there. I did, however, write down the number. At that exact moment, in through the open window came an immense blue butterfly that caught everyone's attention as it fluttered around the room and exited through the same window. The number 2104 was formed—21 for the table and 04 for the butterfly's group. When I told this story, an immediate link was forged between Sr. Artur and me. After all, we had an affinity of fate with the same bicho and thousandth!

Sr. Artur has been playing—daily and all three drawings—that same thousandth since 1976. In the year the research was conducted, he had man-aged to save enough to buy an apartment. At the time, Sr. Artur worked with wagering on horse races. Just when he had decided which apartment to buy, something unforeseen arose. He was stiffed by a friend and, as a question of honor, felt obligated to cover the other man's bad check.

Now unable to purchase the apartment, he bought a taxi with the re-maining savings and installed one of his brothers as driver. The taxi's license plate number was 2104. Artur began playing that number daily. After exactly ten days, it hit and the price of the cab was covered. He persisted with the number, and in 1978 it hit again, "heading the list." He kept the money and traded in the taxi for a newer model with the plate number 6515 (also the butterfly, which "clientelizes" the groups 13, 14, 15, and 16). He played this number and won again. With the capital he bought an apartment much bet-ter than the one he had earlier been unable to acquire.

According to Sr. Artur, the moral of the story is: "Life is like that, we lose now to win later on. That bad debt was a great piece of luck, it doubled my capital!"

This account dramatizes one of the basic principles of aficionados of the animal game: its traditional "law of compensation," which, it is worth recall-ing, looks upon the wager as a sacrifice or present to the bicho.

Truly, when one "chances it," he expects a moral restitution for the un-recompensed undertakings in his life. In this sense, the animal game would also have a redemptory role, for the majority of players hope that the bicho will bring "payback" for the reversals and difficulties of life, by avenging and reconstituting their good luck. This good luck will allow a new beginning, in the framework of a different destiny. From this, without doubt, comes the term *fezinha*—an act of faith—applied to the bet, which allows it to be seen as, and verge upon, the sacrificial gesture. It is an act of confidence in a sign that the routines of the world—"life," as they say in Brazil—gratuitously offer us all. If I lose today, it's a sign that I can win tomorrow. If I'm losing in the "clash of men," I have faith that the "little bicho" will come to my aid and turn my position around, making me a "winner." That combat and that victory have much greater moral than economic or material flavor.

Another possibility of permanent (and extraordinary) relationship with some number lies in the numbers of sepulchers and family birthdays. Such links are examples of the capital importance of kinship relations in the formulation of hunches and bets in the animal game, which, as already stated, is above all a relational, domestic, home-based lottery.

Sr. Gesualdo, manager of a betting site in Copacabana, plays five specific thousandths daily. They are the numbers of the burial niches—also known as "sheep"—of his five deceased children. Sr. Artur has the habit of playing numbers formed by the birth dates of his daughters, all alive and happy, as well as their ages, in a modality of the game that occurs only on the girls' birthdays. He won with the number 0032 (the group of the camel, reference number 8, with "client numbers" 29, 30, 31, and 32) when his youngest daughter had her thirty-second birthday.

Betting on the tomb numbers of friends, relatives, or illustrious figures admired (or even despised) by the player is a rather common practice.

Proving that bankers and players are united and encompassed by a common code, I discovered that one of the biggest bankers of the animal game in Rio de Janeiro bets every day, in all three drawings, on the thousandth 1423 (the group of the goat, reference number 6, "client numbers" or tenths 21, 22, 23, and 24), which corresponds to the tomb number of a member of his family.

Besides this thousandth, he also bets on the eagle and the butterfly "because they fly and are clever and I also like to fly," which, on the real and virtual plane is consistent with the fact that he's a rich banker whose brother is a member of the seven-man high command.

Such a predilection reconfirms the old saying—and sage equation—in the world of the bichos: "a banker is an eagle, a player is a donkey."

It is, however, worthwhile to detail my encounter with a banker. The first fact to observe is the following: if the contact with Sr. Gomes was already one fraught with intermediation, meeting places, and telephone messages, getting close to the banker obviously entailed greater obstacles. And because I had no close relationship with anyone who enjoyed a banker's confidence, I was obliged to follow a different path.

When the animal game marked its centennial, in 1992, a long interview with a banker appeared in a newspaper. I called that paper and asked to speak with the interviewer. After several messages, the journalist got in touch with me.

We set up a meeting at the Brazilian Press Association. The journalist kindly promised to make the contact with the banker. He said it would be easier to introduce me to the banker in a bar where every Thursday he offered a "crab fest" for a group of friends.

The bar was one of those cafés left over from Rio's belle époque, a place that preserved vestiges of beveled mirrors and beautiful chandeliers. The tables were on the sidewalk and, despite the reasonable number of people there, were empty. The people were standing in groups. I found this strange and suggested we sit down and order something to drink while we waited for the banker, who had yet to arrive. The journalist was evasive. So we remained standing. After a time, there was a stir, followed quickly by silence as everyone exchanged glances: "the man" had arrived. Only then did I understand that it was time to sit down. I was summoned to sit with the banker's nephew, next to his girlfriend. My journalist friend commented at the table that "everybody looks like they're waiting for something." The nephew of "the man" disagreed: "I'm not waiting for anything."

Without anyone having ordered anything, the waiters began bringing trays full of glasses, which they distributed among the tables. From inside the bar, the man was giving orders to the waiters. Only after this first round did he begin circulating among the tables, happily greeting those present, who seemed to be acquaintances of long standing. When he came by my table, I was duly introduced: "This is the young woman doing the book I told you about." He greeted me with an almost imperceptible nod and glance, then circled my chair and continued toward the street. Half seated, half on my feet, I hesitated. "Go there," urged the journalist, "go!"

"The man" was waiting for me in the middle of the street, far from the hubbub of the bar. He lowered his head gravely, signaling that he would pay close attention to what I had to say. His face was totally expressionless. I quickly saw I had less than two minutes to state my case. I attempted to make sublime use of this eagle and explained my interest in the most objective manner possible. After two sentences, he had understood and the audience was over. Result: he would gladly grant me an interview, and he invited me to accompany him at a tabulation session, but asked me to return after Carnival—the month was December—as he was very busy with the samba school.

He then immediately resumed his circuit among the tables until he was called by the bar's owner. He reappeared carrying an enormous pot of crabs, which he served with delight on paper plates to each of those present.

When the banquet was over, I said goodbye. My tablemates returned with the banker to his samba school.

Later I found out that the social life of all those people revolved around events sponsored by the banker. This group, made up of friends, relatives, and employees under his "protection," was in fact the banker's "clientele."

I returned three months later to find the same scene. I interviewed the banker, but the only interesting point of the conversation was the discovery that he only bet on "bichos that fly."

Only a detailed description of the practice of the players can bring to life the classificatory schemes studied thus far. Only an analytical description can fill the lacunae that every study of institutional organization necessarily omits.

For this reason we believe it essential to describe in detail an animal game betting site. This area compels the convergence and interaction of inveterate gamblers, occasional players, as well as the professionals who run the animal game industry along with the entire cosmic system that serves as basis of that activity.

As we have already said, there are approximately three thousand animal game betting sites in the city of Rio de Janeiro. I entered several and chose one that would serve as reference for the whole system. Not that it was in any way more "representative" than the others, for I am aware that "representativeness" depends on basically arbitrary criteria and choices. Furthermore, in operation every social institution is a case unto itself, as they only become similar in structure and ideology when we discuss them as maps, diagrams, or value frameworks. It was thus that I chose the site I will now describe.

The chosen site was the locale that I studied most in depth, by listening to employees and players. I stayed there an entire week witnessing the heavy workday of the employees, which began at 7:00 A.M. and ended at 10:00 P.M.

It is not easy to obtain a site manager's permission to spend a week there. Inevitably, someone higher up in the organization must be consulted. And it is easy to perceive, from the frequency of evasive responses, when one is unwelcome. I tried unsuccessfully three times at sites in the districts of Lapa, Santa Teresa, and Ipanema. At the first, after a series of four friendly interviews with the manager, my access was cut off abruptly and without explanation. The affable manager of the day before had become circumspect and distant, as if my presence there were unwanted. His silence seemed to indicate that he had already said enough.

At the second betting site, in Santa Teresa, the refusal was based on the argument that there was little movement there. It would be better for me to look for the main site in the area, where the "chief" worked—the only person, in fact, with the authority to grant permission for my research.

At the Ipanema site, the refusal was straightforward. They lacked the authority to decide on my being there, and it was difficult to locate the "chief," who was always very busy.

Of the contacts with betting sites made for the research, the most promising was one in Copacabana, where I had been introduced by an informant who had been playing there for two decades. Through his friendship with the manager, in the best Brazilian style that the animal game expresses and dramatizes so well, my passage was expedited.

Thus, six months after meeting Sr. Gesualdo, the promise was kept: permission was granted for me to spend a week there. In the cramped space of twenty square meters, I found a spot on a bench beside one of the game's "annotators."

Sr. Gesualdo's site is located in a narrow by-street in the super-populated Copacabana district. It is a street of residential buildings and few business establishments. There is a bar, the usual newsstand on the corner, a cobbler, a hairdresser, a store selling "spiritual items," and the betting site. Despite the cosmopolitanism of Copacabana, the street seems to circumscribe a small community in which everyone knows each other by name, says hello every day, and takes an interest in other people's lives. The betting site is the focal point of this sociability.

The wagers create a common interest and a common denominator, so that it is at the betting site that the assiduous players—approximately one hundred in number—meet to swap experiences with the game and also to chat, vent, and laugh about the others. The site is an obligatory stop, even outside working hours. Like a kind of "gateway institution," and demonstrating its importance, it is at the end (or, if we prefer, the beginning) of the small street, which in turn opens onto a bustling Copacabana. There we invariably find Lindalva, Sr. Artur, Osmar, and more frequently, Sr. Gesualdo, who know about everyone's lives, exchange money, promote raffles, and are always ready to chew the fat.

The vast and diversified clientele comprises housewives, retired persons, businessmen, garage men, street cleaners, and even beggars. All make their leap of faith (including, of course, those who work for the animal game), so that there are eleven invariable wagers daily, those of the four employees of the site and seven by the personnel from the banker's office in the area.

This site is like any other: a narrow door with no sign or other indication on the outside. Inside, a screen prevents the site's activities from being seen from the street. There is a single table with the cashier and a counter at which sit two annotators. In addition, we can see a refrigerator, a television set, several fans, and the narrow entrance to a bathroom.

On the center wall, there is an altar with the classic and beneficent statue of St. George slaying the dragon. Beside it is a votive candle that the site manager himself replaces every morning—proof of the organizers' faith in the system that unites "receivers" (takers) and "debtors" (bettors). On the other walls we see the numbers drawn and pictures of the site's personnel with clients—among them the photo of one of my best female informants.

The manager, Sr. Gesualdo, has been with the game for forty-two years and has had this site for twenty-six. The other sixteen were dedicated to selling the bicho on the street, going from door to door. The site opens at 7:00 A.M., but movement is slow through the morning, as the first drawing closes its bets at 1:30 P.M. and everyone waits till the last minute to play. Only after eleven o'clock, and as the times for the three drawings approach, does the number of bettors increase. But the site does not live by the bicho alone.

An animal game betting site plays an important integrating role for the inhabitants of a large city like Rio de Janeiro. It serves as a reference point and obligatory passage: a place in which one can share one's passion for the game and, through it, translate an entire set of experiences specific to each bettor.

Countless activities parallel to the game take place at the site.

The telephone, the fridge, and the bathroom at the site are virtually public, being used by customers as extensions of their own homes. Telephone calls forbidden at home can be made from the site. Although the small space affords no privacy, a certain discretion is maintained. In the refrigerator the local butcher keeps his customers' orders, leading to a daylong coming and going of packages of meat. It is common to see a customer come in, open the fridge, smile, help himself to water or a soft drink, and go on his way.

The site serves as a community bank, for the customers cash checks and merchants make change. In addition, everything is sold there: from raffles of merchandise smuggled in from Paraguay to the celebrated Avon cosmetics. It also functions as a service center, with information about housepainters, seamstresses, day laborers, and handymen who show up there to look for potential clients.

An older man who sells candy on the corner comes by early to pick up his bench, stool, and umbrella, stored there overnight. He is merely one more of those who benefit from the site's infrastructure. A car watcher and a beggar show up promptly at two o'clock to receive the leftovers from the employees' lunches.

More important, however, than all these acts of kindness and exchange of favors seems to be the site's function as a sure spot for all the idle, lonely, rootless, and poor of the neighborhood.

Widows, the retired, drunks, or simply the lonely are well received there at any hour of the day for a "word or two." They come in, sit, relate their woes, and receive comfort and counsel. Sometimes they remain there for more than an hour, or they make short visits five or six times a day.

On this street is a man who is constantly drunk. He washes cars and, because he is homeless, sleeps in his customers' vehicles. He is called "Boi." During the research, Boi had his sixty-eighth birthday, and the neighborhood organized a birthday party for him. One of his customers baked a cake; the site contributed the soft drinks and, more important, the appropriate spot for the celebration.

A community has developed around "vice." The site also lends itself to promoting romantic encounters, for there is always some widower with his eye on a nurse or a retired man wanting to know if the manicurist broke off her engagement. Besides this, arrangements are made for excursions to cities of touristic interest and trips to the theater in buses or minivans that pick up the elderly at their homes.

Around the betting site, then, meets a necessarily heterogeneous contingent of all sorts of people. During the research we were visited daily by Sr. Reginaldo. At first I thought that this older man worked in the organization, perhaps in the banker's office, for each morning Sr. Reginaldo would come by and ask if someone "wanted something for the bank." He took care of, I soon discovered, all the banking matters for the site's employees. In addition, it was he who organized the site's raffles. Once his banking duties were done, Sr. Reginaldo—who was in reality a retired civil servant—would return to the site and spend long hours chatting. It was obvious that he was good friends with Sr. Gesualdo, Osmar, Lindalva, and Sr. Artur. In the time I was there, he set up a trip to Paraguay, where he bought merchandise to resell to customers of the site or to use as the object of raffles. That was when I understood Sr. Reginaldo's connection to the site: in exchange for small services—"which he did with all goodwill"—he received permission to sell his Paraguayan contraband there. Moreover, the annotators themselves would sell tickets to the raffles that he financed for their customers. In return, Sr. Reginaldo sold them merchandise at cost. As Sr. Artur explained to me, confirming the norm of reciprocity that the animal game reclaims and activates, and denying the anonymity, brutality, and indifference that mark the urban universe, "One hand washes the other; it's all done out of comradeship."

I must emphasize that all of this movement in no way alters the workers' routine. On the contrary, the site reproduces the same order as the animal game—a structure of meetings, a symbolic multivocal encounter that, through an original union of numbers and animals, brings the desire for wealth into contact with fortune itself, and which encompasses every type of person and activity. Thus, while conversations go on and one asks about the other's family, discusses the latest hunch, or speaks of some illness, the scribes jot down the players' bets or simply copy them to the appropriate pad, for many show up with their bets already noted on a piece of paper. The cashier, in turn, is constantly counting money and answering the phone.

The "transporters" also perform their roles ceaselessly, for, like some veritable Hermes of the game, it is they who form the link between the site and the banker's office. Actually, at least six times a day the "transporter" goes from site to site picking up the bets and handing out the prizes already calculated by the tabulation center. They move swiftly, sometimes without exchanging a single word with the personnel at the site as they collect a sealed envelope at the cashier's table and replace it with another. As they are carrying a lot of money, there is always a car with its motor running waiting at the door.

The first result of the day comes out promptly at 2:30 and is transmitted by telephone. However, there is an AM radio station that broadcasts the information five minutes earlier, sometimes with small errors; because of this workers at the site always wait for official confirmation by phone. Some players go to the site to hear the result on the radio, delivered in the tone of a horse race. It begins with the seventh prize, and sometimes there is a commentary on the results.

Once the result is confirmed by phone, the cashier notes the numbers, hands them to the manager, who gives them to the annotator, who sets the stamp to mark the results sheets in a small box on the wall for passersby. All these acts are automatic and are repeated three times a day.

In this site there are two telephones: a standard one, gray in color, which receives the bets of special clients, transmits results, and makes outside calls, and a red telephone that very appropriately only receives calls from the banker's office and operates in code. The gray phone rings once, then the caller hangs up; immediately, the red phone rings, turning on a green light on the wall. The red phone rings some twenty times a day, and it is through it that the cashier finds out the sought-after numbers—those that pay less that day. The red phone also sends word of the close of the game as well as the "unloading": the review (and the banker's compensatory discounting) of the numbers on which there was heavy betting.

Even those who have worked there for decades cannot help but be surprised by certain results, proof of their contact with a truly enchanted universe in which anything can happen: "The monkey hit again today; it hit yesterday and with the same tenth, 67!" (The monkey has 17 as its reference number and the groups 65, 66, 67, and 68 as "client numbers.")

Lindalva says that she could have hit on that same day, in the morning, since she had run into Tião from the bakery, who had asked to borrow money from her. It was obvious that "meeting Tião right away so early" was a clear sign of the monkey, since Tião is black.

At that time the players begin arriving, and almost all of them repeat that "they could have hit . . ." A lady says that she had dreamed about a bunch of blacks starting a revolution. She commented on her indecision: "I get really mad when I ignore the hunch in my head. I didn't think it was going to repeat and it did!" Next to appear is a nurse dearly loved by the group (because, as they told me, she draws everyone's blood, does careful examinations, and never informs about bad results), who said: "Let me see, Sr. Osmar, let me see if my little bicho hit . . ." When she saw that the monkey had repeated, she became indignant, for just that night she had dreamed about a young man exercising on a horizontal bar. It was obvious that dreaming about "acrobatics" was a sign of the monkey, but she had bet on the rooster! Another older man dreamed about a fight in an apartment and lost because—ignoring the "correct interpretation"—he bet on the tiger, when it was obvious that a fight in an enclosed space was a crystal-clear indication of the monkey.

When the result comes out, there is no end of people arriving. Some merely pick up the sheets from the box and leave; others see the result and appear not to believe it. Of them, Sr. Artur asked with interest, as if to confirm his faith in the system of hunches and its hermeneutical traps: "Well then, Sr. So-and-So, how did that monkey treat you?" To which the bettor replied: "Badly, Sr. Artur. But it wasn't him, the fault's with the player. I've never seen anybody make money at this game." Sr. Artur then replied ironically and with verve: "Not at all, Sr. So-and-So, all the bankers are rich!"

This day the players are especially upset with the outcome, for "a repeating bicho" is something no one expects.

From the complaints and commentaries made by the players, I was able to confirm the general relationships of the classificatory framework within which hunches operate. Strategically seated beside an annotator, I was able to hear the justifications that confirmed interpretive errors at the same time they confirmed the guidelines of the system.

In relation to the monkey, for example, they said that dreaming about "a black starting a revolution," "a young man on a horizontal bar," "a fight in an apartment," or "right away running into Tião" (the name of a chimp at the Rio zoo) were signs that would lead to the bicho. Others, however, justifying the error, said that if the monkey hit yesterday, today—by complementary opposition and a matter of "cosmic equilibrium"—it should be the lion, a bicho the very opposite of the monkey. After all, "every dog has his day." Furthermore, we recalled that in the hierarchy of bichos, the lion is "king," standing at the top of the power pyramid or even above it, while the monkey is associated, among other things, with slaves and blacks, situated at the lower end of the scale or even excluded from it altogether, located as it is at the limits of humanity. Thus we see how these principles actually inform the players' actions.

That day, however, there was a single exception in relation to the discontent over the "repeating bicho." The employees of the site commented that "the old lady still hadn't come by to get her prize." They spoke of a lady who bet every day on the thousandth 1667 (the monkey). The lucky elderly lady had won yesterday and repeated the win today. It was a lovely example of reward for assiduousness, read—in this context—as proof of the affinity and loyalty between bicho and player. The assiduousness of inveterate players prompted the site's workers to learn by heart the thousandths "pursued" by some bettors, confirming the totemic or "affinity-sacrifice" relationship between them.

In this case, there were comments about the advantages of "following" a bicho, for if it "hit" for ten days, the player would win ten times! One of the most curious traits of players of the animal game—common, in fact, to all who believe in a cosmology—is precisely the capacity for always finding a rational and virtuous justification for the most widely varying strategies of wagering. To them, only the concrete result of the drawing seemed to be random, anomalous, and demonstrably deceptive. All else confirmed the system of hunches. It was as if, in the game, error and consequent defeat and frustration were fundamental in order to accentuate its deeper reality. For what would the game be if hunches were infallible and players always won?

On one occasion, precisely at noon, the red phone rang. It was the banker's office advising that the thousandth 1000 was "sought-after" that day. I asked Osmar the reason. He said it was likely that the number had appeared in the newspaper or been featured on television.

Discounting a bicho and/or number is a common expedient. Numbers that appear in the great communications media or are associated with telling events in local or national life become dangerous for the bankers, for many players will bet on them. And, if they are drawn, it will represent an enormous loss for the bank.

During the slow hours we would go out one at a time, to walk in the street or get some coffee. On one of these breaks I went to the bar for a snack. Hanging from the ceiling was a cage with a finch that sang a lot. Its owner, the counterman, was trying to sell it. He took down the cage to show the bird to his customers. He placed the cage directly in front of me. I then noticed that the finch had a tag on its leg, on which the number 264 could be clearly seen. It was forming the thousandth 0264. Obeying the canons of the animal game, as soon as I returned to the site I told Sr. Artur I wanted to play it. He advised me to surround the thousandth on all ten sides. A done deal, money lost.

Among the group of regulars was a lady, the friend of my informant, who related that when the dreams of the two of them coincided, winning was a sure thing. That day she had a hot hunch: a thousandth from a receipt. She played it for herself and her friend. This done, she asked to use the telephone, went to Osmar's table, and saw an albino cockroach. Instead of being disgusted, she was jubilant, for that exceptional insect was a sign she would hit in the game. As we have seen, the two privileged sources of hunches are dreams and extraordinary events.

With the exception of fixed numbers—those that are played every day and which in general are taken from tombs and relatives' birth dates—the numbers on which one bets can be anywhere: receipts, identity cards, bank accounts, check numbers, bus numbers, etc.

Recently a player had won by betting on the number of the bus ticket of Sr. Gesualdo, who had just returned from a vacation.

The numbers on betting slips are also much esteemed—they're called "banker's hunches," for they come printed on the ticket. There are customers who only play using this modality: "Play the number of the slip surrounded on twelve sides, 'cause if I don't take money home my wife'll skin me alive," said a certain older man. Others are unable to resist when they see plays by other people tossed on the floor. To find a number or a bicho, any expedient will do. I met players who elaborated the most complicated methods.

Lindalva, for example, submitted the three results of the previous day to complicated mathematical operations from which she would extract a group of three bichos and three thousandths. Although she did the sums with absolute rigor and followed the same method each day, the principles involved were totally arbitrary. For instance, suppose the result of the previous day was the thousandth 1682. To get the group, she added these four digits, obtaining the number 17 as a result, which was the tenth of the dog. Still not satisfied, she would submit the same 1682 to a second operation. Thus, Lindalva added the number 1 to each of the numbers and got the thousandth 2793, the stag. Lindalva had invented this method and employed it daily.

This type of recourse appears to be nothing new. A columnist writing in 1940 relates something similar:

> When I get up in the morning I like to decide on my play, even before breakfast. To get good hunches I usually go to the living room window and look out at the street. If I see a cat, I know the cat's going to come up. It's a good hunch. If I see a dog, I bet on the dog; sometimes it hits. But yesterday I saw neither cat nor dog.
>
> When I got to my window the Vila Isabel trolley, with the number 15, was passing by. At that moment the inspector yelled to the conductor:
>
> "Hey, 22, drop by the house soon!"
>
> That meant the conductor was "badge 22."
>
> In the direction opposite to the trolley came a bread vendor, on whose basket was the number 4.
>
> And, immediately afterward, a handcart with the number 8.
>
> So, adding the 15 from the trolley to the conductor's 22 gives 37; now the 4 from the bread vendor makes it 41, and the handcart's 8 brings it to 49!
>
> 49 is the rooster! But I lost, because I didn't bet on it. I bet on the rabbit. If I had surrounded the rooster on all sides, how much I'd have won (Cavalcanti, 1940:64)!

According to Sr. Artur, the modalities of the game were divided into two large currents. There were players who only bet on groups (1 to 25). This was the easiest type of play and, according to him, the one preferred by women and "little old ladies who love playing on their little group." This was also the game of those least versed in the code of wagers, for all you had to do was choose one of the 25 bichos that maintained a univocal relationship with the 25 numbers.

The other modality included the more sophisticated plays, practiced by experienced gamblers. The options were endless: you could play the thousandth, the surrounded thousandth, the inverted and combined thousandth, the deuces (*duques*), the triple tenths, etc.

According to the annotator, only 10 percent of players knew all the wagering modalities. The most sophisticated plays sometimes wouldn't fit on a single page of the betting pads. These plays, very long and complicated, contain so many lines and inscriptions that they are called "maps."

Some people ask to consult the manuals. One day a young man came in, asked for the manual, and read it very attentively. He was surely seeking the interpretation of a dream. The consultation over, he closed the manual and shrugged. He seemed unconvinced, but he played nonetheless.

Each banker sets the maximum that can be bet. When the value of a wager exceeds his ability to pay, he can pass the bet on to a site with greater capacity or refuse to accept it.

In general, there is a three-day deadline for the player to claim his prize. However, in the case of someone going out of town, the ticket is marked with a thirty-day limit. As a way of controlling the payment of prizes, the annotators keep an up-to-date notebook in which the results of the drawings are listed.

It is not necessary to go to the site to find out the results. Word of the winning bichos passes quickly from mouth to mouth. If we walk down the street after announcement of the result, we perceive a transmission network made up of doormen, the newsstand owner, the bartender. They are telling anyone who doesn't know the result that the turkey, the ostrich, or the lion hit.

And thus pass the week, the month, and the years. Many players have been there since the site opened twenty-six years ago. They maintain a cordial relationship and make the site a meeting place, an extension of their homes. The personnel of the site joke with them, teasing them about their "vice," obviously seen as benign and engendering a pleasurable sociability.

As these thoughts go through my mind, a lady comes in who plays daily. They chaff with her because she is religiously regular in the "little game." In a jocose tone, they tell her that her husband just bet the money from the sale of the electric iron on the monkey and from the washing machine on the butterfly. The lady laughs heartily, and the ribbing continues. They tell her that she and her husband are hopeless, she plays in the "night owl" (the 9:00 P.M. drawing) and her husband, not satisfied with the horse races at the Jockey Club, travels every week to the races in the city of Campos dos Goitacazes, some 180 miles from Rio.

The lady leaves and the "deaf man" enters, an oldster close to ninety who can't hear a thing. Everyone laughs at his expense. They ask, shouting into his ear, when he's going to remarry. Sr. Antônio doesn't play hard to get, saying he has three possibilities lined up.

This is the account of one week at a betting site in Copacabana.

One may think that my presence there occasioned a redoubling of jesting, embellished the details of the stories, and demonstrated more interest in the stories of the players who go there daily. But it can also be argued that perhaps they are just that way, for the animal game promotes communication. It does so because, first, it encourages meetings with friends; second, it is an officially clandestine activity, which engenders a community of semi-illegal aficionados knowledgeable about an art that mixes magic, numerology, and science; and third, because discovering a good hunch is like performing an unusual act on the streets of a great city, for anyone playing the animal game becomes a symbolic hunter. Finally, one who plays has no shame about expressing his hope for changing his position in society and becoming rich.

The study of the site confirms the vocabulary of the hunt employed by the animal game players. Thus they invariably speak of "surrounding," "lassoing," "pursuing," "tracking," "stalking," "hitting," and "catching" the bicho. We noted in these expressions a direct reference to the hunt. We can immediately apprehend that, among other things, the act of betting would describe a rite of the hunt whose prize—once the bicho is "lassoed" or "hit"— would be a proof of legitimacy or a getting even in relation to the position the person occupies in society. A mistake would confirm poverty, inferiority, domination, and social exclusion; a winning wager would correspond to the possibility of trading places. It would be a breach in the closed wall of hierarchy and difference. Error closes, a correct play opens, turning the passive into active and the poor into rich—the hunted becoming the hunter.

The resemblance of this lottery to hunting reaffirms once again the concreteness of the amalgam of numbers and bichos that makes the animal game unique. In contrast with modern lotteries, in which the bettor cannot go beyond the cold universe of numbers, in the animal game one ventures into the magic and happy world of the bichos. Instead of confronting numerical tables and probability charts, the animal game player faces a jungle of heterogeneous animals, all displaced from their original contexts and marked by specific characteristics, which may approach or flee, accept or reject.

As demonstration of this, a certain player comments that he had "lassoed the stag"; another aficionado says it is hard to "catch the bull." When one goes to sleep, he thinks about a bicho that will emerge in his dreams. Someone says that he is "stalking" the pig or the tiger; or hoping to "hit" the peacock or the bear, in a substitution of bichos for numbers. As if it were much easier to have hunches about animals than about numbers.

In referring to the bichos, players may refer more comfortably to themselves and to their interests and fantasies, thus revealing their most intimate experiences and the way they classify and interpret them—whether dreams or events that have captured their attention.

For example: nothing is more clear than associating a bus with an elephant, for the physical dimensions constitute the common element that unites them. A child is a sign of the rabbit and the sheep, as both are white and pure. If we dream about a dog, we must play it and the lion, as both are hunters, the dog being a "miniature lion," in contrast to the feline pair of tiger and cat. Besides which, being loyal bichos, they don't lie. Their appearance would not be a sign of some other bicho but of themselves. One should always bet, as we indicated earlier, on the license plates of cars involved in accidents.

Lindalva told me that in the area of the betting site there couldn't be an automobile accident without the whole street rushing out to write down the plate numbers. She herself never missed a collision, even though she found it worthy of reproof "to benefit from the misfortune of others." This comment reveals her unshakable faith in the animal game as a system that actually does allow becoming rich!

Two Players

During my time at the betting site I was able to observe several players, although none in depth. Many of them proved to be discreet and, perhaps because of having had their bets stolen, leaned over the annotator and whispered their hunches, shielding them from the ears of the other players.

In order for my observations to capture the day-to-day reality of a betting site, I tried to interfere as little as possible in their activities. Seated as always beside the annotator, I observed in detail the movement at the site, waiting for the player to leave before jotting down my observations.

Although the ethnography of the site enhanced my observations about the countless preferences in wagering, as well as about the use of the system by which the animals are classified, I had no means of studying the players in depth. With this as my goal, I spent a year in the company of two assiduous bicho players, Deise and Hércules.

Deise, married to a lawyer, had two children, lived in a comfortable apartment in Copacabana, didn't work outside the home, and was "brought up as a Catholic." Hércules was a twenty-seven-year-old bachelor who lived in São Paulo and worked as an assistant in an office, had completed elementary school, and was a "militant spiritist."

In addition to differences in sex, age, and religious conviction, they had very different life experiences and views of the world. They shared, however, a "passion" for the animal game, which they had played daily for many years.

Deise, who is now fifty, had inherited a passion for the game from her maternal grandmother, who had bet on the game since its inception. She was the only person in the family who played. Sometimes, when accompanying her husband to the interior of Minas Gerais, she had to play surreptitiously, for his very traditional family looked askance at the habit.

Her grandmother would only bet on the cow, but Deise prefers the snake. If she dreams about her husband—who snores and is rich—she plays the pig or the camel. If she dreams about her older son—a successful musician—she plays the lion; if she dreams about her daughter-in-law—the famous musician's wife—she plays the eagle. The eagle that seduced and took away her lion.

I spent a lot of time at Deise's home, where there was always a bountiful table under the direction of Rita, a kind of governess close to seventy years of age. As a girl, Rita had lived in the countryside. In addition to her culinary talents, Rita had "powerful visions in the form of dreams." Deise imputed supernatural powers to her and held in high esteem her hunches about the bicho. She had won the bicho several times thanks to Rita.

Recently, Rita had dreamed she was in an arena where she saw a monkey riding a bull that "pawed" the dirt. Deise put together the triple of monkey-bull-horse—for when you play the bull you always play the horse simultaneously. She won and generously divided the prize with Rita.

She had learned to trust her employee's hunches the day she missed winning a good amount of money by not listening to her. Rita had dreamed about a voice whispering behind her: "Eight thousand, eight thousand." Deise thought the hunch "very clear" but didn't play—and the thousandth 8000 was first on the list.

At times Rita's dreams were very "sophisticated and strange," challenging Deise's hermeneutic intelligence. On one occasion, Rita dreamed about an image of the Sacred Heart of Jesus descending from the sky until it touched her cheek. She spoke of the dream to her employer, who was unable to find the key to interpreting it.

In opposition to Rita's "visions" were the hunches of Deise's husband—always "awful"—to which she gave no credence. It was a long way from the active professional who through rationality successfully braved the jungle of men to the aged servant from the countryside who had surreal dreams. But it was obvious that, in order to win at the animal game, it was best to follow the path of extravagance that—paradoxically but correctly—indicated the true symbolic way.

But, besides the hunches supplied by Rita, Deise also makes use of a large and sophisticated collection of specialized materials. In one of the rooms in her spacious apartment is a desk where Deise keeps a dozen or so "manuals for interpretation of dreams for the animal game." In addition to the manuals, there are Deise's "study notebooks." In them she painstakingly records the three daily results of the drawings and keeps statistics about the bichos that are "overdue"—those that haven't hit in a long time. She explains that she keeps these notebooks for the purpose of arriving at some "conclusion" about the animal game. In another notebook, of what we might call "hermeneutic notes," Deise lists her dreams and transcribes various interpretations gathered from the manuals.

In each manual are numerous comments or notes. Deise has a precise system, which demonstrates the intelligence and seriousness that she brings to the game. She marks with the letter c (meaning "confirmed") the interpretations that prove correct—in other words, that resulted in prizes. In a third notebook she consistently elaborates various methods for hitting the bicho.

The last of these took the days of the month as its base. The point of departure was a day, say the 17th. Well, Deise would play the groups 17, 18, 19, and 20—forming a triple group (of the dog, reference number 5). According to her, this method, as arbitrary as any other, gave good results. However, she herself made fun of a female "acquaintance" who had developed a method that she found completely senseless. The friend lines up vertically the thousandths of the three results of the day before and obtains hundredths. For example, 1234,0000, 1111 converts to 101, 201, 301, and 401.

Despite all this interpretive "rationality," Deise, like most animal game players, was of the opinion that great hunches come from uncontrollable sources such as dreams. Still, parallel to the decipherment of dreams and as proof that magical thinking is not incompatible with empirical observation and rational calculation, she kept her "statistics," creatively complementing the uncontrollable and unconscious stuff of dreams with precise and practical analyses, which resulted in elaborate tables that could likewise be consulted.

These two strategies, which utilitarian and/or rational thought considers incompatible and irreconcilable—for one either believes in the magical message of dreams or one recognizes the probabilistic logic of the drawing and thus resorts to statistics—coexist harmoniously in Deise's mind. On some occasions dreams encompass rational observation, while on others the exact opposite occurs, which shows that magical thinking is more prepared to dialogue with and encompass reality than the other way around.

Besides this, the manuals considered representative of professional knowledge were submitted to rigorous empirical tests. Their contents were not taken as absolute but were worthy or not of a c, in cool confirmation on Deise's part.

According to her, one must have great "imagination" to decide on a number when starting with signs, thus the necessity of always inventing new methods. One must also "always be alert to the signs," which can insinuate themselves at any moment.

Deise makes a distinction that, as I observed, is not rare among players: there is "the old game" and "today's game." Twenty years before, in the days of the "flying bookie"—who walked the streets and went from house to house picking up bets—there was a severe police crackdown and the population of the street covered for that agent of luck and possible change of fate. In the same era—that period of time idealized under the heading "the old days"—dreams were stronger and had "more logic" to them. In addition, "pulls" (or chains of bichos, as it is believed that when a given bicho hits, it can cause another one magically associated with it to come up) worked better.

According to the originator of this observation, Deise, "In the old days it was a sure thing! Everything went right, on track." In her interpretation, "the computer" had messed everything up. She was referring to the method of calculating the results, currently done by computer, with all the doubts that revolve around that hypothesis. In any case, Deise also blamed "modern times" for the decrease in the honesty of the tabulation process. She believed that currently there was a lot of "the hand in the sack" going on, for anyone could look at the outcome and see it was "strange."

This veritable master of logic and hermeneutics taught me many things, among them the brilliant and logically impeccable idea of the existence of "accompanying bichos." If you dream of a crocodile, play it and the snake; the cat and the tiger; the horse and the donkey; the bull and the cow; the dog and the lion; etc. These relationships reveal that the player takes seriously the dimensions of affinity among the animals. This procedure, as I verified from information from Deise, was widely used by players.

Moreover, Deise observed the general precepts of the game. She played the tomb numbers of members of the family and had her lucky bicho—the snake—but she bet on other animals in a scale of favoritism that went through the ostrich, including in descending order the rabbit, the cat, the crocodile, and the pig. She had no sympathy for the tiger, bear, or bull, which she never played. If she bought a new car, she bet on the license plate number; if she found money in the street, she played the serial number on the bill.

Like other assiduous players, Deise also had internalized the classic equations by which: water is crocodile, heat is camel ("which only comes out for man!"), a party is turkey, and a child is rabbit.

Money won at the animal game was, as Machado de Assis had perceived in the aforementioned short story, to "buy silly things, to spend on gifts; if you don't spend it right away, it goes back to the bicho." This norm accentuates the gratuitous nature of the game, which cannot be compromised by any rational end.

Every morning, after seeing her husband off to work, Deise would go to make her "little leap of faith." The danger was running into the doormen from the building, who would "disturb her judgment and divert her hunches with their suggestions." They all had their "sure things" and would insist she play "the tiger, the cat, the eagle, etc.," thus contaminating her fresh intuitions from the morning. Deise would make several trips a day to the site run by Sr. Gesualdo, with whom she had been friends for over twenty years.

The story of Hércules and the animal game is quite different. While still a child, at the age of ten, he lived in the interior of the state with his family. At that time, his parents "wrote bicho" at home—that is, they ran a betting site in the house. His father had seven children and was retired from the army. In the days when he "wrote bicho," he received a commission of 10 percent of the amount wagered. However, he gambled everything he made on the very bichos he wrote, including his pension and commission. He went broke and the family disintegrated. The children left home and only his mother remained with his father, who was an "addict." Hércules blamed him for the "bad path" that many of them had taken.

Despite his unhappy family history and his father's involvement with the game, Hércules plays daily and retains excellent memories of the time when the animal game was "written" in their house.

He agrees with Deise that "in the old days" playing the bicho was much more fun, even when "the police were chasing you." According to him, in the 1970s police repression was very strong but, perhaps because of that, the game was more exciting.

Even with all the scares, Hércules was "happy" working in the game. People came to his house to play or Hércules would go to their houses to pick up the bets, taking the "movement" to the banker's office daily. Once, there was a police raid at the banker's headquarters and Hércules was obliged to flee over the rooftops of neighboring buildings.

As for the game nowadays, Hércules considers it perverted and soulless. According to him, with the growing sophistication of the game's structure, it is no longer possible to have the same "confidence" as in times past. He believes that today's bankers have developed protection mechanisms against very large payoffs by manipulating the results—in other words, by breaking with the common belief in the system, which thus ceases to be the element encompassing players and "takers," poor hunch players and rich bankers.

Like Deise, Hércules also feels that drawing by "machine" makes it easier for bankers to pull a "con." This nostalgia for bygone times can lead us to think that, given the structure of the animal game, the increase in impersonality and automation has led to a diminution of credibility, the opposite of what might be expected. Impersonality—represented here by "the machine" and by automation—enjoys no prestige among players. First, because there is a belief that machines can be manipulated; second, because they in some way "contaminate" with rationality a process experienced as "enchanted," spontaneous, and magical.

Having played the bicho for over fifteen years, Hércules too has developed intricate betting strategies. Like Deise, he keeps a notebook of "statistics" in which he does his studies in order to arrive at a "conclusion" about the logic of the game's results.

Now and then, Hércules also plays Lotto, and although the animal game doesn't award a prize as large as Lotto, it is much more esteemed, precisely because it invites speculation in the formulation of the hunch. In the animal game, the search for a hunch—the symbolic hunt that mobilizes the players' social experiences—seems as exciting as the game itself.

Hércules's major source of hunches was his "lucky numbers," specifically his date of birth—11-17-64—which forms the tenth of the lion (reference number 16; client numbers 61, 62, 63, and 64), along with those of the monkey (reference number 17; client numbers 65, 66, 67, and 68) and of the horse (reference number 11; client numbers 41, 42, 43, and 44). He says these numbers have already won twice for him.

In second place, Hércules privileges dreams. Without the use of manuals, he interprets his dreams in accordance with the people who appear in them. He immediately seeks a correspondence between persons and bichos. For example, if he dreams of his father, he plays the monkey and the bear— the monkey because he feels that his father (a diminutive and agitated man) resembles a "small monkey," and the bear because it is a "false friend." Hércules, who is black and the son of a black, does not argue against the association of the monkey with blacks. If he dreams about his mother, he plays the butterfly or the dog—the butterfly because his mother is a dreamer who's "always in the clouds, and the dog because, in opposition to the bear, it is a "faithful friend," highly reliable. Hércules's hunches, as we see, offer a clear picture of his relationships with his genitors.

As occurs with many players, Hércules plays the animals that are the center of the hunch as well as those associated with them. He uses the "accompanying bichos" process, already described with Deise. If he dreams of a cow, he also plays the bull and the horse; if the dream is about a dog, he immediately bets on the cat, the lion, and the tiger.

Embodying a curious residual perspectivism, referred to in "Initial Hunch," Hércules says he tries "to put himself in the place of the bichos and feel what they feel." Only after this exercise does he place his bet. Thus, if he dreams of falling into a bottomless hole, with the sensation of hurtling rapidly downward, he bets on the eagle, which must feel the same when it launches itself from above.

Hércules remembers and attentively follows his dreams, for he is convinced that they are significant and intervene in the course of his life, predicting, safeguarding, or indicating the necessity for immediate action (the hunch). Certain dreams arouse the "feeling that he has to do something" and that "there is something to settle in relation to the members of his family."

Of the seven brothers and sisters, Hércules claims to have the best judgment, as the other six—like their father—are constantly finding themselves embroiled in difficulties.

Besides being an assiduous player, Hércules is a devout spiritist, so his dreams are interpreted as signals from the other world.

But this double function of dreams—in Hércules's case, dreams are simultaneously a spiritual signal and the source of hunches for the animal game—does not appear to constitute a problem. The game and his beliefs are not in conflict but complement each other. According to him, there are no problems in using these "signals" or "signs" to wager. An exception would be in the instance of the signal being "very serious," in which case he avoids playing and runs to the aid of the person in the dream, thus realizing his "karma," his mission in this life vis-à-vis his fellow man as a means of spiritual ascension, as his religion anticipates.

Moreover, Hércules confirms the classic interpretations that are valid and universally utilized, those that we seek to describe in our classificatory schemata. He insists on mentioning a few examples:

Dreaming about children = rabbit; water = crocodile; woods = horse and cow; clouds or sky = eagle; a woman = cow; a pregnant woman = goat or sheep; a man = stag or bull ("depending"); trees and banana = monkey; flowers and garden = butterfly; water and desert = camel; earth = snake; shouts, chants, or a fight = rooster; scratches from a woman's fingernails = cat or tiger; luxury, a king or queen = lion; the foot = peacock.

Thus, with the starting point of his lucky number 64 (the tenth of the lion), Hércules plays all the tenths of this bicho, "trying to box in the four tenths in combinations of deuces." With the tenths 61, 62, 63, and 64 he works various permutations, avoiding "some other bicho entering" the equation in question. He can thus form the number 6432, whose last two digits are obtained by dividing 64 by 2, although 32 belongs to the tenth of the camel (reference number 8, client numbers 29, 30, 31, and 32).

Or else he forms his betting numbers as follows. He closes his eyes and "sees" (or imagines) the first number that appears. He also plays the number on the betting slip, from which he composes deuces of tenths and thousandths. In addition, he always plays for three consecutive days, following a rigorously prescribed and determined game.

He has won several times but has never pocketed much money. But like every player, he knows people—in this case a childhood friend named Sapo who today manages a betting site—who win every day. Sapo's strategy consists of a secret mathematical operation to which he submits the morning results. With this he selects the numbers to play that night. Hércules knows many people "hooked on the bicho." His aunt, who helped raise him, is always asking him for money to play. She even "takes food money to play and, if she doesn't play, she cries and gets sick." His aunt is very elderly and doesn't know how to read, but her strategy consists of picking up discarded betting slips from the floor and copying their numbers.

These people "obsessed" with the game keep trying to divine a bicho behind anything. If they look at the shape of a cloud and are in doubt as to which of three bichos they see, they bet on all the tenths of the three bichos—all twelve numbers. Like any good magician, Hércules knows that, to one who plays the bicho, "everything has to do with everything," and adds that the "freer" the hunch, the more valuable it is.

He also revealed tactics for inducing hunches. In one of them, his aged aunt places a lit matchstick in a cup of coffee. When it goes out, it leaves a white stain in which she looks for the shape of a bicho. Another infallible practice is this: when someone is sleeping at your house, at exactly midnight place a tuft of grass on his pillow. Then shake the person three times, calling him by name. "So-and-So, So-and-So, what bicho's going to hit today?" (as it is already past midnight). In all certainty, the person will utter the name of one of the 25 bichos, and the hunch is a sure thing.

The last time I spoke with Hércules was just after Carnival week. Commenting on his hunches, which he had kept to show me, he made a curious statement: during Carnival no one wins at the animal game.

Perhaps because it is a ritual alien to any seriousness, Carnival affects even the hierarchy of the bichos. Thus, if the animal game can turn around people's destiny, it is assuredly affected by Carnival.

NOTES

1. Choosing a possible bicho is essential, for some people, ignorant of the list of 25 bichos, want to bet on the duck, the rat, or the toad, as was the case of one intellectual, an M.A. in sociology, who wanted to "experience popular culture"!

2. I played the elephant often without the success of that first magical time when I told my grandmother of a hunch. For the reader who may be an aficionado of the animal game, there is the suggestion of a good hunch. Perhaps the elephant isn't good for me but, who knows, is the "right hunch" for others?

3. We were "ashamed poor" because we had to take care of clothing, schooling, food, and lodging—in sum, of our social standing—though we lacked the income to do so. And, behold the paradox; we couldn't rip away the veil of "appearances" or the playacting that transcended the realm of mere economic reality. See also note 7.

4. A time when the animal game was, as they say in Brazil, "free." On one occasion I was taken by my grandmother to visit the famous Icaraí Casino in Niterói, today the site of a dreary university bureaucracy, with the kindly acquiescence of the doorman, Mr. Mossoró, a neighbor of ours, through its revolving doors, glimpsing the great game room full of elegant people and a statue of a nude woman (a representation of the goddess of Chance?). I recall that the end of gambling in Brazil was met with sadness by my family and felled with a heart attack the unhappy and suddenly unemployed Mr. Mossoró.

5. In chapter 2 of the 1979 book *Carnavais, malandros e heróis* (*Carnivals, Rogues, and Heroes*), the "totemic logic" of the animal game is mentioned in passing.

6. An only son, the late and greatly missed Marcelino Perdigão, shared with her this passion for gambling and even surpassed her, fascinated by horse racing and the women who, to him, constituted the greatest gamble life offered to a handful of courageous men of character. His objective was always to "hit it big" in the game and with the women he would seduce and lose with the same avidity with which he gambled. As was the case with Grandma Emerentina, I never saw him depressed. To him, life was bounded by love, affairs, luck, and—what courage!—never by money or the time clock. Marcelino was the only mortal I've ever met who could have lived in Jorge Luis Borges's Babylon (see note 7).

7. The expression "suicide without death" is that of the character Clappique in the book *The Human Condition,* by Malraux. The idea that gambling is a self-destructive compulsion comes from the Freudian notion that, as Thomas Kavanagh shows, associates the movement of the gambler's hands with masturbatory activity and links gambling to an Oedipal regression in which arise fantasies of parricide that lead to masochism reinforced by repeated and deliberate loss (Kavanagh,

1993:36–37). Functionalist explanations that discuss gambling as a "mechanism of accommodation used by society as a means of channeling protests resulting from frustrations with the basic economic and ethical system" are assessed by James Frey (1984:110ff.). Only Borges could imagine a system in which games of chance would also affect social positions and linkages, bringing fortune and misfortune and producing general social consequences by constructing and dissolving the social structure with each drawing. In Borges's Babylon the lottery was a revolutionary instrument for the distribution of goods and social services and not a compensatory mechanism or compulsion, as modern theories contend (see Borges, 1972).

8. Grandma, like the noble Castiglione, disdained money and assumed that "knowing how to gamble nobly meant knowing how to lose" (Kavanagh, 1993:42). Or, as Norbert Elias (1995:39) clarified, speaking of nobility: it is not the economy (or income) that dictates social position but it is the position and social "role-playing" imposed by society that dictate expenses. It could be said that Emerentina was a bohemian at heart, for she had the same attitude of disdain for money as the literati of the belle époque, as I apprehend Isabel Lustosa (1993). That attitude, which situates people in and out of the world and typifies both roguery and resignation, as I demonstrated in *Carnavais, malandros e heróis* (*Carnivals, Rogues, and Heroes*), appears to have profound implications in Brazil, as we will discuss below, in "Initial Hunch" and in chapter 1.

9. Elena Soárez later broadened the scope of these ideas, transforming them into a film project that won a fellowship from the Fundação Vitae.

10. Lévi-Strauss expands the studies but takes as his starting point the fundamental considerations of his predecessor Émile Durkheim ([1912] 1996), whose ideas cannot be ignored.

11. Which, like the sphere of sports, awaits its Max Weber. Thomas Kavanagh agrees when he observes, in his study of gambling and the Enlightenment, that "gambling does not awaken respect" in the academic world (Kavanagh, 1993:29). Similarly, James H. Frey states: "Sociologists have placed little importance on gambling as an autonomous activity worthy of investigation" (Frey, 1984:108). Roger Caillois, author of a supremely ambitious pioneering essay on gambling, in which the animal game is in fact mentioned, also concurs (Caillois, 1979:162). The great Marcel Mauss comes close to this same opinion in his sociological characterization of the agonistic ritual trading carried out by natives of the North American Northwest. Referring to the potlatch, which makes people give away objects "as are lost in war, by gambling or in running and wrestling" (Mauss, 1990:37), he says in an important footnote: "On this subject it would be necessary to study gambling, which even in French society is not considered to be a contract, but a situation in which honor is committed and in which goods are handed over that, after all, one could refuse to hand over." Gambling, he concludes, "is a form of potlatch and of the gift system" (Mauss, 1990:112, note 139).

12. As I was writing these lines, the magazine *IstoÉ* (2/11/98) published an article that hinted at the demise of the animal game in light of competition, repression, and decadence. In the article, the daughter of the animal game banker Raul Capitão speaks of the decline in betting and states: "The game won't last another five or six years." Further, the bankers were demoralized by imprisonment in 1993; younger people are uninterested in or don't know how to play the animal game and income from the game, according to data from the Federal Savings Bank, was *only* 500 million *reais* of a total of 4.8 billion spent on gambling in general. Along with this death foretold, I read in the newspaper *O Globo* (2/10/98) that a successful police operation, significantly called "Operation Spinning Reel," identified fifty policemen accused of taking payoffs from the animal game. In the same article, the chief of police in Rio de Janeiro was surprised at the meager amount given the policemen, which varied from 3,000 to 10,000 *reais* per month. Admittedly, fifty policemen receiving an average of 5,000 *reais* a month is an impressive sum, especially if we consider that the operation most likely did not identify all the police who continue to receive regular payoffs from the animal game. In the state of São Paulo there are close to ten thousand betting spots in the capital city and close to thirty thousand in the rest of the state, taking in a total of a million and a half dollars per day! At the great samba school parade in 1998—with the governor of the state and the mayor of Rio de Janeiro present—the director of the Caprichosos de Pilares samba school honored the memory of the banker Castor de Andrade with a respectful minute of silence. The glory days may have passed, but wouldn't it be an overstatement to write the animal game's obituary? Wouldn't we be confusing change with extinction? Furthermore, we mustn't forget that the banker may disappear but the system of the animal game remains.

Initial Hunch and Finishing Touch:
The Bichos Are More Important than the Bookies

1. Doubtlessly, these studies were discovered and undertaken as objects of sociological reflection in recent years following the publication of *Carnavais, malandros e heróis* (*Carnivals, Rogues, and Heroes*) in 1979.

2. I believe I was one of the first to stimulate the study of this area on the anthropological plane, in a nonnormative and nonlinear manner, with the object of delving into the dominant historical paradigm in order to read soccer as ritual, drama, and refinement of values. See *Universo do futebol* (Rio: Pinakotheke, 1982), which I organized and in which I published essays by Luís Felipe Baeta Neves Flores, Simoni Lahud Guedes, and Arno Vogel. In this context I cannot leave unmentioned the intelligent essay by Micael Herschmann and Kátia Lerner on soccer, the animal game, and the street; the contributions of Maurício Murad, who founded

the Study Group on Soccer at the State University of Rio de Janeiro (see, for example, the inaugural issue of the Study Group, *Pesquisa de Campo,* published in 1995); the articles by José Sérgio Leite Lopes and those by Luiz Henrique de Toledo about organized rooters; the recent book by Simoni Lahud Guedes (1998); and the classic work by Anatol Rosenfeld. Not to mention the essays of Eduardo Archetti.

3. Despite the efforts of Mário Souto Maior (see Souto Maior, 1985).

4. Among which I distinguish the book by Simone Ferreira Soares (1993), pioneering essays by Machado and Figueiredo (1978) and by Nádia M. A. Silva (n.d.), and the unpublished work by Pedro Agostinho (1979). The one great, noteworthy exception that proves the rule is Gilberto Freyre, who studies the animal game in *Casa grande & senzala* (*The Masters and the Slaves*) (we discuss the scope of his theories in chapter 2); he refers to it twice, in passing, as one of the "vogues" introduced by republican modernity, as the "most Brazilian animal game," which on streetcars led to "democratic" discussions about dreams and hunches, in *Ordem e progresso* (*Order and Progress*) (1959: 124 and 136), an observation that he reiterates in his *Guia prático, histórico e sentimental da cidade do Recife* (1968:104). In a pioneering study published in Paris in 1958, the French essayist Roger Caillois uses the animal game as an example of the undesirable return of games of chance founded on superstition, indolence, and fatalism in societies in transition toward "industrial civilization," the basis of which is work and organized competition, as in Cameroon, Gabon, Cuba, and Brazil, in a text flawed by the generality of its thesis and the ethnocentrism of its perspective. Like many other researchers, he fails to understand the role of ambiguity in the process of modernization (which he surely sees as linear and evolutionary) of certain societies, or the significance of the bichos in their complex relationship with numbers and social acts (Caillois, 1979:152–156).

5. This same logic demands doing away with the bookies but protecting the players in the animal game. It is the same paradox found in the case of drug use, in which the object is desired but the imprisonment of traffickers is demanded. As if one thing could exist without the other, when it is obvious that the only way to contain the traffic would be by understanding the universe of symbols and fantasies engendered by drugs, which motivates users and brings out the suppliers.

6. Differently from the other "social sciences" that assume with greater or lesser naïveté the "natural science" paradigm and believe themselves capable of "explaining" the facts they study, social or cultural anthropology has always oscillated between reductionist models (in which complex phenomena are reduced to a single—usually "material" or "biological" cause or factor) and interpretive, structuralist models in which, as Evans-Pritchard suggested long ago, one *translates* a native model by means of the presumably more encompassing and elegant one of the researcher, leading to the understanding, as Isaiah Berlin says, interpreting Vico, of "why things are as they are and not merely what they are" (Berlin, 1998:56). The fun-

damental aspect of this posture would be to *translate and interpret,* which means—as Louis Dumont observes (1985: chapter 6)—not forgetting that the postulate of the oneness of the human species that is modern and universalistic only makes sense when confronted with its differences or forms of realization and expression, which are always particular.

7. Creatively studied by Lívia Barbosa (1992).

8. As Gellner (1983) reminds us, Renan knew of this and said, as early as 1882, in his classic essay about the nation: "Forgetting and—I would even say—historical error are an essential factor for the creation of a nation." According to a citation in Lúcia Lipp Oliveira's book, this formula is repeated by Karl Mannheim when he says: "For society to continue to exist, social recollection is as important as forgetting" (see Oliveira, 1990). This can be attested by Borges's character Irineu Funes, a youth possessing total recall who "wasn't even able to think," because "thinking is forgetting differences, it's generalizing, abstracting" (Borges, 1972:124). In a world filled with memory or facts accorded equal value, there is no "thought" because there are no acts of forgetting that permit the constituting of identity or the full awareness of self as subject—as a being who makes choices that *values* and imparts order to the world. As Lévi-Strauss states, reiterating Borges's point on another plane and through other materials: "What is true of the constitution of historical facts is no less so of their selection. From this point of view, the historian and the agent of history select, divide, and carve them up, for a truly total history [such as that in the head of Irineu Funes] would confront them with chaos" (Lévi-Strauss, 1966:257). For now, it is enough to emphasize that, for us, identities are governed by the logic of remembering and forgetting, are relatively fixed and variable, being made up of a dialectic and through a complex process of segmentation. I am a carioca as opposed to the paulistas, but cariocas and paulistas are southerners when in Belém do Pará, in contrast to the northerners. Faced with an Argentine, however, northerners and southerners are transformed into Brazilians. Now, the contrast with the United States causes Argentines and Brazilians to unite into another encompassing set—"Latin American" identity—and so on.

9. To be didactic: all human societies appear subject to functional imperatives. All of them must, among other things, produce food, ensure their reproduction as system, and control conflict. The critical point is that not all eat the same things, have the same marriage and kinship systems, and the same styles for legitimizing and exercising what they assume to be legal or politically correct. Variety in habits demonstrates, as Clifford Geertz says, that "Rather than culture acting only to supplement, develop, and extend organically based capacities logically and genetically prior to it, it would seem to be ingredient to those capacities themselves. A cultureless human being would probably turn out to be not only an intrinsically talented though unfulfilled ape, but a wholly mindless and consequently unworkable

monstrosity" (Geertz, 1973:68). In other words: what is usually read as "innate" or "instinctive" is still cultural and dependent on a style of life. As Sahlins reiterates: "The same human motives appear in different cultural forms, and different motives appear in the same forms. A fixed correspondence being lacking between the character of society and the human character, there can be no biological determinism" (1976a:11). Between a postulated primary "universal impulse" and the "ideological response" there is an arbitrary mediation, symbolic or expressive—particular and local—that provokes the difference between the systems. It is this that anthropologists call "style of life" or "culture" and is their object of study and/or commentary.

10. As I have done earlier in relation to a series of Brazilian institutions, beginning with Carnival, military parades, processions, national heroes, *malandragem* (roguishness), "Do you know to whom you're speaking?", the music of Carnival, the system of racial relations, the idea of nature, *saudade* (nostalgia), the house and the street, etc. (see DaMatta, 1973, 1979, 1987a, 1987b, 1989, 1993). As Sahlins would say, developing a style of analysis in which political interests and economic dimensions—the "practical" or "utilitarian" elements of the system—are put in their proper place: Capitalism—with its "practical reason" and utilitarian epistemology— "is no sheer rationality. It is a definite form of cultural order; or a cultural order acting in a particular form" (Sahlins, 1976a:185, and 1995: chapter 4; see also Dumont, 1985: Chapters 6 and 7).

11. The emphasis on "play" and competition, coupled with lack of interest in games of chance, characterizes Huizinga's thesis and, as Caillois (1979:5) points out, has consequences, limiting the scope of this otherwise extraordinary essay.

12. I am fully aware that bourgeois society has various classificatory systems, all of which may be *empirically* treated as totemic systems, such as food and dress— not to mention the advertising so well studied by Everardo Rocha in Brazil (1985)— as suggested by Sahlins (1976a). But the animal game is different, because it does not hide its link with nature, but rather fully acknowledges it as a value. In other words, it is not possible to understand the animal game without penetrating the Brazilian style of conceiving the animals, which makes it akin to the totemisms known to anthropologists.

13. Associated with money, these numbers distinguish our monetary system, making it countable or quantifiable. For us capitalists, the number (and with it the market) incorporates money, permitting quantification of all other social domains because everything can be "measured" and "weighed" by the money spent: from weddings to academic titles, from family goods to religious duties and political loyalties. Even certain social roles can be read numerically, which does away with the traditional division of the so-called "exchange spheres" that divided the social universe into domains adverse to generalized monetary transaction, as Karl Polanyi (1988) and Paul Bohannan (1955) demonstrated. As John Davis correctly observes, this relationship between number and money is not an essential one. There are societies

with numbers but without money, and societies that have money but not "number," as occurs in some Melanesian cultures (J. Davis, 1992:81ff.).

14. See, in this respect, the instructive essay by Matt Cartmill (1993) on the role of the hunt in human evolution.

15. It should be observed that the Monte Carlo casino was founded in 1861, but there was gambling in the pre-revolutionary France of the Louis and in industrializing England since the previous century, as shown by Ashton (1969), Chinn (1991), Clapson (1992), and especially by Dunkley (1985), Freundlich (1995), Grussi (1985), and Kavanagh (1993) for the French case. The first lotteries were established in Italy (see Strazzullo, 1987), England, and Virginia (then an English colony) in the sixteenth and seventeenth centuries. The justification for these lotteries was fundraising for their respective states. John M. Findlay's essay studies gambling in the context of American society, examining Las Vegas as an expression of gambling linked, however, to the idea of the frontier and opportunity. It is obvious that there is a relationship to be sociologically explored between the birth of modern ideology and games of chance in the form of lotteries and casinos.

16. The results of the game are more for Hermes, god of volubility, metamorphosis, ambiguity, than for classical causality, which, I learn from Umberto Eco (1995), admits no subverting of the principle of identity, of noncontradiction. To divine the result of the game, one must make a parallel reading of the world, an anterior reading or one hidden (hermetic) by the "enlightened" linearity of science.

17. In 1969, when I was beginning my studies in anthropology at Harvard, I wrote an audacious letter to the periodical *Man: Journal of the Royal Anthropological Institute,* in which I called attention to the noteworthy similarity of Henri Bergson's and Evans-Pritchard's arguments. Later, Professor Evans-Pritchard, in a letter to the journal, genteelly thanked me for my observation, emphasizing, however, that his dialogue was not with Bergson but with Lucien Lévy-Bruhl (see DaMatta, 1969).

18. The list is inspired by the essential text by Nicolau Sevcenko (1983). The ideal of universal egalitarianism engendered immense difficulties for the police. Traffic, for example, set off a singular occurrence that defies easy classification in a society marked by an aristocratic ethos. The rich, who owned automobiles, had to obey the law, and worse yet, had to come into direct contact with the authority of the police, creating unusual situations in which "Do you know to whom you're speaking?" prevailed. This was not made explicit but can be inferred from the study by Marcos Luís Bretas, which reveals how incidents involving motor vehicles went from 151 cases in 1909 to 497 in 1925 (Bretas, 1997:105–106). See also the works of Rosa Maria de Araújo (1993) and Isabel Lustosa (1993). For a general panorama of the era, we also used the classic by Raymundo Faoro (1975) and the essential works of José Murilo de Carvalho.

19. As if to demonstrate that the world does not proceed in just one direction, Freud published *The Interpretation of Dreams* at the end of 1899 and the animal

game was invented in 1890! This situation recalls the final paragraph of the famous "Anthropophagic Manifesto" written by Oswald de Andrade, one of the leaders of the famous Modern Art Week, launched in 1922 by a handful of intellectuals in the city of São Paulo: "Against the vested and oppressive social reality, registered by Freud—reality without complexes, without madness, without various forms of prostitution, and without the penitentiaries of the Pindorama matriarchy" (Andrade, [1928] 1972:19). To summarize: in Vienna, bichos were locked up, but in Rio de Janeiro they were let loose! In this context, I should mention, as Barbara Tedlock (1995) shows in a valiant effort at synthesis, that in many societies known to anthropologists, dreams are as appreciated and taken seriously as instruments of knowledge, amusement, and creativity as those in the films of Luis Buñuel, and in this Brazil that bets on animals.

20. In her economic history of Rio de Janeiro, Eulália Lobo says that from 1876 to 1886 there was a 1,067 percent increase in stock-market transactions! Alongside this, financial entities increased by 231 percent (Lobo, 1978:460; see also Faoro, 1975: chapter 11, and Sevcenko, 1983: chapter 1).

21. I observe, without any wish to be pedantic, that *encilhamento* comes from *encilhar,* that is, to saddle a horse. This metaphor is more than appropriate to designate the stock-market speculators who, like horse-racing men, were making their investments/gambles, receiving at the site where horses were prepared for races (harnessed and saddled) precious information for their bets on the stock market (Caldeira, 1997:239). I should emphasize that once again we confront a figure of speech based on a code of bichos, in this case that of saddle horses being "mounted" by a thoroughbred aristocrat or by shady speculation. To paraphrase the great poet Manuel Bandeira: the little horses go on running and the big horses go on eating . . .

22. The great academic poet Olavo Bilac also played the animal game, which disappointed the young neophyte intellectual Bastos Tigre, who heard him ask: "Mr. Guima, which bicho hit?" (Lustosa, 1993:37).

23. Traditionally, the bookies fear the "crocodile," which they call "the father of the poor" and which, as we show in chapter 3, is a bicho seen as ambiguous and treacherous. Curiously, the decree that outlawed gambling throughout Brazil, in 1944, was numbered 6,259, which is the group of the crocodile (the crocodile is number 15, which multiplied by 4 yields the tenths 60, 59, 58, and 57, making up the "groups" that it represents or incorporates). The number 6,259, following animal game tradition, was the most played thousandth in Brazil for weeks and was therefore "sought after." The same thing occurred upon the death of the statesman Rui Barbosa, the "eagle of the Hague," and everyone "unloaded" on the eagle, whose number is 2, and on the group formed by the numbers 5, 6, 7, and 8. On St. George's Day, bets on the "horse" increase, which causes the bankers to lower the payoff for its tenths—just as happens with the stock market. We will return to this topic in chapters 2, 3, and 4.

24. Thick recently published volumes about "private life in Brazil" attest to this point by never mentioning the animal game, except for a single sentence in volume 3 of the work organized by Nicolau Sevcenko (1998:554).

25. The speculative mania seen as an avatar of modernity arises from the pen of Francisco Otaviano two decades before the invention of the animal game, providing an illustration of the social terrain in which this lottery would flourish: "To the game, citizens! To the game! To the game in the full light of day, to the game in the public square, to the game with no fear of the police, to the legal, commercial, industrial, and moral game. . . . To the game, citizens, to the game! All good instincts, the idea of justice, strict customs will lay down their arms until the dizziness calms and the fever of usury yields to the lancet of the lowering of the reward" (Faoro, 1975:427).

26. Octavio Paz (1979: chapter 2) was among those who best reflected on this link, typical of a premarket conceptualization, in which saving money would be like accumulating excrement. Louis Dumont summarizes this mentality well when he says, alluding to the Marx of *Grundisse* and the first chapter of *Capital*: "With the moderns, a revolution occurred . . . : the relationship between real estate and power over other men was broken and movable wealth became autonomous, as a superior aspect of wealth in general, while land-based wealth became an inferior, less perfect aspect" (Dumont, 1977:6ff., and also Dumont, 1985). The relationship between excrement and money leads to a "transmodern" dimension of our society, which accepts money but is aware of its malign power and its ability to stimulate selfishness, arrogance, and the rejection of a generous feeling of totality as capital. This malignancy, as Michael Taussig relates, in a text in which philosophical confusion attempts to replace the tradition of anthropological studies, appears in other places, such as the Cauca valley in southern Colombia, associated with a baptism of money that is thought to have magical properties, causing it to grow and return to the pocket of its "godfather" (see Taussig, 1980). Money is good, but dangerous, they say in Colombia (and in Brazil), which in part denies its sacralization and its Calvinist capitalist independence. The "profane" attitude toward capital promoted the operation of Brazilian society against both a hyperinflationary economy and corrupt, clientelistic governments in the final period of the military regime (see DaMatta, 1993: chapter 6), which would probably have been impossible in a system of "advanced capitalism" in which, as Karl Polanyi (1988) showed, the society is subsumed by the market.

27. The expression "political capitalism" is that of Raymundo Faoro and comes from his penetrating and little-read study of the work of Machado de Assis as participant-observer of the Brazilian social scene. The term "political capitalism" attempts to reveal the links between business and politics, in which personal relationships, kinship, ritual co-parenthood, and, naturally, reciprocity are the fundamental elements (Faoro, 1976:24ff.). In another context, Otávio Velho uses the expression "authoritarian capitalism" to clarify the same group of phenomena (see Velho, 1976).

28. The entire issue of Camilo is the imbalance of the structural (and structuring) relationship between fondness and personalism that ruled social relations in Brazil, marked by expectations of reciprocity, the "give and get," or the favor, as Roberto Schwarz (1977) emphasizes, projected onto the chosen bichos, and also the uncertainty of the results that allows the bichos to escape from that web of personal feelings and dispositions. It is this paradox between the impersonality of the outcome and the personalness of the bet that characterizes and popularizes the game. See the story "Jogo do Bicho," published in 1904 and collected in the volume *Outros Contos* (Machado de Assis, *Obra Completa*. Rio de Janeiro: Editora Aguilar, 1979).

29. Could this disenchantment with the world be that which Machado de Assis called, in true Brazilian fashion, *calundu,* the melancholia resulting from awareness of the difficulties of wanting to be like the "advanced foreigners" while, however, living in a mulatto, ambiguous, slave society? Would that *calundu* be curable only by the proverbial anti-hypochondriac plaster invented by his character Brás Cubas? For fundamental considerations about this subject, see Sá Rego (1989).

30. I am convinced that the coming of Dom João VI to Brazil in 1808, at the beginning of a century marked by the most profound sociopolitical transformation, has significant consequences for the formation and the aristocratic, hierarchical modeling of the Brazilian elite. In an ironic note, Raymundo Faoro helps characterize this aristocratic trait of a Brazil that adopts the letter of the law in liberalism but has a virtually untouched social hierarchical organization and practice: "Thanks to nobility-creating munificence," Faoro says, "the Republic took by surprise 7 marquises, 10 counts, 54 viscounts, and 316 barons, landowners, money men, politicians, and writers" (Faoro, 1975:488). By different routes, Roberto Schwarz and I point to the same issue.

31. In a revealing essay, Albert Hirschman (1961) says that political experimentation is a marked characteristic of Latin American institutional life. We always prefer to innovate on the formal plane, in institutional design, by formally modifying the premises of the system, even when the results may be incoherent or even tragic vis-à-vis the most established social practices and beliefs. Thus the idealized vision of the elites, according to which things from "outside" would always be exemplary but which, once adopted, generally add one more frustration to those already in existence. What is interesting, both in the case of the animal game and in that of soccer (just to mention a rich and successful cousin), is that, left alone—because, after all, they were of no importance to the elites—these institutions followed an adaptive sociological path of their own, adjusting to the values of society.

32. In 1944, the jurist José Duarte called this prohibition "the most outrageous injustice," as recalled by Pedro Falabella T. de Lima in an article in the *Folha de S. Paulo* for May 8, 1994.

33. This disharmony between the national state and society is a common phenomenon. It is worth recalling a passage by Clifford Geertz dedicated to a similar

"game" practiced by the people of Bali, the highly popular cockfight, also made illegal by the elites. "The elite, which is not itself so very puritan, worries about the poor, ignorant peasant gambling all his money away, about what foreigners will think, about the waste of time better devoted to building up the country" (Geertz, 1973:414). In other words, in Bali as in Brazil, the elites "know" what is good for the people and try to "educate" them through the law, which, obviously, has no value for them. For a study of the paradoxical relations between "Afro-Brazilian" religiosity and the state, brought about because the police, whose aim was to repress and discipline "macumba" and sorcery, believed in it, see Yvonne Maggie (1992).

34. I prefer "trans" and "anti" to the trivial and misleading "postmodern," which in the bourgeois world of the individualistic societies of advanced capitalism has a gothic, funereal connotation and lends itself to lifeless, pessimistic, decadent linkages. Now, there is nothing more vibrant and vital than this "Brazilian transmodernity," which rejects indifference and believes in sensuality, love, and reciprocity at the level of the house, and of celebration, friendship, and family. For an appreciation of the pessimism that typifies Western cosmology (or, it is worth specifying, the cosmology of countries that find their ideological fulfillment in liberal individualism), see the elegant essay by Sahlins (1996), which appears to be an outgrowth from Sahlins (1995), especially chapter 4.

35. It is clear that some players have an acute awareness of numbers that, for them, possess mystical and magical properties, like 3, 7, 10, and 12 (respectively, donkey, sheep, rabbit, and elephant), which represent, respectively, the Holy Trinity, the three temptations of Christ, or the three days he remained in the tomb; the number of the Gospels, the days God took to create the world (sacrosanct in the cabbala [see Dines, 1992:38]); the Ten Commandments; and the number of disciples. In addition, other players delve into the formal properties of the numbers by creating tables to guarantee correct hunches, which allows the assertion that the animal game engenders a popular numerology and could have some relationship to the cabbala. In fact, the search for hidden meaning in numbers is common, both in the cabbala and in the animal game. About the cabbala, consult the presentation by Alberto Dines and the commentaries by Elias Lipiner in the book by D. Francisco Manuel de Mello, originally published in 1724 (Mello, 1997). See also the book by Alberto Dines (1992), which deals with the repression of Jews in Brazil. But, as we are speaking of Brazilian society, we cannot forget that the ultrasacred number 7 also represents ambiguous, intermediate, multivocal entities—like Exu and "Seu" Sete, beings of the surprise, the accident, the crossroads, the encounter, mediation, and vitality— in the popular religions (Roger Bastide, 1960:349); for the case of *umbanda,* see the important book by Diana Brown (1986). Robert H. Lowie, in a text devoted to establishing ethnology as a distinct mode of interpretation of social phenomena, speaks of numbers with a "peculiar character of sanctity" like 7 in certain regions of Asia, 3 in European folklore, 5 for certain American tribes, 6 among the Ainu of Japan,

9 among the Yakut, 10 among Pythagorean philosophers, and 4 for the Crow of Montana, whom he studied (Lowie, 1966 [1917]:18–19). Lévi-Strauss mentions that among the Osage the number 13 represents the totality of society, having the ability to "symbolize the union of two terms": 6 and 7, heaven and earth, etc. (Lévi-Strauss, 1966:145). Such numbers would be "sacred," as Rodney Needham confirms, citing R. Allendy (a reference, however, absent from his bibliography), and are always composed of small digits like 2, 3, 4, 6, or 7 (Needham, 1978:10). These cases demonstrate that numbers are useful for placing a value on things and events and for distinguishing people and institutions, as Needham states and every player of the animal game knows. Needham also informs us that among the Nyoro of eastern Africa (Uganda) odd numbers are associated with the feminine universe, contingency, the extraordinary, and the mystical dimension in general; even numbers are masculine, regular, linked to formality and to secular or profane positions. A preliminary inquiry shows that such associations also occur in Brazil. The first anthropological look at this topic was probably that of Edward Burnett Tylor in chapter 7 of his celebrated *The Origin of Culture,* where he considers the evolution of the "art of storytelling" with intelligence and sophistication, grounding his thinking in the Victorian evolutionary hypothesis by which primitives equated numbers with natural concrete elements because, lacking a well-developed faculty of abstraction, they could not think of numbers as pure figures. For an abstruse, but certainly intriguing "anthropology of numbers," see Thomas Crump (1990), who, incidentally, is unacquainted with the efforts of Tylor and Lowie. Georg Simmel indicates that numbers can be used as symbols of certain groups and/or social identities. Thus, the Barcelona senate was known as "the 100" and the numbers 6 and 8 designated the masters of certain guilds in Europe (Simmel: 1950:107). In the text of Vincent Foster Hopper (1938) I found, despite the tinge of evolutionism, some lucid explanations of the symbolism of numbers in Western society, from the Pythagoreans to Dante.

36. Here is the complete list of the "master," leader, reference, or original numbers, and the "followers" or adjunct numbers that form the hundredths and the thousandths in the animal game. The numbers 01, 02, 03, and 04 are encompassed by the number 1 = the ostrich (*avestruz*); 05, 06, 07, and 08 by the number 2 = the eagle (*águia*); 09, 10, 11, and 12 by the number 3 = the donkey (*burro*); 13, 14, 15, and 16 by the number 4 = the butterfly (*borboleta*); 17, 18, 19, and 20 by the number 5 = the dog (*cachorro*); 21, 22, 23, and 24 by the number 6 = the goat (*cabra*); 25, 26, 27, and 28 by the number 7 = the sheep (*carneiro*); 29, 30, 31, and 32 by the number 8 = the camel (*camelo*); 33, 34, 35, and 36 by the number 9 = the snake (*cobra*); 37, 38, 39, and 40 by the number 10 = the rabbit (*coelho*); 41, 42, 43, and 44 by the number 11 = the horse (*cavalo*); 45, 46, 47, and 48 by the number 12 = the elephant (*elefante*); 49, 50, 51, and 52 by the number 13 = the rooster (*galo*); 53, 54, 55, and 56 by the number 14 = the cat (*gato*); 57, 58, 59, and 60 by the number 15 = the crocodile (*jacaré*); 61, 62, 63, and 64 by the number 16 = the lion (*leão*); 65, 66, 67, and 68 by the number 17 = the mon-

key (*macaco*); 69, 70, 71, and 72 by the number 18 = the pig (*porco*); 73, 74, 75, and 76 by the number 19 = the peacock (*pavão*); 77, 78, 79, and 80 by the number 20 = the turkey (*peru*); 81, 82, 83, and 84 by the number 21 = the bull (*touro*); 85, 86, 87, and 88 by the number 22 = the tiger (*tigre*); 89, 90, 91, and 92 by the number 23 = the bear (*urso*); 93, 94, 95, and 96 by the number 24 = the stag (*veado*); 97, 98, 99, and 100 by the number 25 = the cow (*vaca*). Adding a digit to the left of any number forms thousandths.

37. Which shows that the natives of South America espouse a culturalist (or romantic) attitude relative to the nonhuman universe. It is worth noting that the expression "perspectivism" is used (without, however, Viveiros de Castro's fundamental theoretical implications) by Todorov (1996:187) and Sahlins (1995: introduction) as a sign of cultural particularism—a property simply unknown to and rejected by an enlightened, empiricist, and/or evolutionist anthropology founded on the notion of "civilization," which, as Sahlins (1995:12) shows, is singular and manifested in degrees (one can be more or less "civilized") and not on the idea of "culture," which is a plural concept and given once and for all (we all have a culture).

38. It is known that in the Middle Ages animals were excommunicated, blessed, and judged, and could be punished for their shortcomings and/or crimes. Thus, E. P. Evans lists several cases of excommunication, accusation, and condemnation of various animals, the great majority of them pigs, mares and mules, cows, rats, goats, bulls, dogs, and various insects (such as locusts, flies, and, for Brazilians using this classification, lizards)—that is, animals with some significant relationship to society—from 824 until 1906, when in New York City one Mr. Marger was killed and robbed by a man named Scherer in collaboration with his son and his dog. The men were sentenced to life imprisonment and the dog was put to death (Evans, 1906:313–334).

39. I remember, in this context, what Guimarães Rosa says about the backland in *Grande sertão: Veredas*: "The backland is this: you push it back, but suddenly it surrounds you on all sides again. The backland is when you least expect it; that's what I say."

40. As occurs in the expression, "So-and-so is a bicho!" One should note that the thresholds at the gates of residences were guarded by figures of lions, cats, dogs, and tigers, which, as Gilberto Freyre emphasizes, were the "great animals virtually symbolic of patriarchal domination in Brazil" (Freyre, 1961:xxii). Or, we would say, expanding upon Freyre's always acute thinking, those animals mark ambiguous zones situated precisely between house and street. They make possible the integration and passage between the impersonal world of the street and the intimate world of home and family, providing the necessary mediation between the bureaucratic rules, uncontrollable and federal, that should apply to all, in the street, and the particularistic rules of living together amicably in the home, which apply only to our relatives and friends. Located on the thresholds, these lions, cats, dogs, and tigers—

all, significantly, personages in the animal game—would be, as we shall see later, in chapter 3, equally ambiguous. For an exemplary study of the ambiguity of the figures that guard temple gates, see Leach, 1983.

41. In Brazil, as pointed out to me by José Ronaldo Fassheber and Antônio Pimentel Pontes Filho, master's candidates in anthropology at the Federal University of Santa Catarina, there are also associations between certain soccer teams and animals. Flamengo is sometimes equated to the vulture, Palmeiras to the pig and the parrot, Santos to the fish, Atlético of Minas Gerais to the rooster, Cruzeiro to the fox, América of Minas Gerais to the rabbit, Corinthians to the falcon, Criciúma to the tiger, and Vasco to the cod. The difference is that these relationships are residual and not always positive. In these cases nature is not read as an example or ideal to be followed or imitated, as occurs in the majority of totemisms and in the American case. In this context, I cannot help but observe that when Marshall Sahlins studies Western bourgeois society as culture he focuses on food, dress, and traffic lights, ignoring this very broad totemism of social groups. This proves an old anthropological dictum by which no one is a good ethnologist of his own culture.

42. Thomas Nast was born in 1840 in Germany and was also the creator, in 1870, of the first modern Santa Claus, in the same *Harper's Weekly,* thereby Americanizing and humanizing in definitive fashion a Saint Nicholas born in Europe.

43. It is as if these animals were in the bosom of American society, naturalizing it and establishing a "real" bond between the domains of nature and culture. Mickey Mouse is an "extreme right-wing Republican (some say even a John Bircher). Actively campaigned for Barry Goldwater and Ronald Reagan (an old friend from Hollywood days). A recluse ever since his stroke, he is said to have helped finance Buchanan's campaign" (see www.unknown.nu/cartoon). Of Donald Duck it is said, confirming Vianna Moog's interpretations, that he is "too paranoid to vote. Frequently mouths off with convoluted theories about the Masons, the Illuminati, and the Trilateralists, but nobody can understand him due to his speech impediment." Goofy "votes for whoever Mickey Mouse tells him to vote for." Bugs Bunny and Porky Pig, however, are card-carrying Democrats, while Felix the Cat is "a strict libertarian. Against censorship, taxes, workplace safety laws, minimum wage, etc." The "culturalization" of these characters is confirmed by their evolution in the sense of their becoming more and more human and American. Robert De Roos states that the success of Mickey Mouse began when he became a talking rat. That is: when he began to speak English and thus humanized himself completely, becoming transparent and equal to all Americans. Several critics have pointed out that Mickey lost his primitive, sharp-edged, animal-like air and became—in the famous demonstration by Stephen Jay Gould—more juvenile, "babified," and rounded. Such a neonatalization, in Gould's view, makes the character powerfully attractive (it is known that we humans—so goes the American biological theory of "natural linkages"—like the large eyes with dilated, open pupils and the small rounded bodies of infants), but

such a process is at the same time an extreme means of humanizing the prototypical animal—a rat—by transforming it into a character close to American society, a being that produces a strange and therefore positive ambiguity: a mixture of animal endowed with good sentiments, of a child capable of behaving like an adult, and of a well-behaved and ingenious adult aware of his civic duties and obedient to social norms. In an essay written in 1934 (Peary and Peary, 1980:239), the great English novelist E. M. Forster asks whether Mickey is really a rat (see also www.jps.net/xephyr/rich/dzone/hoozoo/hzlist.html).

44. Of Mickey Mouse, it says on the "Mickey Mouse" page on the Internet that he is "synonymous with all that is good and benign; he is the ultimate symbol of happiness and delight. Mickey has survived through the ravages of World War II (where his name was the code word for the entire Allied mission) as well as the different trends that the world has followed." Of him, the columnist Bob Greene said, "Mickey is the quintessence of the symbol of innocence. Subliminally, he represents a lot of things we've lost. He shows how things used to be simple and fun and free of darkness" (see www.geocities.com/Hollywood/Set/1344/histo.html).

45. The species closest to or most admired by humanity, surely because they can be read more anthropocentrically—like mammals and birds—are preferred in this hierarchical citizenship, from which are excluded certain fishes like the herring and the cod (Descola, 1998:24).

46. For the dialectic between egalitarianism and hierarchy and individual and person, absent from Dumont's work, see DaMatta, 1979 and 1989.

47. See also the pertinent criticism by Sahlins (1978). If it were not going too far, it would be valid to say that in America Diderot's concepts have become part of the national ideology (see Todorov, 1993).

48. It could be said, following the suggestion by Sahlins (1972: chapter 4), that the ideology of the gift recaptured by the animal game levels and reinterprets the individualism of the Hobbesian contract inaugurated by the modernization that came with the proclamation of the republic in 1889, by proposing a residual social pact based on the reciprocity of dream and hunch, of numbers and animals.

49. In the story by Machado de Assis, mentioned above, Camilo (or Camilinho), from so often playing the animal game, becomes friends with the bookie who takes his bets and has long conversations with him about the strategy of the game, consoling him when he loses and always feeding his hope of victory.

50. In relation to that commitment, the unimpeachable dean of Brazilian economy, Eugênio Gudin, commented in his classic book *Inflação, crédito e desenvolvimento:* "The private bankers more easily lend a million *cruzeiros* to a bookie than to a metalworker or a farmer. There's a better guarantee" (see the magazine *Realidade,* June 1966).

51. In Brazil there is a belief that rich people don't steal and are fundamentally generous. It is a matter of the aristocratization of money, in a cultural construction

in which the moral value of money is emphasized. This belief is very frequently applied to candidates for public office, in the foolish supposition that the rich—believe it or not will not plunder the state treasury.

52. In fact, in Brazilian society "businessmen," "capitalists," and "politicians"—who form the core of the upper levels, making up the world of the "rich"—can be read, respectively, as "eagles," "cats," "pigs," and "horses" (as in the previously mentioned poem by Manuel Bandeira). And the destitute can be read as "donkeys," "sheep," "goats," and "dogs." The cosmopolitan and/or refined are "butterflies"; the large and slow, "elephants"; the fat, "pigs"; the vain, "peacocks"; the homosexual, "stags"; the brave, "lions"; the clowns, "monkeys"; and so on. This shows how, besides profession, residence, skin color, educational level, salary, money in the bank (and other modern criteria), society represents itself *also* by the language of totems and castes that, for Lévi-Strauss, are mutually transformable codes.

Chapter 1.   History and Sociology of the Animal Game

1. This estimate was furnished by one of the "bankers" best informed about the movement of bets, as he is part of the so-called "group of seven" responsible for running the animal game in the entire country, in an interview in March 1992. In an interview with the researcher Simone Simões Ferreira Soares and published in the book *O jogo do bicho,* in May 1990, Sr. José Petros (Zinho), at the time spokesman for the animal game bankers of Rio de Janeiro, said that, after the arrangements provided by the administrations of Leonel Brizola and Moreira Franco (former state governors), the animal game employed "more or less 60,000 people" in Rio (Soares, 1993:77).

2. The biographical information for Baron de Drummond was enhanced by interviews with Sérvulo Drummond, his great-grandson, whose help we gratefully acknowledge. For a biography of the baron, see Renato Pacheco (1957).

3. See the article, reproduced in part below, published in the *Jornal da Cidade do Rio* (October 30, 1889), written by its editor, José do Patrocínio, a leading figure of the Brazilian abolitionist movement.

4. We did not find, however, in the most complete biographical study of the Baron of Mauá, written by Jorge Caldeira (1995), any reference to João Baptista Vianna Drummond.

5. Vila Isabel anticipated the "modernist" projects of which Brasília would be the paradigm. In both Drummond's Vila Isabel and Lúcio Costa and Oscar Niemeyer's Brasília, streets lose their function as places of encounter, business, leisure, and sociability and are transformed into channels of access, transit, or outflow. The great change from the traditional city to the "modernist city" speaks—among other

things—to the transformation of the street from symbolic space (where the street was simultaneously means and end) into rational space (where it is reduced to merely a means of outflow for vehicles and people). For a discussion of the street in the Brazilian case, see Freyre (1961) and DaMatta (1979, and especially 1987a). For a study of Brasília, see Holston (1993).

6. The zoo was apparently a success. The memoirs and diary of the businessman Cristiano Carlos J. Wehrs, of German descent, a piano maker and musician, has the following entry for the month of March 1888: "When we were all ready, we left for Vila Isabel to visit the reopened Zoological Garden. But the streetcars going there were so full that we had to hang onto the outside. We traveled that way as far as Mangue, when we thought it best to give up, as the other passengers appeared to be headed for the Zoo also, reducing the hope of someone getting off en route and giving us a seat" (Wehrs, 1980:216).

7. In this petition signed by the baron and Manuel de Segadas Vianna, co-director of the zoo, there is a noticeable effort to harmonize with proposals that prioritized the modernization of agriculture, a basic theme and political preoccupation at the turn of the century when the slaves were freed. It can also be seen that the baron was sensitive to the political tone necessary to appeal to the deputies.

8. Regarding this matter, the American missionary Thomas Ewbank, who visited Brazil in 1840, said: "*Lotteries.*—Gambling in these is universal. Granted for all sorts of things, fresh ones are perpetually announced. Boys run about peddling tickets; they enter stores, visit the markets, and even stop you in the street; nay, women are sent out as agents by the dealers. . . . The Diario of the 9th contained the plan of the *fifth* one granted for the 'Beneficio do Obra da Nova Igreja do Senhor Bom Jesus de Iguape' [Benefit of the work of the new Church of the Senhor do Bom Jesus de Iguape], and advertised another for the 'Beneficio de Igreja Matriz do Ceará' [Benefit of the Mother Church of Ceará]" (Ewbank 1856:197). In 1878, according to Mello Barreto Filho and Hermeto Lima: "Gambling reigned in the city." Fortunes were made at roulette, cards, lansquenet, baccarat, dice, and lotto, with much stealing in favor of the bankers (Barreto Filho and Lima, 1944, vol. 3:96–97). The police, serving the moral code of the upper segments, tried as always to "order," "discipline," and protect the citizen.

9. Article published on the front page of the *Jornal da Cidade do Rio,* October 30, 1889, which shows well the modernizing rhetoric that dominated the republican and monarchist elites of the time. It must be noted that the baron—along with Viscount Nogueira da Gama, Roberto Jorge Haddock Lobo, Leopoldo Augusto de Câmara Amoroso Lima, Joaquim Manuel Monteiro, Homem de Melo, Tomás Quartim, Fernando Mendes de Almeida, and many other wealthy men, high-placed public functionaries, landowners, businessmen, professional politicians, bankers, and investors, who made up the small and highly concentrated Brazilian elite of the

period—was also a member of the famous and aristocratic Fluminense Casino, the locale where they would meet to read, eat, exchange information, and, of course, *gamble* (Needell, 1993:89ff, and also the appendix)!

10. There exists, however, the suspicion, raised especially by Pereira de Mello in his important study of the social history of games of chance in Rio de Janeiro, that at that time the baron had established a partnership with Luis Galvez, a well-known Rio promoter of games of chance (Pereira de Mello, 1989:57).

11. Data obtained from the page http://www.alternex.com.br/~solidario, which reproduces notes collected by João Marcos Weguelin from Rio newspapers of the end of the nineteenth century.

12. The newspaper *O Tempo* for July 3, 1892, says in regard to this participation by Zevada: "This important establishment created by the illustrious baron of Drummond will inaugurate today different amusements for the people of Rio de Janeiro, who will find there a daily pastime. Sr. M. I. Zevada, the manager of the firm and knowledgeable about various European and American establishments identical to the Zoological Park, has hopes of enlarging that meritorious Brazilian institution. There is an inaugural dinner, the invitation to which we gratefully acknowledge." With some exaggeration it is possible to raise the hypothesis that the "flower game" found its inspiration in the popularity that the "language of flowers," originated in Paris, must have enjoyed in Brazil and by which lovers could exchange messages (see Goody, 1993). The Frenchman Charles Expilly, who visited Brazil around 1850, speaks of a message sent by means of a bunch of flowers (a *selam*) by her lover to the wife of a slave trader, decoded by a female slave as follows: " . . . this *selam* is as clear as day. The thorn and the hyacinth, which express pain, take on a more precise meaning beside this sprig of rosemary, which means faithful love, and this bitter almond, which signifies violent love. Therefore it is an unhappy heart speaking, unhappier still because of separation, as this twig from a lemon tree indicates. This is so true," the slave continued, "that I discover here a pineapple leaf between a golden hibiscus and a carnation. The pineapple leaf recalls the hours of happiness because of love, as the carnation states, while the lover begs his beautiful lady, by sending her the hibiscus, to take pity on his torments and grant him another meeting. An answer is requested in an insistent way through this small white carnation bud. That's the decoding of the *selam*, Master." The message presages the deceived husband's revenge, and the fact of its having been deciphered by a slave shows the possible extent of its diffusion (Expilly, 1977:146; see also Goody, 1993:237, 239). In sum: flowers are better for communicating and giving than for gambling. I cannot help but point out that in his encyclopedic book about what he calls the "culture of flowers," Goody does not mention this lottery-related use of flowers in Brazil.

13. The data on the "flower game" come from the works of Cabral (n.d.) and of Pacheco (1957).

14. Flowers, though they have other distinct traits, like color, perfume, and shape—and therefore an immense evocative, symbolic power—serve more as gifts, ornaments, and decorative objects, acting almost always as objects of contemplation. In the tradition of our society, flowers are offering and sacrificial object—a passive object, a means of exchange, or a "still life," as a genre of painting in which they predominate so aptly puts it. When they are represented as agents, they embody the virtues of passivity, such as purity, virginity, and even the Virgin Mary, and need to be protected in gardens, as Goody (1993) informs us.

15. The piano builder Cristiano Carlos J. Wehrs saw the elephant dance in 1891, mentioning it in his diary: "Sunday. At 11 A.M. we left for Vila Isabel, where I was invited to visit the Zoological Park, in the company of Dreisler and his future wife and family. . . . The Park has not improved much since my last visit there, but it has received many new animals from Europe. Around four o'clock we went to the restaurant in the interior of the park, and drank some bottles of Staten beer, which cost Dreisler (who insisted on paying) 14$900, an exorbitance. A dinner there costs 6$000 and a lunch, without wine, 4$000. When we traversed the Park again, we met Sr. Brück and his young wife (*née* Göldner), Mussel (president of the Gas Company), and Sauer, with whom we attended the demonstrations of a trained elephant. The large animal was seated next to a plate, from which he ate; having previously rung a small bell asking for food, next he paid the waiter and then began performing tricks, walking backwards and forwards on wooden cones, playing a hurdy-gurdy, beating a drum, stepping over his trainer, etc." Wehrs added that there was also "A boy with half a body, which we chose not to see" (Wehrs, 1980:262). Such notes indicate that the baron's zoo operated like a circus, presenting anomalous figures (a boy with half a body), which reveals the desire to maintain an audience and raise funds. On the other hand, the text shows that the park was well attended, with a very expensive restaurant, confirming the baron's commercial sense.

16. Perhaps these words were printed on the old tickets. The photograph of a ticket from 1895, in a documented book by Jaime Larry Benchimol about Pereira Passos, shows the following: dominating the left side is the name of the animal, in the case in question a lion, printed in large letters. In the body of the ticket, in the upper right, is its number and, just below, this text: "Admission to the Zoological Park." On the right side is the stamp of the lion and in the lower part is written: "One *mil-réis*." Below, in smaller letters, is: "This admission gives the bearer the right to a prize twenty times the value of same, if the depicted animal is drawn. Valid for 4 days." And finally, there is a typically bureaucratic and very Brazilian notice: "This ticket cannot be altered in any way." It is worth noting that the lion is called not "bicho" but "animal," which allows us to say there was official language that spoke of "animals" and another, popular one that referred to "bichos" (see Benchimol, 1990: illustrations).

17. This information about the original system was provided by Sérvulo Drummond.

18. The animal game was common even among slaves, who through it could possibly buy their freedom (cf. Karasch, 1987:359).

19. In Brazil, as already mentioned by one of us (DaMatta, 1991), there is an important distinction between "foodstuffs" (*alimento*), a category that includes everything edible and nutritional, and "food" (*comida*), a category that connotes everything that is eaten regularly and with gusto in Brazil. The first category is universal; the second is local, referring to culturally approved and desired "foodstuffs" endowed with social value. In Brazil, as in other societies, not everything that is a foodstuff is considered food. Because of that, food marks feelings and identities. The *feijoada* is a national symbol and also a "dish" denoting an open, egalitarian environment free of ceremony. So it is our guess that if the food game had dealt less with ingredients and raw materials and more with foods (*peixada, rabada, feijoada, vatapá, angu, cozido*), it would have been more popular.

20. Thus the English word *bookmaker* entered the Brazilian vocabulary. It is worth noting that the bookmaker is strictly an intermediate, just like the taker of bets, who with his list of written hunches kept the cashbooks of those banking the game. The bookmaker is necessary for modalities of gambling that operate at a distance from the bettors, such as horse racing (the activity that established the expression) and, at that time, the animal game.

21. In 1900, João Ferreira da Costa had his house searched by a policeman from the 10th District because the officer understood that Costa was "a seller for the animal game." He therefore pursued the suspect and, in obedience to the unwritten rule in a hierarchical society (in which if a family produces one criminal, all its members are viewed as lawbreakers), he would not leave João Ferreira da Costa's family alone. Because of this, the family protested to the *Jornal do Brasil* (E. Silva, 1988:110).

Chapter 2. The Animal Game as Totem and Sacrificial Rite

1. It should be pointed out, however, as I previously noted in the "Initial Hunch," that in *Ordem e progresso* (*Order and Progress*) Gilberto Freyre presents, in passing, a more sociological and theoretically productive reading of the animal game—a reading, however, upon which he never expanded. In this work, Freyre mentions that lottery as one more code capable of promoting integration and intimacy among individuals of different social levels in a modern vehicle, the streetcar, when they spoke of dreams and hunches. In this sense, the animal game is a typically Brazilian mechanism for opening space *between* differentiated social segments.

2. By the way, this is not the case with the indigenous societies about which we have detailed information in Brazil. Among the Ge-speaking societies, for example, there are elaborate initiation rituals but no totemic relationship between initiates and eponymous animals, as Freyre states (see DaMatta, 1976). For a much more precise and elaborate study of these systems, see Melatti (1978). The same occurs in the case of the Tupi-Guarani groups, as the monograph by Viveiros de Castro (1986) shows. Judging by his bibliographical references, it is possible that when he mentions "Amerindians" Freyre was projecting onto Brazil attitudes relative to the animals present among the indigenous peoples of North America.

3. Even more because, in *Casa grande & senzala* (*The Masters and the Slaves*), Freyre dialogues extensively about concepts of "race," and, as I learned through Ricardo Benzaquen de Araújo (1994:38ff.) in his important and balanced reading of Freyre, about "physical setting." Today, it is known that there is no "physical setting" distinct from the ideology, value, or culture that classifies, defines, and permits its operationalization in distinct social practices.

4. In this context, it is worth recalling what Erving Goffman says about the game of poker: "Each player . . . must assess what is going on with the opponent and act accordingly. But, of course, the opponent is concerned to misdirect this assessment so that he himself can defeat the assessor. The assessor, knowing this, must see that the picture he obtains of the opponent's situation may be one that has been specifically designed to produce a false impression. The participant, then, by virtue of the structure of the game, is forced to determine a considerable part of his own situation on the basis of the events and material immediately associated with the opponent, and all of this he is right to feel may be organized to misdirect this assessment—in brief, to contain him" (Goffman, 1974:455). This means that in cards—and I would add, roulette and dice—a lot depends on those subtle performances that inform the action and engender a special situation in which contracts, losses, gains, and redefinitions of character take place. It is where, as Goffman says, the "action" is: conduct that, besides being problematic, has its own plane or sphere and, in addition, has consequences for the life of the actor (Goffman, 1967:149–270). Gambling, in Goffman's contractual and individualistic thesis, is not a work-disdaining mode of disregarding money and challenging the system in order, paradoxically, to use it better as a gambler. To him, gambling is a test of character and a way of staying whole despite pressures.

5. Helena Morley, as far back as 1895, informs us about this: "I only regret not having the money to play every day. Mr. Costa is so nice that when I complained I couldn't play every day, he said I could play on credit. I don't do that; but how good it would be if I had the courage" (Morley, 1971:262).

6. Exactly as happened with the lottery and "900" phone numbers, now forbidden, on television, in which people played at home, anonymously, attracted by

appealing figures on TV. In relation to this, in its edition of June 30, 1998, the newspaper *Jornal da Tarde* wrote that the Federal Savings Bank (Caixa Econômica Federal) had reported a drop in income for the federal lotteries, surely caused by the World Cup soccer championship, used to attract players to that televised form of gambling, which would justify its outlawing, a move already under way at this writing.

7. In an original and well-elaborated master's thesis, Cláudia Matos uses a literary slant and interprets this same samba. To her, unlike us, the subject of the musical plot is an idler and a gambler. Further, she interprets the expression "I hit the thousandths" as a win in the lottery when, in fact, the samba refers clearly and obviously to the animal game (Matos, 1982:114–117). In the lottery you don't "hit," you "win." In it, the player has a much more passive role, for he cannot establish when he is going to play or the means of combining the numbers that express his hunch.

8. This is demonstrated by the countless manuals dedicated to deciphering and interpreting dreams, such as those of Aknaton-Ra, *O antigo e verdadeiro livro dos sonhos* (Rio de Janeiro: Editora Eco, 1962); Ben Samir, *O livro dos sonhos e da sorte* (São Paulo: Ed. Livreiro, 1960); Mahal Bathan, *O livro completo dos sonhos* (Rio de Janeiro: Editora Eco, 1973); Rahm Agamenon, *O livro dos sonhos, da sorte e dos orixás* (Rio de Janeiro: Editora Eco); and many others.

9. In this context of the relationships between the living and the dead in Brazil, it is worth remembering a classic passage by Gilberto Freyre in the preface to the first edition of *Casa grande & senzala* (*The Masters and the Slaves*): "The custom of burying the dead inside the house—in the chapel, which was an extension of the house—is quite characteristic of the patriarchal spirit of family cohesion. The dead continued under the same roof with the living. Among the saints and the devotional flowers. Saints and the dead were, after all, part of the family" (lviii). And a bit further on, Freyre defines more precisely the outlines of an "ancestor cult": "Below the saints and above the living were, in hierarchical order, the dead, governing and watching over to the greatest extent possible the lives of children, grandchildren, and great-grandchildren. In many plantation owners' houses their portraits were kept in the shrine, among the images of the saints, with the right to the same votive light from the oil lamp and the same devotional flowers. Sometimes braids of hair from the ladies, as well as curls from the little children who had died as angels, were also preserved. A domestic cult of the dead that recalls that of the ancient Greeks and Romans" (lix).

10. A friend of one of the authors, having fought with a swindling, lowlife, scheming, and dishonest cripple, won a few times by betting on 18 (the pig), 9 (the snake), and 15 (the treacherous crocodile).

11. There are countless lists of prayers of the same kind, all aimed at "hitting the bicho." They are rather curious and would merit a study of their own. See Pacheco (1957), Ramos (1942), and H. Carvalho (1966).

Chapter 3.   Who Are the Bichos?

1. In the book *Carnavais, malandros e heróis* (*Carnivals, Rogues, and Heroes*), one of us mentions this type of complementarity, which some tend to read exclusively as conflict or historical discontinuity. Thus, "Do you know to whom you're speaking?" and the "way around something" (*jeitinho*) would be complementary to the anonymity and egalitarianism fostered by the liberal, modern dimension of Brazilian social life.

2. We have pointed out above that it is impossible to reconstruct the baron's list. But one cannot help mentioning this absence of wild animals (such as the jaguar and the leopard) and the overwhelming presence of tame and domesticated animals, apparently with no zoological value but of obvious usefulness, as well as enormous evocative or symbolic power. This ideological power serves, among other things, to establish social differentiations, entering along with everything else—from clothes to gestures, handwriting, styles of eating and drinking, type of dwelling—into the hierarchy that orders the system. Pedigreed dogs and cats, thoroughbred horses and cows are notorious symbols of social superiority, in contrast, respectively, with mongrel dogs, mules, and goats, as Veblen (1965) and Freyre (1961:139) pointed out.

3. In the seventh century, St. Isidore of Seville also used these same categories and divided animals into "cattle" (domesticated animals) and "beasts" (wild animals). See Joyce E. Salisbury (1994:14).

4. This would characterize the tiger in an openly negative way, as a common predator. At the risk of exaggeration, I wonder whether this view could be implicitly associated with the fact that "tiger" is the name given to slaves who, in Rio de Janeiro and other Brazilian cities of the nineteenth century, hauled the barrels containing fecal matter, a term that later came to designate the barrel in which the filth was transported. In Recife, the expression served to designate "bullies," "bodyguards," or hired guns of a certain strongman, as Câmara Cascudo (1988:737) and Vivaldo Coracy (1988:145) show. It is unnecessary to emphasize that carrying a barrel of excrement on one's back demonstrates a great deal of courage and the complete absence of choice—total obedience as when one is a "bodyguard."

5. The American historian Robert Darnton (1985: chapter 2) reveals that at the dawn of modern times, cats were an indispensable part of certain rituals, like the charivari (in which they were tortured), and in the cycle of St. John the Baptist (when they were hung from ropes and burned). He also stresses, like Câmara Cascudo before him (1988), the autonomy of cats, which, as the public says, are more friends of the house they live in than of its owners, have an uncontrollable reproductive cycle, have nine lives, and can bring on asthma attacks and cause bad luck. Cats possess attributes that afford them a certain perspectivism: an independent and particular view of men and of society. As Darnton says, "[T]here is an indefinable *je ne sais quoi* about cats . . . one can sense a quasi-human intelligence behind a cat's eyes.

One can mistake a cat's howl in the night for a human scream" (1985:89). Cats, with their proverbial ambiguity, are tied to the diabolical arts and were important in popular medicine. In Brazil, it is known that cat excrement had miraculous curative properties against certain diseases such as the evil eye. Cats were also walled in to bring good luck to new dwellings, an element that appears in reverse form in Edgar Allan Poe's "The Black Cat" (see DaMatta, 1973).

6. Which confirms observations by Gilberto Freyre, published over sixty years ago, in *Sobrados e mucambos* (*The Mansions and the Shanties*): "The pureblood dog—large, ferocious, barking, fat, well fed . . . was the characteristic animal of the *sobrado:* a kind of living, masculine, useful expression of the porcelain lions or dragons displayed at the doors of the seigniorial gates" (Freyre [1936], 1961:139).

7. Since the Middle Ages it has been said that crocodiles were hypocrites because, after savoring their human victims, they cried "crocodile tears" (Salisbury, 1994:111). Completing this picture of ambiguities, Câmara Cascudo (1988:382) informs us that crocodiles protect teething infants and are considered responsible for earthquakes.

8. For a stimulating study of the place of the monkey in contemporary Japanese culture, where it occupies a prominent place as clown and mythological-dramatic character and as an important vehicle for criticism the society makes of itself, see Emiko Ohnuki-Tierney (1987).

9. It is worth remembering that on August 21, 1997, a lively and well-attended vote was taken at the zoo in Rio de Janeiro to determine which of two monkeys, Pipo or Paulinho, would replace the famous Tião, an elderly chimp that had died in December 1996 from diabetes. Able to maintain a characteristic relationship with visitors, Tião had garnered four hundred thousand votes for mayor of the city in 1988. Supporting the secular ambiguity of monkeys, Camilinho, a character of Machado de Assis's, begins his career as a player in the animal game by winning with the monkey, but immediately afterward "the half-human animal fell short of the hopes of the first day" (see Machado de Assis, "O jogo do bicho," in *Outros contos. Obra completa*, vol. 2, Rio de Janeiro: Aguilar). In her *Minha vida de menina*, Helena Morley speaks of a monkey named Chico, who, scalded by a malicious neighbor, awakens feelings of sympathy in everyone, precisely because of his ambiguous humanity: "You don't know what we have been suffering. And it's that also which has put Inhá [the simian's owner] in such a state, the poor woman! You know that to her Chico isn't an animal, he's a son. Just imagine a son of yours scalded by boiling water" (Morley, 1971:140).

10. As always, it is Câmara Cascudo who informs us that Aesop, Crates of Thebes, Scarron, Santeul, and Pope were all sages and hunchbacks. On the other hand, it is known that a hunchback's house never catches on fire and that hunchbacks, such as the Nibelungen, watch over incalculable enchanted treasures (Câmara Cascudo, 1988:250).

11. Not to mention the legends of the Enchanted Sheep, which appeared in the Brazilian backlands between the states of Maranhão and Piauí, in a place called Passagem de Santo Antônio (Câmara Cascudo, 1988:199). It is also interesting to mention that 7, the number of the sheep, is blessed in the cabbala as the sum of 6 + 1, which, according to Alberto Dines, "corresponds to the letter *Zain*, the initial of *Zman*, time—the week has seven days, the last of them dedicated to rest and to communing with the Lord; the distance between 6 and 7 is that existing between man and the Creator. Seven is the absolute" (Dines, 1992:38).

12. In Bali, the rooster—called *sabung*—has the metaphorical function of hero, champion, warrior, candidate to public office, dandy, conqueror, and tough guy, images similar to those in Brazil (Geertz, 1973:418; see also Câmara Cascudo, 1988).

Chapter 4.   Final Reflections: Describing the World of the Bichos

1. At the risk of intellectual mannerism, we cannot overlook the considerations of Umberto Eco (1995:24ff.) in relation to the cabbala, alchemy, and other modalities of "hermetic semioses," all ruled by a compact, totalized, or hierarchical view of the world.

2. This can change, in view of the death of Castor de Andrade and the actions of the police vis-à-vis the game. See, for example, the *Jornal do Brasil,* City section, for June 20, 1997.

3. In its edition of May 8, 1994, the *Jornal do Brasil* published a list of thirty-nine personalities and politicians, the majority active on the power scene—such as governors, members of congress, and candidates—who were receiving aid from the bankers of Rio de Janeiro. The magazine *Veja,* in its issue for April 13, 1994, made these linkages its cover story.

4. Obviously, all names are fictitious.

REFERENCES

Agostinho, Pedro

(1979) "Código, tática e divinação no jogo do bicho." Unpublished essay, Museu Nacional, Rio de Janeiro.

Andrade, Oswald de

(1972 [1928]) *Do Pau-Brasil à antropofagia e às utopias.* Rio de Janeiro: Civilização Brasileira.

Araújo, Ricardo Benzaquen

(1994) *Guerra e paz: Casa Grande & Senzala e a obra de Gilberto Freyre nos anos 30.* Rio de Janeiro: Editora 34.

Araújo, Rosa Maria Barbosa de

(1993) *A vocação do prazer: A cidade e a família no Rio de Janeiro republicano.* Rio de Janeiro: Rocco.

Ashton, John

(1969 [1898]) *The History of Gambling in England.* Montclair, N.J.: Patterson Smith.

Bakhtin, Mikhail

(1989) *A cultura popular na Idade Média e no Renascimento: O contexto de François Rabelais.* São Paulo: Hucitec.

Barbosa, Lívia

(1992) *O jeitinho brasileiro.* Rio de Janeiro: Editora Campus.

Barreto Filho, Mello, and Hermeto Lima

(1944) *História da polícia do Rio de Janeiro: Aspectos da cidade e da vida carioca (1870–1889).* Rio de Janeiro: Editora A Noite.

Bastide, Roger

(1960) *As religiões africanas no Brasil: Contribuição a uma sociologia das interpenetrações de civilizações.* 2 vols. São Paulo: Livraria Pioneira Editora/Editora da Universidade de São Paulo.

Benchimol, Jaime Larry
(1990) *Pereira Passos: Um Haussmann tropical: A renovação urbana da cidade do Rio de Janeiro no início do século XX*. Prefeitura da Cidade do Rio de Janeiro: Biblioteca Carioca.

Bergson, Henri
(1978 [1932]) *As duas fontes da moral e da religião*. Translated by Nathaniel C. Caixeiro. Rio de Janeiro: Zahar Editores.

Berlin, Isaiah
(1991) *Limites da utopia: Capítulos da história das idéias*. Translated by Valter Siqueira. São Paulo: Companhia das Letras.
(1998) "The First and the Last," *The New York Review of Books*. Vol. 45, no. 8, May 14.

Bohannan, Paul
(1955) "Some Principles of Exchange and Investment Among the Tiv," in *American Anthropologist* 57:60–70.

Borges, Jorge Luis
(1972) *Ficções*. Translated by Carlos Nejar. São Paulo: Abril Cultural.

Bretas, Marcos Luís
(1997) *Ordem na cidade: O exercício cotidiano da autoridade policial no Rio de Janeiro: 1907–1930*. Rio de Janeiro: Rocco.

Brown, Diana
(1986) *Umbanda, Religion, and Politics in Urban Brazil*. Ann Arbor: UMI Research Press.

Cabral, Oswaldo R.
(n.d.) *O folclore do jogo do bicho*. Porto: Tipografia da Livraria Simões Lopes.

Caillois, Roger
(1979) *Man, Play, and Games*. Translated by Meyer Barash. New York: Shocken Books.

Caldeira, Jorge
(1995) *Mauá: Empresário do Império*. São Paulo: Companhia das Letras.
(1997) *História do Brasil*. São Paulo: Companhia das Letras.

Carelli, Mario
(1994) *Culturas cruzadas: Intercâmbios culturais entre França e Brasil*. São Paulo: Papirus.

Cartmill, Matt
(1993) *A View to a Death in the Morning: Hunting and Nature Through History*. Cambridge, Mass., and London: Harvard University Press.

Carvalho, Hernane
(1966) *No mundo maravilhoso do folclore*. Rio de Janeiro: Tipografia Batista de Souza.

Carvalho, José Murilo de
(1990) *A formação das almas: O imaginário da República no Brasil*. São Paulo: Companhia das Letras.
(1991) *Os bestializados: O Rio de Janeiro e a República que não foi*. São Paulo: Companhia das Letras.

Cascudo, Luís da Câmara
(1985) *Superstição no Brasil*. Belo Horizonte and São Paulo: Editora Itatiaia/Editora da Universidade de São Paulo.
(1988) *Dicionário do folclore brasileiro*. Belo Horizonte: Editora Itatiaia.

Cavalcanti, Eugênio C.
(1940) *Os bicheiros*. Rio de Janeiro: Editora A Noite.

Chinn, Carl
(1991) *Better Betting with a Decent Feller: Bookmaking, Betting and the British Working Class, 1750–1900*. New York and London: Harvester-Wheatsheaf.

Clapson, Mark
(1992) *A Bit of a Flutter: Popular Gambling and English Society, c. 1823–1961*. Manchester and New York: Manchester University Press.

Coracy, Vivaldo
(1988) *Memórias da cidade do Rio de Janeiro*. São Paulo e Belo Horizonte: Editora Itatiaia and Editora da Universidade de São Paulo.

Crump, Thomas
(1990) *The Anthropology of Numbers*. Cambridge: Cambridge University Press.

DaMatta, Roberto
(1969) "Intuitional, Emotional and Intellectual Explanation. Richard Tohrn, Roberto DaMatta," in *Man. The Journal of the Royal Anthropological Institute.* New Series, vol. 4, no. 3. September, p. 454.
(1973) *Ensaios de antropologia estrutural.* Petrópolis: Editora Vozes.
(1976) *Um mundo dividido: A estrutura social dos índios Apinayé.* Petrópolis: Editora Vozes.
(1979) *Carnavais, malandros e heróis.* Rio de Janeiro: Zahar. English translation, *Carnivals, Rogues, and Heroes: An Interpretation of the Brazilian Dilemma.* 1991. Translated by John Drury. Notre Dame, Ind.: University of Notre Dame Press.
(1987a) *A casa & a rua.* Rio de Janeiro: Editora Guanabara.
(1987b) *Relativizando: Uma introdução à antropologia social.* Rio de Janeiro: Editora Rocco.
(1989) *O que faz o brasil, Brasil?* Rio de Janeiro: Editora Rocco.
(1993) *Conta de mentiroso: Sete ensaios de antropologia brasileira.* Rio de Janeiro: Editora Rocco.
(1996) "Um rei fora do lugar." Review of *Dom João VI no Brasil,* by Manuel de Oliveira Lima. *O Globo,* Caderno Prosa & Verso, June 29.

Darnton, Robert
(1985) *The Great Cat Massacre and Other Episodes in French Cultural History.* New York: Vintage.

Davis, John
(1992) *Exchange.* Minneapolis: University of Minnesota Press.

Davis, Natalie
(1990) *Culturas do povo: Sociedade e cultura no início da França moderna.* Translated by Mariza Corrêa. Rio de Janeiro: Paz e Terra.

De Roos, Robert
(1994) "The Magic Worlds of Walt Disney," in *Disney Discourse: Producing the Magic Kingdom.* Edited by Eric Smoodin. New York and London: Routledge.

Descola, Philippe
(1998) "Estrutura ou sentimento: A relação com o animal na Amazônia," in *Mana: Estudos de Antropologia Social,* vol. 4, no. 1.

Dines, Alberto
(1992) *Vínculos do fogo.* Banco Safra Projeto Cultural. São Paulo: Companhia das Letras.

Douglas, Mary
(1976) *Pureza e perigo*. São Paulo: Editora Perspectiva.

Dumont, Louis
(1977) *From Mandeville to Marx: Genesis and Triumph of Economic Ideology*. Chicago and London: University of Chicago Press.
(1980) *Homo Hierarchicus: The Caste System and Its Implications*. Chicago: University of Chicago Press.
(1985) *O individualismo*. Rio de Janeiro: Editora Rocco.

Dunkley, John
(1985) *Gambling: A Social and Moral Problem in France, 1685–1792*. Oxford: Voltaire Foundation.

Durkheim, Émile
(1996 [1912]) *As formas elementares da vida religiosa: O sistema totêmico na Austrália*. Translated by Paulo Neves. São Paulo: Martins Fontes.

Eco, Umberto
(1995) *Os limites da interpretação*. São Paulo: Editora Perspectiva.

Edmundo, Luiz
(1938) *O Rio de Janeiro do meu tempo*. Especially vol. 3. Belo Horizonte: Editora Itatiaia.

Elias, Norbert
(1995) *A sociedade de corte*. Lisbon: Editorial Estampa.

Evans, E. P.
(1906) *The Criminal Prosecution and Capital Punishment of Animals*. New York: E. P. Dutton and Company.

Evans-Pritchard, E. E.
(1937) *Witchcraft, Oracles and Magic among the Azande*. Oxford: Clarendon Press.
(1957) *Antropología social*. Buenos Aires: Editorial Nueva Visión.
(1978) *Os Nuer*. São Paulo: Editora Perspectiva.

Ewbank, Thomas
(1856) *Life in Brazil*. New York: Harper and Brothers.

Expilly, Charles
(1977) *Mulheres e costumes do Brasil*. São Paulo: Companhia Editora Nacional.

Faoro, Raymundo

(1975) *Os donos do poder: Formação do patronato político brasileiro.* Editora Globo/ Editora da Universidade de São Paulo.

(1976) *Machado de Assis: A pirâmide e o trapézio.* São Paulo: Companhia Editora Nacional: Brasiliana, vol. 356.

Findlay, John M.

(1986) *People of Chance: Gambling in American Society from Jamestown to Las Vegas.* New York and Oxford: Oxford University Press.

Freundlich, Francis

(1995) *Le Monde du jeu à Paris (1715–1800).* Paris: Bibliothèque Albin Michel - Histoire.

Frey, James H.

(1984) "Gambling: A Sociological Review," in *The Annals of the American Academy of Political and Social Sciences.* Vol. 474, July.

Freyre, Gilberto

(1984 [1933]) *Casa grande & senzala.* Rio de Janeiro: José Olympio Editora. English translation, *The Masters and the Slaves.* 1946. Translated by Samuel Putnam. New York: Alfred A. Knopf.

(1961 [1936]) *Sobrados e mucambos.* Rio de Janeiro: José Olympio Editora. English translation, *The Mansions and the Shanties.* 1963. Translated by Harriet de Onís. New York: Alfred A. Knopf.

(1959 [1959]) *Ordem e progresso.* Rio de Janeiro: José Olympio Editora. English translation, *Order and Progress.* 1970. Translated by Rod W. Horton. New York: Alfred A. Knopf.

(1968) *Guia prático, histórico e sentimental da cidade do Recife.* Rio de Janeiro: José Olympio Editora.

(1979) *O escravo nos anúncios de jornais brasileiros do século XIX.* Coleção Brasiliana, vol. 37. São Paulo and Recife: Companhia Editora Nacional/Instituto Joaquim Nabuco de Pesquisas Sociais.

Geertz, Clifford

(1973) "The Growth of Culture and the Evolution of the Mind," in *The Interpretation of Cultures.* New York and London: Basic Books.

Gellner, Ernest

(1983) *Nations and Nationalism.* Ithaca and New York: Cornell University Press.

Goffman, Erving
(1967) *Interaction Ritual: Essays on Face-to-face Behavior.* Garden City, N.Y.: Anchor Books.
(1974) *Frame Analysis: An Essay on the Organization of Experience.* New York: Harper Colophon Books.

Goody, Jack
(1993) *The Culture of Flowers.* Cambridge: Cambridge University Press.

Gould, Stephen Jay
(1979) "Mickey Mouse Meets Konrad Lorenz," in *Natural History,* May.

Grussi, Olivier
(1985) *La vie quotidienne des joueurs sous L'Ancien Régime à Paris et à la cour.* Paris: Hachette.

Guedes, Simoni Lahud
(1998) *O Brasil no campo de futebol: Estudos antropológicos sobre os significados do futebol brasileiro.* Niterói: Editora da Universidade Federal Fluminense.

Harris, Marvin
(1974) *Cows, Pigs, Wars and Witches: The Riddles of Culture.* New York: Random House.
(1978) *Cannibals and Kings.* New York: Vintage.

Herschmann, Micael, and Kátia Lerner
(1993) *Lance de sorte: O futebol e o jogo do bicho na Belle Époque carioca.* Rio de Janeiro: Diadorim Editora Ltda.

Hirschman, Albert
(1961) "Ideologies of Economic Development in Latin America," in *Latin American Issues,* org. by Albert Hirschman. New York: Twentieth Century Fund.

Holston, James
(1989) *The Modernist City: An Anthropological Critique of Brasília.* Chicago: University of Chicago Press.

Hopper, Vincent Foster
(1938) *Medieval Number Symbolism: Its Sources, Meaning, and Influence on Thought and Expression.* New York: Columbia University Press.

Huizinga, Johan
(1950) *Homo Ludens: A Study of the Play Element in Culture*. Boston: Beacon Press.

Karasch, Mary
(1987) *Slave Life in Rio de Janeiro: 1808–1850*. Princeton, N.J.: Princeton University Press.

Kavanagh, Thomas M.
(1993) *Enlightenment and the Shadows of Chance*. Baltimore and London: The Johns Hopkins University Press.

Leach, Edmund R.
(1983) *Edmund Leach, Coleção Grandes Cientistas Sociais,* dir. Florestan Fernandes. Edited by Roberto DaMatta. São Paulo: Editora Ática.

Lee, Raymond
(1970) *Not So Dumb: The Life and Times of the Animal Actors*. South Brunswick, N.J., and New York: A. S. Barnes.

Leite Lopes, José Sérgio
(1994) "A vitória do futebol que incorporou a pelada," in "Dossiê Futebol," *Revista da USP,* no. 22.

Lévi-Strauss, Claude
(1963) *Totemism*. Translated by Rodney Needham. Boston: Beacon Press.
(1966) *The Savage Mind*. Chicago: University of Chicago Press.
(1986) *O totemismo hoje*. Lisbon: Edições 70.

Lima, Manuel de Oliveira
(1996) *Dom João VI no Brasil*. Rio de Janeiro: Topbooks.

Lobo, Eulália Maria Lehmeyer
(1978) *História do Rio de Janeiro: Do capital comercial ao capital industrial e financeiro*. Rio de Janeiro: IBMEC. 2 vols.

Lowie, Robert H.
(1966 [1917]) *Culture and Ethnology*. New York and London: Basic Books.

Lustosa, Isabel
(1993) *Brasil pelo método confuso: Humor e boemia em Mendes Fradique*. Rio de Janeiro: Bertrand Brasil.

Machado da Silva, L. A., and A. Figueiredo
(1978) "A partir de um ponto do jogo do bicho," São Paulo, *Anais da 30° Reunião Anual da SBPC.*

Maggie, Yvonne
(1992) *Medo do feitiço: Relações entre magia e poder no Brasil.* Rio de Janeiro: Arquivo Nacional/Ministério da Justiça.

Matos, Claudia
(1982) *Acertei no milhar: Samba e malandragem no tempo de Getúlio.* Rio de Janeiro: Paz e Terra.

Mauss, Marcel
(1990) *The Gift: The Form and Reason for Exchange in Archaic Societies.* Translated by W. D. Halls. New York and London: W. W. Norton.

Mauss, Marcel, and Henri Hubert
(1972) *A General Theory of Magic.* Translated by Robert Brain, foreword by D. F. Pocock. London and New York: Routledge.

Melatti, Julio Cezar
(1978) *Ritos de uma tribo Timbira.* São Paulo: Ática.

Mello, D. Francisco Manuel de
(1997) *Tratado da ciência Cabala.* Rio de Janeiro: Imago.

Moog, Vianna
(1955) *Bandeirantes e pioneiros.* São Paulo: Editora Globo. English translation, *Bandeirantes and Pioneers.* 1964. New York: G. Braziller.

Morley, Helena
(1971) *Minha vida de menina: Diário de Helena Morley.* Rio de Janeiro: José Olympio Editora/Instituto Nacional do Livro.

Neal, Arthur G.
(1985) "Animism and Totemism in Popular Culture," in *Journal of Popular Culture,* vol. 19.

Needell, Jeffrey D.
(1993) *Belle Époque tropical: Sociedade e cultura de elite no Rio de Janeiro na virada do século.* Translated by Celso Nogueira. São Paulo: Companhia das Letras.

Needham, Rodney
(1978) *Primordial Characters*. Charlottesville: University of Virginia Press.

Nogueira, Oracy
(1954) "Preconceito de marca e preconceito de origem: Sugestão de um quadro de referência para a interpretação do material sobre relações raciais no Brasil," in *Anais do XXXI Congresso Internacional dos Americanistas*. São Paulo, August, vol. 1:409–434.

Ohnuki-Tierney, Emiko
(1987) *The Monkey as Mirror: Symbolic Transformations in Japanese History and Ritual*. Princeton, N.J.: Princeton University Press.

Oliveira, Lúcia Lipp
(1990) *A questão nacional da Primeira República*. São Paulo: CNPq/Editora Brasiliense.

Ortner, Sherry B.
(1991) "Reading America: Preliminary Notes on Class and Culture," in *Recapturing Anthropology: Working in the Present*. Richard G. Fox (org.). Santa Fe, N.M.: School of American Research Press.

Pacheco, Renato J. C.
(1951) *Antologia do jogo do bicho*. Rio de Janeiro: Organização Simões.

Paraguassu, Camilo
(1954) *Memórias sobre o jogo do bicho*. Rio de Janeiro: Pongetti Editora.

Paz, Octavio
(1979) *Conjunções e disjunções*. São Paulo: Editora Perspectiva.

Peary, Danny, and Gerald Peary
(1980) *The American Animated Cartoon: A Critical Anthology*. New York: E. P. Dutton.

Pereira de Mello, Marcelo
(1989) *A história social dos jogos de azar no Rio de Janeiro: 1808/1946*. Rio de Janeiro, IUPERJ, unpublished ms.

Polanyi, Karl
(1988) *A grande transformação*. Rio de Janeiro: Editora Campus.

Ramos, Arthur
(1942) *Aculturação negra no Brasil.* São Paulo: Companhia Editora Nacional.

Ribeiro, João
(1919) *Livro da interpretação dos sonhos.* Rio de Janeiro: n.p.

Rocha, Everardo
(1985) *Magia e capitalismo.* São Paulo: Editora Brasiliense.

Rosenfeld, Anatol
(1993) *Negro, macumba e futebol.* São Paulo: Editora Perspectiva.

Sá Rego, Enylton de
(1989) *O calundu e a panacéia: Machado de Assis, a sátira menipéia e a tradição luciânica.* Rio de Janeiro: Forense Universitária.

Sahlins, Marshall
(1972) "The Spirit of the Gift," chapter 4 of *Stone Age Economics.* New York: Aldine de Gruyter.
(1976a) *Culture and Practical Reason.* Chicago and London: University of Chicago Press.
(1976b) *The Use and Abuse of Biology: An Anthropological Critique of Sociobiology.* Ann Arbor: University of Michigan Press.
(1978) "Culture as Protein and Profit," *The New York Review of Books,* November 23.
(1995) *How "Natives" Think: About Captain Cook, for Example.* Chicago and London: University of Chicago Press.
(1996) "The Sadness of Sweetness: The Native Anthropology of Western Cosmology," Sidney Mintz Lecture for 1994, in *Current Anthropology,* vol. 31, no. 5:395–428.

Saldanha, Gehisa
(1986) *O jogo do bicho: Como jogar e ganhar.* Rio de Janeiro: Fênix Editora.

Salisbury, Joyce E.
(1994) *The Beast Within: Animals in the Middle Ages.* London and New York: Routledge.

Sandler, Kevin S.
(1998) "Gendered Evasion," in *Reading the Rabbit: Explorations in Warner Bros. Animation.* New Jersey and London: Rutgers University Press.

Schwarz, Roberto
(1977) *Ao vencedor as batatas: Forma literária e processo social nos inícios do romance brasileiro.* São Paulo. Duas Cidades

Seagle, William
(1948) "Gambling," in *Encyclopaedia of the Social Sciences.* New York: Macmillan. Vol. 5.

Sevcenko, Nicolau
(1983) *Literatura como missão: Tensões sociais e criação cultural na Primeira República.* São Paulo: Brasiliense.
(1998) "A capital; irradiante: Técnica, ritmos e ritos do Rio," chapter 7 of *História da vida privada no Brasil. República: da Belle Époque à era do rádio.* São Paulo: Companhia das Letras.

Silva, Eduardo
(1988) *As queixas do povo.* Rio de Janeiro: Paz e Terra.

Silva, Nádia M. A.
(n.d.) *A resolução de problemas aritméticos no trabalho: O caso do jogo do bicho.* Recife: Universidade Federal de Pernambuco.

Simmel, Georg
(1950) *The Sociology of Georg Simmel.* Translated and org. by Kurt H. Wolff. New York: Free Press.

Soares, Simone Simões Ferreira
(1993) *O jogo do bicho: A saga de um fato social brasileiro.* Rio de Janeiro: Bertrand Brasil.

Souto Maior, Mário
(1985) *Dicionário folclórico da cachaça.* Recife: Fundação Joaquim Nabuco/Editora Massangana.

Strazzullo, Franco
(1987) *I Giochi d'Azzardo e il Lotto a Napoli. Divagazioni storichi.* Naples: Liguori Editore.

Tambiah, Stanley Jeyaraja
(1985) *Culture, Thought, and Social Action: An Anthropological Perspective.* Cambridge, Mass., and London: Harvard University Press.

Taussig, Michael
(1980) *The Devil and Commodity Fetishism in South America*. Durham: University of North Carolina Press.

Tedlock, Barbara
(1995) "La Cultura del Sueño en las Américas," in *De palabra y obra en el Nuevo Mundo: 4. Tramas de la identidad*. Org. by J. Jorge Klor de Alva, Gary Gossen, Miguel León Portilla, and Manuel Gutiérrez Estévez. Mexico and Spain: Siglo Veintiuno Editores.

Tocqueville, Alexis de
(2000 [1840]) *Democracy in America*. Translated, edited, and with an introduction by Harvey C. Mansfield and Delba Winthrop. Chicago and London: University of Chicago Press.

Todorov, Tzetan
(1993) *Nós e os outros: A reflexão francesa sobre a diversidade humana 1*. Rio de Janeiro: Jorge Zahar Editor.
(1996) *A conquista da América: A questão do outro*. Translated by Beatriz Perrone Moisés. São Paulo: Martins Fontes.

Toledo, Luiz Henrique de
(1994) "Transgressão e violência entre torcedores de futebol," in "Dossiê Futebol," *Revista da USP*, no. 22.

Troeltsch, Ernst
(1950) "Lecture on the Ideas of Natural Law and Humanity," in Otto Gierke, *Natural Law and the Theory of Society: 1500–1800*. Cambridge: Cambridge University Press.

Tylor, Edward Burnett
(1958 [1871]) *The Origins of Culture*. New York and Evanston: Harper & Row.

Valeri, Valerio
(1985) *Kinship and Sacrifice: Ritual and Society in Ancient Hawaii*. Translated by Paula Wissing. Chicago and London: University of Chicago Press.

Veblen, Thorstein
(1965) *A teoria da classe ociosa (Um estudo econômico das instituições)*. Translated by Olivia Krahenbühl. São Paulo: Livraria Pioneira Editora.

Velho, Otávio
(1976) *Capitalismo autoritário e campesinato*. São Paulo: DIFEL.

Veríssimo de Melo
(1951) *Orações propiciatórias para o jogo do bicho*. Natal: n.p.

Viveiros de Castro, Eduardo
(1986) *Araweté: Os deuses canibais*. Rio de Janeiro: Jorge Zahar Editor/ANPOCS.
(1996) "Os pronomes cosmológicos e o perspectivismo ameríndio," in *Mana: Estudos de Antropologia Social*, vol. 2, no. 2, October.

Weber, Max
(1981) *A ética protestante e o espirito do capitalismo*. São Paulo: Editora Pioneira.

Wehrs, C. Carlos J.
(1980) *O Rio antigo - Pitoresco & musical: Memórias e diário*. Rio de Janeiro: n.p.

Whiting, John W. M.
(1964) "Effects of Climate on Certain Cultural Practices," in *Explorations in Cultural Anthropology: Essays in Honor of George Peter Murdock*, org. by Ward H. Goodenough. New York: McGraw-Hill Book Company.

INDEX

ROBERTO DaMATTA

is professor emeritus of anthropology at the University of Notre Dame and is presently teaching at the Catholic University in Rio de Janeiro, Brazil.

ELENA SOÁREZ

is a script writer.